to Antonio with heartfelt
apologies for a 14-year
absence from our family,
a family that meant, and
always will, everything worth
while in life. Unknowing,
you were much of that
which kept me from becoming
spiritually handicapped.
Sons are a great institution!
And to Dominique and
my first grandchild, Nathen,
as well. To all with
love.

October 1980

LEAVE ME MY SPIRIT

by

Lawrence K. Lunt

ЛWЛ

Affiliated Writers of America/Publishers
Tempe, Arizona

Printed in the United States of America
by Ben Franklin Press/Tempe

Edited by Jay Fraser

Copyright © 1990 by Lawrence K. Lunt

Published by

Affiliated Writers of America, Inc.
P.O. Box 2006
Tempe, Arizona 85281
U.S.A.

Distribution Office and Permissions Editor:
Affiliated Writers of America, Inc.
P.O. Box 343
Encampment, Wyoming 82325
U.S.A.

ISBN: 0-918080-58-4
Library of Congress Catalog Card Number: 90-82568

Cover Design and Illustration by Randy Galloway

DEDICATION

Why do so many authors dedicate their books to their wives? It must be something more than gratitude to them for years of wondering why their men don't take up more remunerative work and behave like other husbands. The author's unsung silent half must have faith in the intangible, the incomprehensible, the innumerable rejects. Faith in a companion whose thoughts are often on another tangent rather than on her, off on business of their own, in another world. My wife was all of this and more.

With love and gratitude to Beatrice.

ACKNOWLEDGMENTS

Marie & Billy Hoyt, steadfast friends during my prison years and
after, invaluable editors of all my mumblings in pencil, and though
geographically far apart, remaining very close indeed.

Nina Lobanov for first introducing me to the intricacies of editing,
followed by years of encouragement, help and friendship.

Faith Titus, my sister, who has read and edited this book and others,
and been of inestimable help.

JoAnn Bromley, Gary Weesner, Ron Clark, and Randy Galloway.

And to all the countless, some unknown, people who prayed for me
and other political prisoners everywhere, and helped stir
bureaucracies into helpful action.

Table of Contents

Publisher's Note

This story is the true-life experience of the author although some names have been changed to protect persons and their families.

ATLANTIC
OCEAN

CARIBBEAN
SEA

CUBA

Havana
Pinar del Río
Santa Clara
Bay of Pig
(Cochinas Bay)
Escambray Mountains
Isle of Pines
Birán
Sierra Sierra Cristal
Bayamo Maestra
Mtns.
La Plata
Guantánamo
Granma
Alegría de Pío
Santiago

❶ Finca San Andrés (Ranch)
❷ Guanajay Prison
❸ La Cabaña Prison
❹ Combinado del Este Prison
❺ Taco Taco Prison
❻ Isle of Pines Prison
❼ Moa
❽ Baracoa

Foreword

What is perhaps the most striking aspect of style in this story is the compassionate tone in which it is written. Lunt, rather than reflect bitterness, has portrayed a sense of humanity and inner spirit which continued to survive, and even flourished, against completely overwhelming odds. Against brutality. Against totalitarianism. Against communism. And a similar sense of humanity within the people of Cuba survived and flourished in total opposition to Castro's communist regime, a force he could suppress but not destroy.

Lunt's tone and vivid detail captures Cuba in its totality—a portmanteau of political repression and brutal prison life against a light, colorful prose suggesting transcendentalism through nature and spirit. Lunt demonstrates a rare ability to see through the harshest of environments to find nature, beauty, and humanity. Thus, the extreme contrasts in the portrayal of people and images reveal deeper meanings and conflicts than one might expect in an outwardly political story.

Amidst Castro's forces which dictate nearly every aspect of life in Cuba, Lunt demonstrates a distinction between *enduring* and *prevailing* in terms of human spirit. One is reminded of the words of

William Faulkner in his Nobel Peace Prize Acceptance Speech (1950): ". . . the old verities and truths of the heart, the old universal truths lacking which any story is ephemeral and doomed—love and honor and pity and pride and compassion and sacrifice . . . . I believe that man will not merely endure: he will prevail. He is immortal . . . because he has a soul, a spirit . . . ."

Survival is portrayed in terms of humanity and tradition. As people the world over argue where it is that humanity comes from, it should be noted that the first and foremost goal of communist thought is to destroy tradition. A news picture of Castro dated 1958 shows him open-mouthed with the caption, "We're not communists." Of course, it is not difficult to see the humor in that today. But Eisenhower didn't see it then. Within the political community, these things are all shifting and grey, people form strange alliances—then these alliances disappear—and these same people become opposed to each other. And when you get to the intelligence community, things are done outside of government. In the end, whatever the reasons, Carter did what was right.

Lunt credits his best preparation in life for survival to "the rough and tumble Wyoming life, broadening one's perspective, and teaching self-reliance." JoAnn Bromley, of Encampment, remembers him well: "There he was, bareback on a pony, he always seemed to ride bareback, herding cattle, and he looked up at a jet in the sky and said, 'This is as far off the ground as I want to be.' That was just after he returned from the Korean War." William Middendorf remembers him well also: "To those of us in the diplomatic core working for his release, we heard that every time Larry Lunt's name came up, Castro would go into apoplexy because of Larry's unshakable idealism . . . . Once a fellow prisoner had said that Larry jumped in front of a guard who was trying to bayonet him and Larry took the knife wound. I have the utmost respect for Larry Lunt."

This is not only a great story about Cuba, it is a story with implications for the entire world, for all of mankind, wherever common decency, individuality, and traditional values are threatened by totalitarian forces or communism. As John Steinbeck once said of *The Grapes of Wrath*, "Throughout I've tried to make the reader participate in the actuality; what he takes from it will be scaled entirely on his own depth or hollowness."

—JAY FRASER

Chapter 1

"You!"

Like a pistol shot in the quiet of the soundproofed room.

I remember that voice as if it were yesterday. And strangely, I remember the content of that voice's raving foulness, although at the time it passed me by, protective shock diluting the insults into meaningless jabber. Crude reference to my mother's antecedents, and my father's, leaving me without a name. My wife's many infidelities were shouted in my ear to reduce my claim to manhood, to prove my inadequacy with women. I had been badly put together in a brothel. I was a bastard, a pimp, a whoremonger. I was lewd, unchaste, unfaithful. I was also homosexual. In short, I had absolutely nothing going for me and would do well to opt for absolution and confess my many sins. Here the voice dropped to decibels manageable to the ear and hissed.

"You! Who are you? A nobody, an extra nothing—to me, to anyone, and after I'm through not even to yourself. You beginning to understand?"

After pissing all over my family tree, splintering branches, axing roots, the voice droned on, cataloguing my crimes against the working class, against the state, against all humanity. The voice knew every atrocity I had ever committed. I would never leave this stifling windowless box of a low-ceilinged room. I'd not escape the hateful grey dungeoned walls outside at some unknown Havana address, away from this soldier-garbed creature playing God with my genealogy.

My genealogy. How had I, a Boston wasp, married to a Belgian Catholic (also a wasp in their eyes), ever come to this mid-nightmare arrest? Traumatized by the night's events, I had forgotten. The voice across the grey metal desk was right. In defensive shock, I did not know then who or what I was—like not immediately feeling the pain of a severed limb. And why for Christ's sake couldn't he douse those blinding lights? He must have read my mind.

"Those lights bothering you? Here, I'll adjust 'em for you."

And he turned them even brighter. And hotter. His voice, too, rose in intensity.

"You don't answer. Well then, I'll tell you who you are. Sired by an imperialist bastard, mothered by a whoring bastard, you-are-a-bastard!"

Why all that verbal abuse when he must have known I was anesthetized for the moment against all insults? He ranted on.

"Right now you don't even have a name. You have become a number. 1256, that's who you are. And if you're expecting any mail, your address is cell 59, G-2 Headquarters, Havana, Cuba. You got two bunks to lie on and electricity and running water and a piss pot and single occupancy. You're living in luxury, 1256. We got some of your cock-sucking buddies here living in the dark, eight to a cell the size of yours. See this file here? The story of your life. Episcopalian. That mean you believe in some gussied-up society God, a Sunday excuse to dress up fancy so all your mother-fucking friends can see how much inherited money you got? Oh—maybe forgot to mention—we're shooting gringos nowadays for less than you've done."

And I'd done quite a lot in five years to destabilize Castro's communist regime. But now, more than anything in the world, I wanted to rasp that mosquito bite on my arm. For one brief moment the exquisite torment of that itch obliterated the hurt in my wrists, the hangover throb in my head, and the dull ache in back and thighs from hours in the devil's own chair I sat on—that inverse curve to the back which makes any position untenable. Involuntarily my

2

arms came up—and fell again to my lap. The mosquito, undoubtedly a militant member of G-2, and paid in blood, was to be suffered along with the aches and pains and the handcuffs imprisoning my wrists. He mistook my attempt to scratch for a complaint against the handcuffs.

"Those *esposas* bothering you? Here, let me adjust 'em."

He eased out of his scuffed, leather-padded chair (from the office of some long-departed sugar baron?) to inspect my wrists, and manacled them a notch tighter. I loved the guy's sense of humor. At least the itch of the mosquito bite was forgotten with the new pain of cold steel pressing bone.

As I had lost my name for a number, the voice across the desk was just The Man to me. I knew nothing at all about him, although later I would. I had never seen him before and never wanted to again. I would though, through many weary nights and days, through many miserable months. I would grow as tired of that face as I'm sure he did of mine. A handsome face but for the too small, sensuous mouth. Some impassioned poet might have immortalized his lips as a damsel's rosebud labium. I found them repulsive. Mouth aside, his features were cast from Tyrone Power. Latin good-looks with a teak tan, long thick eyelashes over hazel eyes. Eyes that, according to the role he played, altered from soft compelling to compelling hard. A lot of lithe black cat in his six feet. He might have been a tennis player or ballet dancer. Long-fingered hands well manicured—a player of piano or guitar. With his well-pressed uniform he wore foreign shoes, Bally perhaps. A man of fastidious taste.

With no file before me on The Man's life to flip through, I felt the need to know my inquisitor as he knew me. I had to put together the bits and pieces as I could, deduce his character from his speech, mannerisms, physical aspect, the clothes he wore. All this became important to me. I don't know why.

I'd have to form my own opinion. There weren't any other opinions going. Animals don't consult each other about other animals. There's a look, a mutual scenting, and they make their noises. In love and hate and everything in between, these are the only opinions that matter.

"Hey, 1256, whatcha thinking? Answer me! You know you've had it, don't you? If I want I can fold you up real small and put you in a pocket with my cigarettes. Maybe you'd like a cigarette?"

He flipped a Cuban brand half out of the package in his hand and held it out. Textbook perfect, I neither replied nor moved. Textbook perfect, my mind was saying, "Shove it up your ass, bimbo."

Chapter 2

Thursday, May 5, ~~1956~~ *1965* Rancho Boyeros Airport, Havana, Cuba. A terminal empty of travelers except those on Iberia's weekly nine A.M. flight to Madrid via Bermuda. By eight, all passengers checked in, but departure postponed again and again. "Technical difficulties," they said. Difficulties synonymous with Castro's Cuba.

The passengers were emigrating Cubans, a few government officials, European embassy secretaries with their diplomatic pouches, and myself, an American, Cuban resident since 1955. I was leaving the plane in Bermuda to connect with a flight to the States for my parents' fiftieth wedding anniversary in Santa Fe, New Mexico.

The plane had been before the terminal all morning, loading ramp in position, baggage loaded, the only plane to fly out that day. Before the Revolution, Rancho Boyeros had been a busy airport, crowded with noisy, laughing people, arriving and leaving. After January 1959, the Revolution brought doubt, then fear. Incoming flights brought few. Not an empty seat on departing planes. The once-gay terminal became somber with sad and tearful farewells.

At noon, the airline offered lunch in the airport restaurant. Chewing on a tough *biftec*, I heard my name on the loudspeaker. Would I please come to the Iberia check-in counter right away? An apologetic Iberian employee said my name had been struck from the manifest. I could not board the plane. With undisguised worry, I asked, "Do you know the reason for this?"

"No, *señor*, I am sorry. I know nothing."

"Am I the only passenger bumped from the flight?"

"*Sí, señor*, the only one—so far."

I thought I read in his eyes a knowing sadness, as if he had told many people before me the same unhappy news: that at the very last moment, they were not to be allowed to leave this tragic island for the freedom just beyond its beaches.

My first annoyance gave way to dread as I half walked, half ran to the office from which the order had come. The loudspeakers, echoing through the near-empty terminal, blared out the flight. Finally, I reached the right door to the right office, my heart beating fast, a sour taste in my mouth.

The long, narrow room with glass-door opening onto the tarmac had once been a dark corridor, converted now into a military command post. The only furniture was one overstuffed chair, well past its prime, two straight-backed chairs, and a battered desk. No space for more. From a hole punched through the wall, a cable snaked to a cracked phone on the desk, mostly buried by drifts of forms and official papers, unwashed coffee cups, a dented hubcap overflowing cigarette stubs and half-smoked cigars, and a pair of scuffed boots on the feet of a lieutenant not many years into shaving. He was bored. He was unshaven. And unpressed and unimpressed with my problem.

"Why can I not leave on that plane?"

Inspecting his dirty fingernails, "I do not know."

"They told me you were in charge here."

"That is true."

"Then can you tell me what I must do? Please, I am in a hurry."

"One can do nothing. You will have to talk with the ministry."

"What ministry?"

Looking me in the eyes for the first time, he shrugged, the gesture of bureaucracy everywhere. Why did I bother? In my heart I knew the answer.

Recognizing a stone wall, I pleaded for a phone call. He grunted, and I fell back on a ploy used successfully in other binds.

6

Showing the lieutenant a telephone number in my address book for one of the Revolution's most respected and loved combatants, Che Guevara, I demanded a call to clarify my position. The name of el Che seldom failed to impress Cuban bureaucracy. My unwilling friend picked up the phone and dialed some three-digit number within the airport. He didn't ask my name.

"I have *el Americano* here. He wants to know why he cannot leave."

Then something indistinguishable about el Che. Tiredly dropping the receiver back into its cradle, he said, "You cannot leave."

I wished he'd tell me something I didn't already know. "Why?"

"You have a ranch in Pinar del Río?"

"Yes."

"You have a mortgage on that ranch?"

"Yes."

"*Bueno*, that is why you cannot leave." And he looked rather pleased with himself.

Realizing the futility of argument, I tore back to the check-in counter to get my bags off the plane, still in position, ramp withdrawn, propellers turning. My two bags were there at the counter where they must have been all morning. If never loaded, my restraining order had been known since check-in. Had the plane been held all those hours for some bureaucratic tug of war as to whether or not I should leave? I didn't buy the story of the mortgage. My mental alarm sounded louder still.

Resigned to losing my flight, I took a cab to the central office of the Banco Nacional. One of the senior officers, a lady I knew from embassy receptions, took my problem in hand. After three phone calls, she said the ranch mortgage was no obstacle; the bank had issued no holding order. The only other ministry interested in prohibiting departures from the country was the Ministry of the Interior, or G-2, the security forces. I could no longer pretend other reasons. I had no more doubts. From a pay phone outside, I called an embassy number and set off for my apartment, wondering what, perhaps who, I might find there.

My *pied-à-terre* in Havana was at 464 San Lazaro in one of the three penthouses sharing the top of a crumbling nine-story office-apartment building fronting the ocean. From the street, all seemed normal. With a taste of pennies in my mouth I took the ancient lift to the eighth floor and climbed the last flight of stairs, spiraling around the rusty iron grill enclosing the wheels, cables and levers of the old

Otis elevator. My two suitcases were heavy. I was tired and afraid and held back from unlocking the door, standing there listening. The rustle of paper, the squeak of a chair, heavy breathing? No, the breathing was mine, otherwise silence. I turned the key and opened the door to the stagnant air of closed windows. All as I had left it twelve hours before.

I double locked the door, and with a knife from the kitchen pried loose the third tile from the left directly under the window sill in the bathroom. Behind this tile was a four-inch-deep cavity, an imperfection in the building I had discovered. I pulled out the few pages of coded names hidden there. With copies in the States, and no further need of them, I carefully burned them one by one in an oversized ashtray, and flushed many years of hard work down the toilet. From the mop cupboard I took a can of baking soda containing cement, made a mixture of cement and toothpaste in the same ashtray, and remorticed the tile. I opened windows and the terrace door. Perhaps the ocean breeze would clear the pre-thunder atmosphere of the stuffy apartment. I skimmed the top off my suitcase for immediate needs and showered. With a towel around me, I took a strong Bacardi and lime to my rooftop garden to sort out my thoughts.

The entanglement in my self-spun web of intrigue had turned into a third war for me. This turned back the pages to the Second World War and the three years in the Pacific with the U.S. Army Air Corps, flying radar-navigator in a night-fighter squadron. Participation in the invasions of Iwo Jima and Okinawa brought some pretty ribbons, a few grey hairs, and a new maturity that nudged me in the mistaken direction of higher education.

In college, my new maturity proved unripe. I weathered the freshman year badly at Harvard. The women's college of Radcliffe was too nearby and Boston and New York debutantes much too attractive. My studies suffered. So did I. Post-war restlessness had mental discipline on hold, and I thought it wise to exchange grey flannels for Levis, Boston for Wyoming and the family ranch.

Much of remote-mountain ranching is horses. No hardship for one who mistrusts mechanical things, feeling helpless when they stop, as so often they do. Contrary-wise, with a horse—a moment's rest to attend to the mechanics of nature, and he's off again with no tinkering at all. A horse is warm friend, a machine only cold Detroit. I can love a horse, not a McCormick-Deering hay baler.

Happy ranching was interrupted by Air Force reserve status recalling me for two years in the Korean War. Based in Japan, our night-fighter squadron flew missions over the Sea of Japan at the intriguing confluence of Korea, China and Russia. With few targets on my radar scope, my pilot and I, to stay awake, were reduced to word games over our intercom. I won still another pretty ribbon.

Soon after my return from Japan the Wyoming property was sold. By 1955, I was scouting land for a cattle ranch in Cuba. Married to a Belgian girl a year later, my father-in-law became interested in a Cuban investment. A ranch lain fallow half a century or more, Finca San Andrés became our property in my father-in-law's name, the only Belgian property in Cuba. From Bainfaic, a government bank, I secured a long-term mortgage on the land to improve the property and purchase cattle.

Our ranch straddled la Sierra de los Organos, the east-west mountain range forming the backbone of Cuba's westernmost province of Pinar del Río. We built high in these hills against the very base of a massive rock formation. Ten miles to the north, across valleys green with royal palms, sugar cane, and pineapples, was the Gulf of Mexico. To east and west, the serrated tops of lesser hills carried the eye to two horizons. To the south was Pico Grande, that rock escarpment against which we had our house. Each passing hour of sun modified this panorama with changing colors. Wandering rainstorms changed it too, while the night worked yet another metamorphosis on this wonderous land below us. The ranch was all up and down with scarcely a level bit to it, but from its fertile earth grew guinea and pangola grass, excellent for cattle. It was a generous land that we loved and respected, as we did the gentle Cubans, who worked for us and made the whole endeavor possible. The years were good to us. We had three sons, and the ranch with its Brahma cows and calves prospered.

But now, sitting alone on my Havana rooftop, a threatened CIA operative, I thought of what I'd accomplished. I had not used Castro's tactics in tumbling his predecessor, the corrupt dictator Fulgencio Batista. Not the random slaughter of innocents with bombs in restaurants and movie theaters. Not the rape and castration of mountain peasants, who, through real property refused their meager rations to Castro's troops. My tactics, orchestrated by the CIA, were first, establishment of cells: a foreman in construction, a voice in the restaurant syndicate, a naval officer, a man in Protocol, and another in the foreign office. Later, coordination of airdrops of arms and ammunition and explosives, counterfeit pesos, medicines, and on one memorable occasion, the hysterical *novia* (girlfriend) of an anti-Castro guerrilla chief.

9

It was not with any idea of espionage that I had taken the apartment. Only later did I see its advantages for contacts. The numerous people who lived and worked in the building gave anonymity to anyone coming in from the street. Whenever I met with one of my informants we sat on the terrace talking with the background music of a radio. No higher buildings from which to train binoculars or cameras on us, and as for my neighbors on either side, it was easier to see them than they me due to my arrangement of potted plants.

Why had I volunteered for espionage? In the beginning, the great patriotism of even greater youth, leading to a view of the spy trade as a fast lane to glamour, a chance to live on the edge rather than ease through life as an observer. My own decision, my own life, no arm twisting. At any time I might have cried quits. I didn't.

My time of reckoning had come. Yet why had I not been arrested at the airport? Bait to catch others? To get rid of a troublesome American did they expect, or want, me to seek embassy asylum? While I worried my thoughts, the sun set. The short twilight of the tropics passed into night, and I shivered. I found no answers, but I made a decision.

Chapter 3

There was no phone on the ranch. A telegram, relayed by rented jeep from the nearest town of Consolación del Norte, was the only manner of communication—and often arrived as if wrung through a word scrambler. My wife, Beatrice, was expecting for the weekend our good friends the Norwegian Ambassador and his wife, Lars and Clara Onsager. They would be leaving Havana early Saturday. I would see them the following morning, Friday, to explain the imbroglio and to let Beatrice know to expect me on Saturday. I intended to spend the next day and a half at the Ministry of the Interior sorting things out with the help of acquaintances there—if they still acknowledged me as friend.

Instead of a day and a half, I spent five thousand two hundred and thirty days and nights with the Ministry of the Interior.

Chapter 4

At seven thirty, Friday morning, I retrieved my Opel station wagon from the garage and met the Onsagers for breakfast. I declined their kind offer of embassy asylum. I never saw them again. They got as far as our ranch gate and were turned back by rifle-toting soldiers.

At nine thirty, I was at the reception desk in the Ministry of the Interior asking for Humberto Pessino, a soft-spoken, well-educated man from a previously wealthy family. As a university student, disillusioned with Batista's corruption, he had taken part in the March 13, 1957 palace attack. The poorly planned assault to kill Batista failed, and Humberto escaped to join Castro's guerrillas. With most of my Cuban friends long since exiled, I had fraternized more and more with the diplomatic crowd, both east and west, and had come to know Pessino through embassy receptions. We occasionally met for lunch in Havana at Floridita or Zaragozana where you could still have a decent meal and a proper daiquiri and chat each other up.

With his total abandon before food and drink, it was hard to imagine him soldiering in the mountains of Cuba, sleeping on the ground and playing cops and robbers with demoralized Batista forces. If ever trim and fit, it was hidden now under collops of fat on flanks and sideburned jowls. Suety, I guess you'd call him, except for the brain. There he was whippy and quick.

Humberto received me most cordially, proffering the customary *cafecito*, that strong aromatic Cuban coffee, perhaps the best in the world. I explained my problem.

Without a word he picked up his phone. The man he wanted was unavailable, but another heard him out and the reply was unfavorable. Frowning, Humberto replaced the phone, held up his hand indicating patience, and began writing. I was puzzled until he shoved the paper across the desk, simultaneously putting finger to lips for silence and waving his other hand around the room. A Big Brother warning.

I read his message: Comandante Mendieta not in till after four —lieutenant on phone knows your case—says only under suspicion as *contra-revolucionario*—do not try to see me again (this last underlined twice)—give me number to call at six tonight after I see Mendieta—strongly suggest embassy asylum—luck.

I scribbled under this the telephone of my apartment and pushed the pad of paper back at him. He looked at the number, tore off the page, and folded it carefully into his wallet.

"*Muchas gracias*, Humberto, for the coffee and telephone call. *Hasta luego*."

With less warmth in his voice than on my arrival, "It's nothing. *Hasta luego*."

Before the news of my infection should spread, I called José Luis Gallo in the protocol office of the Foreign Ministry. Through the Belgian Ambassador I had come to know Raul Roa, the Foreign Minister, whose ministry granted Cuba's entry and exit permits. Grasping at the smallest of straws, I thought to get Roa to reissue my exit permit and overrule the Ministry of the Interior's holding order. I might still leave on a Sunday flight to Mexico. Time was short. It was the beginning of a weekend, and odds were long for an overruling of the Ministry of the Interior where a suspected *contra-revolucionario* was concerned. But I remembered my father's poker lessons: never compound a weak hand with timidity.

José Luis was of the same background as Humberto, a family grown rich through Batista patronage and special trading privileges.

14

He had been schooled in the States. Later, he spent a year in prison for his anti-Batista political activities, and cooperated with Castro. Unable to see me until three that afternoon, I asked on the phone for an appointment with Roa Saturday morning.

"Larry, for Christ's sake, why don't you ask for something easy? Like bedding Roa's wife. O.K., I'll give it a whirl. Let you know at three."

What to do in the interim? The apartment repelled me, in my mind a trap. The idea of eating lunch repelled me, too. In times of stress, physical action is the thing. Had I been on the ranch I would have taken to my horse and gone off into the remedial solitude of the hills. In Havana I took to my feet and walked two miles of seafront along the Malecón, scanning my rooftop from the water's edge.

At three o'clock, the customary *cafecito* in José Luis' office, never dreaming in what radically different circumstances I would see him next in two-and-a-half-month's time. He would be in the same ivy league suit with black tassled loafers, but his wide smile and friendly countenance would be replaced with cold correctness.

"Well, now that you know what's happened, what do you think? Were you able to get me to Roa?"

"Impossible! He was with Fidel last night and must have had a royal flushing out. In such a lousy mood today he even cancelled an appointment with the Russian Ambassador. And no one in Cuba does that without one helluva good reason. Forget Roa today. Maybe tomorrow. I'm real sorry, Larry, but that's all I can do. Call me Saturday around ten. If I were you, I wouldn't wait to see Roa. I'd get my ass into an embassy. Quick."

"*Gracias, viejo*, I'll think about it." It was the third time that day I'd had that advice.

For over twenty-four hours I'd lived with the threat of arrest, but with the idea there was still something I might do, someone I might see, to avert the catastrophe. Now there was nothing more to be done, no one else of influence to see, and the nervous energy that had kept me going dissolved like the sugar in all the *cafecitos* I had had that day. The trauma of the last twenty-four hours weighed on me like undigested food. I felt tired and dirty and hungry. Two sandwiches and a beer on the way back to San Lazaro and I felt better. And better still after a shower and another beer on my terrace watching the sun set—my last for many months.

15

I waited till eight. Humberto never called, and really I had not expected him to. I didn't suppose there was more to be said, and had he talked with Comandante Mendieta, he had probably been told to stay away from me. I dressed, turned out all the lights, and left the windows open to the clear sky and ocean breeze. Closing and locking the door behind me as I left had been a truly prophetic act, had I but known it.

There was a French movie, *La Belle Americaine*, I had long wanted to see, and a comedy seemed the logical choice on a night like this. Good entertainment, but nothing could hold my attention. Returning home, I parked close to a corner cantina, a nightcap habit of mine. No inclination tonight for the false solace of a bar. I passed it by with a *buenas noches* to the young barkeep at the door with whom I'd uncapped so many beers. He returned my greeting strangely, raising both arms above his head, hands clasped. Only in retrospect did I recognize it for the kiss of Judas, the sign to those waiting in the shadows that their man had arrived. His gesture was blotted from my mind thirty seconds later.

A chronic shortage of power produced a partial blackout on the street, giving a midnight pedestrian the impression of navigating a forbidding coastline with shadows jutting into headlands and others receding into shallow coves. From one of these black and sinister headlands they pounced. One moment alone, the next surrounded by four civilians with drawn pistols. Instinctively my right hand went to protect the wallet in my hip pocket. At once my arms were mobilized from behind and bent sharply upwards, suggesting more pressure in reserve. A frisking produced the wallet. My arms were released. I stood quietly, strangely unafraid, and asked who they were. There seemed no doubt in their minds as to who I was. In the beam of a pencil flash the older of the four presented his G-2 identity card, Lt. Juan García Pérez, and formally arrested me. They led me to their '59 Mercury sedan under the wide-eyed stares of the bar's late customers. There was no one else around. I had parked directly behind their car without giving it a glance. It resembled all the cars of Cuba, tired, disreputable and falling apart. It carried no special plate or insignia and passed incognito on its official rounds of arrest and harassment. I was shoved into the back seat between two of the young toughs, pistols in one hand, free arms linked with mine as if the best of friends. The third took the wheel with the lieutenant beside him. In true gangster style, the souped-up Mercury accelerated in seconds to fifty on the deserted narrow streets while the lieutenant extracted a radio transmitter from the glove compartment to announce mission accomplished.

From the first, my reaction was more outrage than fear, and as the car swerved around late traffic I remember shouting, "What a stupid way to get us killed. Must you show off your crazy driving just 'cause you've captured an *Americano*?"

And to the lieutenant, "It's just as stupid as arresting a man on the streets of Havana with four drawn pistols."

To my surprise he said something in a low voice. We slowed down. My two buddies in the back seat clutched me tighter. This *gringo* wasn't behaving according to the book. It upset them. I suppose my completely irrational outburst was reaction to shock, although unconsciously I had been prepared for this finale to what Kipling called "the great game that never ceases day or night and only ends when everyone is dead." I was far from dead, and at forty-two had no wish to die in one of G-2's old rustmobiles.

Wearing my outrage as protection against cold reality, something quite unbidden came to help me, and was to stand me in good stead for many years. I began to feel a clear, detached curiosity about my fate and looked with interest at my companions and the route we followed to the headquarters of Castro's secret police. My indignant outburst left me nothing more to say, and we drove in silence through the sleeping city. I felt the tension in the arms that circled mine. Sensing my lack of fear, they seemed more nervous than I. This lack or lapse of fear surprised me, perhaps only held in abeyance by the adrenaline stimulating my whole being. Perhaps as outrage gave way to passivity, fear would yet come in.

As if time had any importance now. I remember looking at my watch when bundled into the car. Eleven twenty. On arriving at G-2, I inadvertently checked again. Eleven forty. Not very important this piece of information. A point of reference all the same, providing a tenuous line of continuity from a past I knew to the uncertain present. In the months ahead I was often to wonder what hour it was, trying for a glimpse of my interrogator's watch. It made me feel no better to know for I used the knowledge to place my family in their accustomed activities at that time, visualizing each at play or work or sleep. A futile exercise in nostalgia that did nothing positive for my morale. I was a neophyte in the game of prison survival and had the whole course to run.

G-2 in Havana, national headquarters, occupying a block of residential suburb. The land originally a summer retreat for some wealthy family. The Victorian mansion still stood, administrative offices and two containment suites for VIPs under investigation. Newly attached to this, a three-story cement structure with cells for the men and women detained there, interrogation and visiting rooms. I learned the layout later. Two gates breached a high brick wall imprisoning the land within: one to the north for officials and visitors, another to the south for the busy traffic of paddy wagons, souped-up Mercuries such as I was in, and other vehicles concerned with the business of security.

The lieutenant radioed in two blocks south. The heavy chain across the gate was down and we shot past the sentries and their submachine guns into a walled compound of trees and flowers and manicured lawns—cosmetics to hide the ravaged countenance of secret police headquarters and the misery within. Outside the glass doors to the receiving room, clean smell of grass and flowers. Inside, white tiles, hospital antiseptic. Only the motley mismatch of chairs and benches suggested the lobby of some third-rate hotel— furniture requisitioned from imprisoned or fleeing Cubans. At the tiled check-in counter I filled in a form with name and address and next of kin. Above my name, a typed number, 1256—my first loss of identity. On a large manila envelope the soldier in charge wrote my new identification and the contents: everything from my pockets, my wallet with the money scrupulously counted, and my watch. The watch showed eleven forty-five.

Then, fingerprinting and photographs, and on through a small wooden door into a low, tunnel-like corridor no wider than a man's shoulders, leading to narrow stairs for the floor above. Here, the second loss of identity, exchange of civilian clothes for prison uniform. In my own underwear, socks and shoes, I pulled on a khaki-colored one-piece jumper, big enough for two.

With a soldier fore and aft, I was taken down a wide, clean, brightly lit hall, iron doors to either side, each with its judas window for spying on the prisoners, an eight-by-twelve-inch metal flap. The door to 59 stood open, half blocking the corridor. In contrast to the

18

corridor's bright lights, my cell was dark and ominous (how quickly one can think possessively).

For the first time that night I acknowledged fear. The door slammed shut—a super percussion effect that set my ears to ringing. My senses reeled and brought on that ghastly claustrophobia long forgotten: my childhood nightmares of burial in a collapsing tunnel. With the closing of the door, in a rush, the nightmares returned across the years to panic me again.

The feeling lasted as long as it took to pivot on my heels and raise both arms to face the iron. I remained frozen in that position for, I suppose, seconds, although minutes it could as well have been. Time had little meaning now. Panic subsided, sanity returned, and my arms dropped to my sides. I leaned against the guardian door and pressed my forehead to the coolness of the iron. Suddenly and wearily overwhelmed, my reserve of adrenaline-given courage ran low. I felt crushed by helplessness. I felt lost and already forgotten. Then through the blackness of depression and self-pity came a spark of that cold, detached curiosity that had supported me earlier. The psychological effect of sudden and total isolation gradually gave way to reason and I looked beyond myself at the tight confines of my cell.

It didn't take long to see the poverty. Six-feet-by-ten-feet with one half the width taken up by two wooden bunks, suspended by wall chains one above the other, and a shower with the open drain as toilet. Three-feet-by-ten-feet of floor space remained for movement, four short paces from door to far wall, four back again. Above the door, behind heavy mesh wire, a low-wattage bulb accentuated the dreariness. Above that, three inverted-V cement louvres admitted a drizzle of light from the hall, complementing what little daylight came from similar louvres in the outside wall. I could see nothing through these louvres, but I tried a dozen different ways to catch a glimpse of sky. The spoon-chipped edges testified to the futile efforts of others to free at least the eye. The walls were covered with names and initials, dates and crude calendars, prayer fragments, verbal defecations on Fidel and other traitors, and as always, where man must advertise himself, a heart or two pierced by arrows.

That first night I noticed none of this in detail. There would be time, and time again, to examine this cement box until I knew intimately every square inch. After the initial inventory I fell to pacing wall to door, door to wall.

Under such conditions the power to imagine accelerates and exaggerates every thought beyond reality. The fate of family and employees loomed larger than the surrounding gloom. Memory, unaccustomedly sharp and clear, brought back the counter-revolutionaries hidden at one time or another on the ranch, implicating my foreman, one of the *vaqueros*, and the gardener, all of whom had carried them food and clothing. Only one of these counterrevolutionaries had been caught, but I wondered if before being shot he had broken and told of the good Samaritan efforts of ourselves and others.

Chapter 5

Batista fled Cuba on New Year's Eve, 1958. On the back of the Revolution, Castro mounted the ex-dictator's saddle January 1, 1959. Within one year, his political drift to the left was chartered and the first counterrevolutionaries appeared. My initial enthusiasm for "the new broom" changed to disgust, and when from time to time I was asked to hide a local peasant fallen foul of the regime, I willingly agreed. Part of our property was *magote*, a rough and tumble rocky jungle that neither horse nor cow could penetrate. There were many natural caves, and even a spring or two, so that with the benign tropical climate it was ideal terrain for hiding out in—if one had food. This we provided. Whenever a man we knew wanted hiding he had only to come to my foreman to be taken into the refuge of the *magote*, and shown some landmark, a certain tree or stone, for the daily food drop. With a burlap sack of cooked food on our saddle, either I or another would provision him for as long as he stayed. A frond from the mountain palm hung upside down at the food drop was signal that our man had gone.

Out of the dozen or so counterrevolutionaries we had sheltered, the only one caught was Chicho Suárez. He had owned his own few acres and a two-ton truck, earning sufficient money to maintain two women in two homes, each with her gaggle of children, and *una querida* on the side, a comely girl of fifteen miraculously unfertilized by this mountain Lothario. Through a Havana agent of ex-President Prío, Chicho had been recruited for sabotage. From Florida, Prío sent light planes by night to parachute arms, ammunition and explosives onto the north-coast savanna where Chicho retrieved them to cache on his farm. Harem jealousy was his undoing. The oldest, and therefore the least attended, informed on him and he sought refuge with us. He stayed a fortnight before we found the palm frond hanging upside down, undoubtedly the longest period of sexual abstinence Chicho had ever endured. G-2 caught up with him at his *querida's* house. Two weeks later he was shot. None knew what he had confessed. Now I wondered if this were my dyke's first hole. And a radio operator in one of my groups, arrested several months before me? Was he the second?

Chapter 6

A sharp report and blinding corridor light shattered my trance-like state. The drawing of the heavy iron bolt and opening of the door was simultaneous. Rubber-soled boots gave no warning of patrolling guards. With a jerk of the thumb I was motioned out and back in the direction I'd come earlier that night. A walk I was to know all too well. Only the destination changed according to the psychological play of the moment. Down the hall and to the left to that rabbit warren of windowless interrogation rooms. Most of them small with space for a desk and padded chair for the interrogator. For the prisoner, that devil's chair with the back's imperceptible inverse curve. There were two larger rooms, each with four comfortable chairs grouped around a low table, and one library with lounge chairs and curtained windows. For my second interrogation one of the larger rooms had been chosen, but not with any idea of putting me at ease.

As if on remote control, always walking ahead of the guard, turning left or right as directed, I stopped just beyond a closed door, face to the wall. Confused by the tongue-clicking and short, sharp whistles from the guard on our brief walk, I later discovered they were identifying sounds to warn other prisoner-herding guards. To avoid confrontation, an incoming prisoner stood face-to-the-wall until the other had passed. A peek was a truncheon across the back, a wide, dull pain that made you gasp for breath. My keeper knocked. A muffled voice commanded, "Enter."

The door was flung wide with a, "*Señor*, prisoner 1256."

Three of the four chairs were occupied by men in uniform, but as was then the custom, no sign of rank. The Man was not among them. One, with long nasal hair and heavy-lidded lizard eyes, motioned to the fourth chair. As I eased into its softness he gave a supercilious laugh, intended, I supposed, to increase my already intense sense of doom. I looked first at one unpleasant face, then the other, finally at my shoes. A carefully prepared script, but not for me to break the silence. Tiring of my shoes, I looked at each of them again, returning stare for stare. When the time came, they opted for a frontal attack. It came with a roar from the man who had seated me with the point of his chin, and so startled me I understood not a word, and remember wondering what language he had used. Another roar from one of the others, echoed by the third, and back again to Number One. A fugue in Spanish played fortissimo so that the recurrent theme escaped me until I caught the word *guapo* many times repeated, and realized they were harping on my *bold* outburst in the car. My *presumptuousness* had been reported and was to be their opening theme in that first of so many interrogations.

"So you think you're *guapo*, hey?"

"Nobody's *guapo* here."

"Your days of giving orders are over, *Americano*."

"From now on you'll take the orders."

"You don't like taking orders, do you, *Americano*?"

"You can't play the *guapo* with us."

"How you feeling, *Americano*?"

"Still feeling *guapo*?"

"Not so nice taking orders from a *Latino*, hey?"

"Were you *guapo* with your *peones*? Hey, *Americano*, speak up."

"What's the matter? Not feeling so *guapo* anymore?"

"Come on *maricón*, talk to us."

Having set the stage with *guapo*, they moved on to the natural arrogance of North Americans and their superiority complex towards the Latins. My sense of national superiority established,

24

they began to tear it down with their victory at Playa Girón, or the Bay of Pigs as gringos liked to call it. They harped on their moral victory following the missile crisis (Kennedy had been unable to make on-the-spot inspections). The racial problems we would not solve, the low morality of the American people, the lies of our presidents (Eisenhower promising the Russians we had no overflights at the time of Power's U-2 incident). And other topics, their roots in truth, but grafted with the branches of scurrilous innuendos, Marxist hypocrisy, lies and propaganda. So far, it had been a three-pronged harangue aimed at my Yankee conscience demanding no reply. Once or twice I had ventured an interruption.

"No, that's not true. It's not possible. You're wrong. How—"

They juxtaposed unrelated melodies, coming together in discordant clashes. They were a shout band and I was shouted down. I settled myself more comfortably to wait them out. My gesture caused a change in tactics, or the other side of the record they were playing. Abruptly the melody switched from national attack to personal. They knew everything about me, my friends and contacts, my subversive work, everything. No sweat though. The Revolution was humane. With cooperation I'd get off smelling like a rose. Without cooperation it'd be lilies. I'd not be the first American to die by their firing squads, nor the last they assured me. The threat of death, then and later, never bothered me. The only proof of anything warranting such a sentence lay safely outside of Cuba.

They seemed at last to be winding down. I tried my voice.

"You're making a mistake with me. I don't know what you're talking about. If you know so much about me I've nothing more to add. I want to see the Swiss Ambassador."

"No ambassador is going to see you. No ambassador is going to save you. Only a full confession. Start talking, *Americano*, start talking."

This turned into a chant of the three, first one and then the other. An effective team that must have practiced often, for with no apparent sign between them, the chant ended as suddenly as it began. With a disgusted and tired gesture, Number One called the guard to click and whistle me home.

Returning to 59 was not the earlier traumatic experience. No longer unknown, the cell represented the only thing for the moment that *was* known, that belonged to me, barren and forbidding though it was. I felt bone tired, fell onto the lower bunk, and slept immediately, neither caring about nor noting the lack of mattress.

Was it a minute or an hour before that infernal noise of iron on iron rattled me awake? A guard at the open door, slamming the handle back and forth, telling me to hurry. Prison was always hurry, hurry, an integral part of discipline. Much later I would learn to hurry slowly. Still half drugged, I followed directions from behind to be parked face-to-the-wall before a different door. Eventually I would know them all. This was one of the smaller interrogation rooms, and only Number One awaited me there behind the desk. Alone he seemed less foreboding.

He gestured towards the chair. On the desk beside an ashtray were Cuban cigarettes, the kind for export only, and matches. He pushed them to me. Had he done his homework on my file before him, he'd have known I didn't smoke. Or perhaps he did know and this was just part of the ritual to establish a false sense of camaraderie between prisoner and interrogator. I didn't like this new *let's be buddies* approach.

"Look, Larry, at this file we've got on you. A good four inches thick and this is only a part of it. Be sensible and we'll go easy on you. I don't like treating an intelligent man this way."

In Spanish, always in Spanish, my interrogations. A mistake. I soon learned the small privilege of a foreign language: *I don't understand.* In the case of Number One, as I later learned, he had no choice, with no command of the English language.

"Look, I'm sorry we had to stick you in that cell. All we've got for the moment. Tomorrow we'll see if we can't make you more comfortable. What do you need?"

"Everything."

And not yet knowing the game, I enumerated my necessities from toothpaste to mattress, a department store shopping list. He assured me it would all be forthcoming. *Mañana*, always *mañana*. Promise the prisoner everything and give him nothing. Raise his hopes, dash them down. Give him a whole package of cigarettes in his cell—but no matches. Keep him off balance. Break down his self-confidence and morale, his morals, too, if you can. Humiliate him, lie to him, promise salvation. Keep the pendulum swinging from bad to good, from hard to soft, sharp to dull, from the heat of hell to the cool of respite. I had all of this to learn.

He continued in his role of friendly advisor, not inquiring too deeply into any one subject, advising man-to-man cooperation for my own good. I nodded acquiescence, keeping thoughts and determination to myself.

"You know, Larry, this isn't your revolution. No reason to suffer the consequences of a few misguided Cubans. Cooperate with us and you'll be back on that beautiful ranch with your wife and kids where we need you for raising beef by the way how did you know Cara Linda?"

This was to become a common tactic. A question quite irrelevant to the preceding subject, loaded with dynamite. An interjection with no change of voice, a single sentence without continuity of meaning. Later, through exhaustion, I acquired a *prison lag*, and noting its effectiveness with the sudden question, nurtured it to protect me from surprise.

The name Cara Linda shocked my dulled senses into fresh awareness of where I was and what I was up against. The first fear, the first knowledge that involvement was real and personal and far removed from any ho-hum life. The astonishment on my face I tried to pass off as injured innocence, admitting I'd heard of the man, as who hadn't in our province, but denying acquaintance. Unexpectedly this new direction was not continued, and still relaxed, he said, "Well, I guess we've had enough for one night. You must be tired. I'll see you again tomorrow."

I saw him maybe half a dozen times after that, but never alone and never again the "friendly advisor."

Chapter 7

Ignacio Sánchez, alias Cara Linda, Pretty Face, had been a captain in Batista's army and the right-hand man of the sadistic and repressive General Menocal, chief of the army in Pinar del Río province. Of peasant stock, Cara Linda learned to read and write, but little more of intellectual value. To escape the hopeless poverty of his class, he took the army uniform, and with brute intelligence climbed to officer rank. He earned the esteem of his superiors until repression and corruption came to him as naturally as hunting prey came to a barracuda. During these years of insurrection against Batista he won a certain notoriety as torturer and murderer. On the Revolution's hit list, he was among the first to be arrested in January 1959. His record: one hundred and eight proven killings, fifty-three more under investigation, and an undetermined number of rapes and castrations. Before he could be shot, he escaped, taking to the hills with stolen arms and ammunition to live the only way he knew, by violence. As a gangster he was feared, but sheltered by those who saw in him their champion against a new detested dictatorship.

Cara Linda knew well our mountain range, la Sierra de los Organos, and fit comfortably into its peaks, valleys and forests. With ammunition supplied for his M-3 submachine gun by sympathizers in the army, and food and clothing from family and friends, he roved his territory at will, shooting up government trucks and official cars, setting fire to cane fields, burning depots of government supplies, and a house or two of military personnel. He drew the line at shooting soldiers. With time, he hoped some of them would join him. His was a lone voice in a society of fear, and though many admired his guts, few threw in with him.

He had almost been caught one night when a prearranged rendezvous with his girlfriend from Los Pozos had somehow been leaked to the military and the trysting ground surrounded. But his cool thinking and the stupidity of the troop commander had saved him. He had fired at the voice in the night demanding surrender and then lain quiet while the troops caught each other in their crossfire, leaving him to slip away in the confusion. He became more cautious and for safety's sake gave up his girlfriend.

In the summer of 1961, he sent a message through Lino, local taxi-jeep driver, asking to meet with me. My reply that he come to the ranch was countered with an invitation to meet on his turf—twenty miles by road, four as the bird flies. I felt uncertain about making contact with this amoral man, but the sabotage he practiced and his continual harassment of Castro's forces put him squarely on my side of the political fence. He was an ally of the moment and therefore to be cultivated.

Three nights later I sat in a palm-thatched hut not far from the north coast and drank coffee with an old peasant couple, whom Lino had introduced as *mi familia*. The word *family* in Latin society can be all-encompassing, gathering in close friends, the respected old and loved ones, and denoting a true closeness and confidence—the intention of this introduction.

The light smoke from green guayaba leaves, crisping at the edge of the charcoal fire, gave relief from mosquitos as we awaited the arrival of their son to guide us to Cara Linda. Perhaps the *cafecito* was providing time to check that none had followed me. When the old lady had half finished her home-rolled cigar, black and pungent enough by itself to rid the small shack of mosquitos, the dogs barked welcome to her son, according him more recognition than either parent did. The old lady, tipped in her chair against the wall, seemed only intent on sending her thoughts upwards with the smoke from her cigar, while the old man remained hunkered on the dirt floor by the kerosene lantern mending some leather. The son acknowledged my presence with an appraising glance, said something to Lino, and motioned us to follow. I had brought a flashlight he didn't want. I left it in the jeep and we filed out Indian fashion into the pine woods, the dogs obediently remaining behind. A five-minute walk brought us to an abandoned corral. Our guide's whistle materialized Cara Linda from the obscurity of the moonless night.

Lino, the old and trusted friend, received a strong embrace, while my welcome was a firm hand clasp, held longer than usual, perhaps to gain confidence in this *Americano*. The man's total lack of morals, his hands stained with the blood of innocents, represented all I hated, and yet here I was, my hand in his, greeting him as friend. Hypocrisy too I hated, and yet, I played it to the full. Espionage is a dirty game. Despite my preconceived dislike, while our hands held contact, I sensed a strength of character and a strange affinity with this anti-communist guerrilla. The spell lasted as long as our hands touched. And in that moment there had been strong chemistry between us. If he were the means to further the breach in Castro's wall, then I hoped to help him.

Only vague outlines gave substance to the scene, like a charcoal-surrealistic drawing. I could not make out his face, only a sturdy, bulky six-foot height, dressed like any peasant in loose-fitting trousers and shirt of indeterminate color. He wore no hat, and slung over his shoulder was his M-3, his left hand never leaving the grip. Had he not drawn attention to his boots I'd not have noticed. He proudly explained he had them from a foreign technician, ambushed the previous month in his jeep.

He said he desperately needed fully automatic arms of a heavier caliber, and ammunition. With an updated arsenal he thought to hold the few men he had and attract more, building a guerrilla force in the mountains as had Castro. I longed to explain the difference between his fight and Castro's. How there had never been any real test of force between Castro and Batista because of the U.S. State Department's arms embargo, and the general ineptness of Batista's army, and how *The New York Times* had manipulated public opinion with their pro-Castro reporting while the Revolution was still in its infancy. To explain how conditions now were totally different, that he was only a Don Quijote, with inadequate Sanchos to help him tilt at hammer-and-sickle windmills.

Sure of Cara Linda's ignorance of the hypocrisy in international politics, I felt ashamed to play armsbroker and a part in what might well be his death. But if not me, someone else, and at least in me he had an honest agent, one who would do his best. I lied that I had no connection with the U.S. Government, but would inquire through embassy friends about all he asked for and report results through Lino. Our handclasp of *adiós* brought back the magnetism of this man, only dimly seen but strongly felt. I wished him well before he disappeared into the night. I never saw him again.

To my request for Cara Linda's arms came a terse negative. I had either bruised another's toes or trod on turf not mine. But at least Washington was aware of his needs. I don't know if he got his arms, but without ever attracting more than ten or fifteen men he continued operating in our hills until 1962 before being ambushed and killed. He was twenty-nine.

Chapter 8

Back again to the hard bunk and instant sleep that even this new worry of Cara Linda couldn't keep me from. Two minutes or two hours later, that unbearable alarm of iron-on-iron rampaging into sleep. Half awake, I took the now-familiar route, my clicking, whistling guard in tow, back to the room of the first troika encounter. The three sat as before, comfortable in their soft chairs. Three sets of eyes held me standing to the lash of voices rising from easy conversation to infuriated roar. No let-up in questions and accusations, sometimes from one, sometimes from two or three together. The real tiredness of hallucinations was getting to me when Number One sprang up to push me with a glance into the fourth chair. I relished the comfort only momentarily before being engulfed in questions already asked.

"Just tell us who got you into this. Tell us who you worked with. This isn't your country. This isn't your affair. Leave it to the Cubans. Tell us all you know and you're out of here like that." And he snapped his fingers.

Like jacks-in-the-box one jumped up to question or refute while he who had just been shouting sat. And so it went till my head spun and my thoughts became a jumble. Still they persisted, at times leaning over me, eyes only inches from mine, or talking with backs turned to change the tempo of the play. My "no" had become an automatic and comfortable litany, broken at last by the guard. In a daze I returned to my cell, this time to find a diffused light seeping in through outside louvres. Dawn, or midmorning? No idea. And I was asleep before my head hit the hard pine boards.

As my unwound watch no more marked the hours from somewhere in its manila envelope, neither did I. I was taken from the cell at all times of the day and night for interviews that might last minutes, or hours. I would return from them to find a tray of lunch or supper, or the aluminum cup of watered breakfast milk, or even two of these together on the floor inside the door. I ate or drank without noticing what it was, more famished for sleep than any food.

And then I thought I was mistaken, for there seemed to be longer lapses between interrogations. I was being allowed to sleep. But no, it was so, and with respite from the drugged state of extreme fatigue came a clearing of my mind, a sense of fear and desperation born anew at recognizing the hopelessness of my case. Where was my initial bravado on being arrested, the curiosity detaching my mind from its surroundings to allow a kind of objectivity? To escape the insupportable present I drifted into the past, despite some inner voice warning me against meaningless retrospective dreaming. My salvation lay not in living on remembered things but for the future, putting my mind to this, *to think*.

Convalescing from the nightmare of the interrogation marathon, I began to think more rationally, to compose myself for the tilting match to come. I thought I had left no loose ends from which G-2 might plait a noose for me, though remembering the communist motto, "Give us the man and we'll find the charge." There were names and happenings to forget, and others to remember.

There was the name of my CIA handler, John Brightheim, and the Virginia address to which I had sent my coded letters. In my mind he became Robert Warner with the address of my Boston lawyer. I must forget the CIA "safe houses" in Washington and Arlington, Virginia where I had learned the rudiments of espionage. Mickey Mouse stuff for what came later. I must erase from memory the western embassy contacts in Havana, the case of the Russian in the Czech Embassy, whose name I never knew, my informants in three ministries, the location of the radio—and so much more. But above all, I must admit to nothing until the proof was brought before me.

Part of my CIA training had dealt with behavior under cross-examination. Compartment the mind and concentrate on imagined people or occurances to cover someone or something you wish to hide. With what facility the rules and regulations of The Game came back to me. Now to see if I could put them into practice. But as comprehensive as this training had been, I was still unprepared for the experience and the highly professional manner in which these investigators worked. And I could understand now how some weaken under the strain, lose all hope and begin thinking in terms of limited immediate advantages—a bit of information in exchange for a mattress, toilet articles, better food, anything to sweeten their bitter lot.

With more time in the cell, I saw the necessity to organize not only my mind, but my new life. How many days had I been there? Judging by the calendars and hash marks on the wall, man's first inclination on being imprisoned is to establish his place in time. I was no exception. I had been under more or less constant interrogation without real sleep for five, perhaps six, nights and days. I opted for five, and when the next tray arrived, as quickly as possible I etched with the spoon onto a clear space on the wall the thirty-one days of May. I crossed off the first six as free, the next five as prisoner. Like a wild animal I had made my mark.

And with that mark it was as if an epoch of my youth had ended, a revolution in my way of life breaking up the old to give way to the new, to the growth of character and the recognition of influences yet to be understood.

Chapter 9

How to fathom the spiritual workings of the mind? How to *know* there is greater being than ourselves? A million theories with one simple proof not everyone can accept. The proof is in things unseen, but sensed. Sensed with such a force that none can doubt its genesis from a source beyond our comprehension, beyond our physical world. And now, suddenly, from some mysterious source came this greatest of revolutions. With no warning, no preamble, God came into my life.

It was as if I had spent my forty-two years in a false dawn awaiting this moment of sudden light-headedness, a true fullness of the heart and soul, a wondrous happening in the mind, a spiritual ecstasy. Unthinking, I fell to my knees before the outside wall and completely naturally and unbidden cried as I had never cried before. I cried unashamedly, wholeheartedly as if my heart would break. Without sadness, with a deep remedial strength-giving happiness. A true pouring out of the spirit, a baptism of the tears that coursed so freely down my face. My emotions spent, a lovely calm pervaded soul and cell and God seemed very close.

What triggered this sudden appearance of God? My religious inheritance had been poor. My family lived by the precepts of the Ten Commandments, though none of us could recite them. In most people, atheists or believers, there exists an innate goodness, or Godness, and perhaps one's daily life lived decently and well by His standards is all that is demanded until our spiritual maturity reaches harvest and we need Him and He is there. And yet, I had not wittingly called on God. He had called on me.

"Be thou obedient to this call, and be silent before the Lord, sitting alone with Him in thy inmost and most hidden cell—-So shall thy light break forth as the morning, and after the redness thereof is passed, the sun himself which thou waitest for shall arise unto thee, and under this most healing wings thou shalt rejoice." Jacob Boehme, a German, wrote this of inner meditation in the sixteenth century. My light had broken forth as the morning and I greatly rejoiced and was silent before the Lord.

I no more feared my jailers. I felt above them and realized with something of a shock that confinement was more a state of mind than physical condition. G-2 had my body, God had my soul.

Chapter 10

Before my arrest I'd only been involved. Now I was committed. Like ham and eggs. The pig's committed, the chicken's involved. My chicken days began in the early fifties through a chance encounter in New York with the owner of a small chemical company, George Gallowhur. Although divorced and a dozen years my senior, we found much in common and became good friends. In 1954, George wanted to complement his business with a cattle ranch in the Bahamas and invited me to Nassau as prospective ranch investor-partner.

George was an extrovert with an infectious 360° enthusiasm. Usually his blue eyes sparkled with the pleasure of living, but they could also turn cobalt hard when business demanded. And fair hair and Nordic features gave him an edge with women, an advantage he capitalized on outrageously. A keen mind gave him an edge in commerce and, as soon became evident, in another field as well—espionage.

While prospecting islands on a chartered cruiser, the real motive surfaced for inviting me to Nassau. The spin-off from questions and innuendos was an offer to join The Game, the CIA, to gather sociopolitical information in the Bahamas and adjacent islands, to use the ranch as a cover and a base for future espionage. The long-term planners in the State Department, the CIA, and others in the alphabet-soup hierachy, were increasingly aware of the nascent political unrest in the Caribbean, but lacked trained observers rooted there.

Why me? The coddled life of eastern preparatory schools and one college year had better prepared me for the social problems of Boston and New York than evaluating those of the Bahamas. Fancy decorations from two wars were of little use. What came closest to preparation was the rough and tumble Wyoming life, broadening one's perspective, and teaching self-reliance. Flattered to be considered intelligence material, I ignored that even a six-year-old child can have his use in The Game. The James Bond syndrome attracted me. A fallacy. The popular concept of intelligence work is so completely colored by the paperback that the black and white of it is less easy to believe. All the same, I was genuinely pleased to be a part of it.

Two weeks of checking the more promising islands decided us on Eleuthera where a dairy herd was flourishing. Negotiations were begun, then mysteriously terminated. Government doors, hospitably open, suddenly closed. Puzzled and annoyed, we objected. The property we wanted was no longer available. From Washington came the advice to forget the Bahamas and try the Dominican Republic. A second no-go. Much later it was explained that the two governments got wind of our intentions and wanted no part of our clandestine operations. A case of the British lion showing a rare bit of solidarity with the Dominican fox, or a mole in our hole? We suspected the latter and turned to Cuba.

It didn't matter so much to the CIA on which island I established a ranch, as long as it was in that Caribbean corner. They had not foreseen the problems to be encountered in Cuba.

I went alone to Cuba. As before, my first concern was land. A banker's letter of introduction led me to speculators, realtors, and ranchers wanting partners. One of these was Dave Gilbey, with large inherited holdings on the north coast of Oriente, Cuba's easternmost province, a ranch accessible only by boat, consisting mainly of forest. Land rich, money poor, he wanted a partner to harvest timber and develop pasture.

The ranch met the maritime requirements of easy access for CIA ships, and my own for the remoteness and challenge of these still-wild mountains. Through the banker I made the necessary arrangements. There was no telephone. Weather permitting, communication and travel were by a fifty-foot motor launch plying the ocean between the small fishing village of Baracoa and United Fruit's sugar refinery at Moa Bay.

The launch was primitive, like a rural Mexican bus, each passenger with his or her garden produce, livestock, multitudinous children, and ample nourishment for the journey. The only cabin was small and stank of petrol. A tarpolin roofed the after-deck and covered a sand box at the stern for anyone wishing to cook over charcoal during the day-long run.

There were no docks at the small bays we entered to load and off-load. Our waterbus rolled and pitched while skiffs lightened or added to our passenger-baggage manifest, and at the same time offered all sorts of tempting food: fruits, tortillas wrapped in the fresh leaves of the corn from which they were cooked, eggs hardboiled and fried, and rice and beans with chunks of pork. Prices were minimal for one's choice of menu, deftly wrapped in huge plantan leaves that served as plate, napkin, and disposal unit. Proffered too were shot-size cups of very strong aromatic coffee, coconut water in its shell, and, at fifty cents, an amber liter of robust local rum.

At each bay we touched, the same performance was repeated. The menu never varied, only the decor of nature's restaurants, and when the sea was smooth there were few better places to eat and drink.

A most practical innovation on this public transport was the lack of any sanitary facility. An exercise in restraint for the proud, an exercise in hanging over the side, the lee side, for all others.

Late afternoon the launch turned in toward a high cliff with no visible anchorage in the restless sea at its base. Closer in, I made out a narrow pass, opening into a quiet inlet beyond, my destination. In the hill-sheltered lagoon the launch's dinghy set me ashore on a bit of sand beach with the directions, "Follow the path, you can't miss the house." I set off through frangipani trees with a Pan American flight bag, my only baggage, weighted more with my gift of two bottles of bourbon than with clothes. The exercise was welcome after

41

nine hours on a small boat, and, interested in the growth supported by the sandy soil underfoot, I came on the house by surprise.

A man was sitting outside in a kitchen chair tipped against the wall, staring south towards the mountains, one foot on an empty case of rum, the other lying beside him on the ground—a wooden stump. My "hello" brought his head around with no sign of welcome to the face. He rarely smiled. He didn't find life amusing, even after a liter of the local rum. Perhaps his wooden leg had something to do with it. I don't know. I never did hear how he lost it.

He brightened slightly at my self-introduction, bawled into space for another glass, and kicked his footrest in my direction.

"Sit down, sit down. Heard the boat. Didn't think it'd be bringing anyone for us. Never does. Where the hell's that glass?" And he bawled again.

A woman ambled out in faded Levis, army surplus shirt, and tennis shoes. She handed me a jelly glass and introduced herself at the same time.

"Hi, I'm the better half of that one-legged giant over there." And she jutted her chin in the man's direction.

Dave Gilbey paid his wife not the slightest attention, just held his hand out to me for the glass and filled it from a bottle at his feet. Mrs. Gilbey had her own inside. With neither electricity nor ice, they drank it neat, their first liter broached at eight, a second after lunch, the third around five. I had arrived opportunely on the crest of the wave when tempers were even and the marinated livers had not yet reached their daily saturation point, bringing on the bilious attacks of evening.

Dave Gilbey was in his fifties, his wife too, I thought, though she'd not stood the years as well. Women seem to take the hard knocks harder. Years best forgotten were etched on hands and face and around her eyes. Tropical dry rot had set into the soul of this climate-withered lady with the sun-worried skin. She'd given up a long time ago.

If Mrs. Gilbey looked the defeated, low-rent farm wife, Mr. Gilbey looked to be the landlord—and acted it, particularly when his wooden leg lay severed by his chair. With leg attached, he was as quick as their lean grey cat. Easier though to be one-limbed with a wife to run the errands. He had once been handsome. His strong features were a clone of an old Spencer Tracy, sunburned a deep mahogany brown. Tongue was a satirical scalpel to match eyes veined with red, eyes of furious dissipation, either blank and vague or staring at you malevolently, a man of violent mood swings, angry with his destiny.

Both college graduates, the Gilbeys had known better living than the two-bedroom, zinc-roofed shack they now inhabited. Giving up the furniture design business in Florida, they had come to Cuba in the thirties to manage the ten thousand acres of woodland her father had bought. The difficulty of lumbering in the remoteness of this bay, and the small demand for Cuban timber, had eaten away most of their capital through the years. But they had stayed on, always hoping for a road along their coast, bringing the anticipated fortune. Empty hopes kept alive with cheap rum, the classic case of the Anglo-Saxon gone to tropical seed.

My second evening there, a man in his thirties of light step and hard physique burned dark from the sun, walked into the Gilbeys' kitchen during our supper of fried eggs and rice. Dave Gilbey looked annoyed, his wife, delighted, and she knocked over a chair in her haste to fry more eggs. Only at my self-introduction did his name come out: John Polansky. It was a Polish name, though he claimed to be Italian. His backpack held the clothes and tools of a geologist. Swinging his pack to a peg on the wall without a by-your-leave suggested an intimacy with host and house alike, though they pretended otherwise. He and I shared the same room that night, but I learned no more than that he was a government geologist on the trail of manganese deposits. Finding him guarded and evasive to questions on his work, I accepted his turn to music and books, and thought no more about him until our next encounter four years later.

I stayed five days. After one I could have left, convinced there was nothing here for me with such a partner. I stayed longer only to walk the beauty of the mountains with their clear running streams, to swim off the white-sand beaches, and to cast a rod in the surf to augment the meager table fare. My two bottles of bourbon had broken their reserve more than my being potential partner. To their credit their welcome outlasted the bourbon. The bourbon was gone in two days. The welcome survived for five.

Soon after my trip to Oriente, and following a courtship of eight years, Beatrice and I were married. With George Gallowhur's tacit understanding, "we would stay in touch," my father-in-law replaced him as ranch partner. Towards the end of 1956, I found the property I wanted, Finca San Andrés, and within a year, began a house and land improvements.

Beatrice and I were happy there, although there were aspects of life I found distasteful to my Scottish-mother, Puritan-father upbringing. Foremost was the accepted practice of bribery from the president on down to rural guard, still riding the countryside on his American calvary horse. What rankled me more was the insensitivity and stupidity of many wealthy landowners toward the man with no land of his own, living from hand-to-mouth on the periphery of *el patrón's* vast and often unused, or ill-used, property. At pathetic pay, he was hired when needed, laid off when not, and dispossessed of his shack and square yards of ground at will. No rights. Law was on the side of money, morality be damned.

We heard of rebels, led by a man called Fidel Castro, fighting at the other end of the island in the Sierra Maestra Mountains. Over seven hundred miles away, it had no effect on our lives in 1957 and 1958. Most Cubans discounted this handful of guerrillas in eastern Cuba, as did most of the personnel in the American Embassy, except those who remembered the role this rebel leader played in Columbia in April l948, a rebellion known as the "Bogotazo."

The communists were threatening to disrupt the 9th International Conference of the American States in Bogotá with an anti-American show of force. Castro was among the organizers, actively participating in the four days of rioting that came close to toppling Columbia's democratic government. He fled Columbia with his anti-American, pro-communist convictions well established.

The history of the communist intelligence apparatus in the western hemisphere dates back to 1928 when Stalin's secret service, Tcheka, then in its infancy but with remarkable foresight, first dispatched an agent to Havana: a Pole, Fabio Grobart, with proven capacity in Russia's October Revolution, and personally chosen by Stalin. Even then the communists had recognized Cuba as ideal ground from which to infiltrate their agents north and south. Grobart had soon taken out Cuban citizenship and lived in Havana as an inconspicuous businessman, while increasingly active in the service of the Russians. With Castro's triumph in January 1959, he was still in place, unknown to all but a handful of loyal lieutenants and American Intelligence. By 1960, Grobart had organized "Bureau 13," the neophyte Cuban intelligence corps, within which is G-2, trained and equipped in Russia and East Germany. In 1954, Tcheka was reorganized to become the KGB. It is the KGB today which is very much in the driver's seat of the Cuban secret service and the more important ministries.

On first arriving in Cuba, my relationship with the U.S. Embassy had been purely social, and I'd not attempted to build on it, having no wish to plug myself into the Havana cocktail circuit. In the fall of 1957, a telegram invited me to call on one of the embassy attachés. In his office the following week, he cut quickly through the small talk.

"I believe we have a mutual friend, George Gallowhur."

Not quite sure where this was leading, "Yes, we were in the Bahamas together."

"And in the Dominican Republic as well, no?"

Understanding the drift, uncertain of the intent, "Yes, we were both there."

Now I better understood George's parting shot, "Since your father-in-law is backing you, I'm sorry we won't be ranching together, but *we'll stay in touch.*"

The attaché's next question came to the point. "I wonder if from time to time you'd mind dropping by to clue me in on conditions in your part of the island? For example, is there evidence of Castro's partisans operating in your hills, sympathy for his cause, or even an awareness of the man?"

These informal conversations took place until broken relations forced the closure of the U.S. Embassy in January 1961. My reports were of small importance in themselves, but gave substance and a differing interpretation to the composite picture. Information growing from my first report in 1957 on the people's ignorance of Castro to their increasing awareness, and then to almost total sympathy in late 1958.

My first direct involvement with the Revolution came unexpectedly in November 1958, the month of presidential elections. To no one's surprise, the government-supported candidate stole the show. The day before the elections I was returning from a hardware-buying trip. The sun was setting as I turned off the Central Highway onto the gravel road. It was fifteen miles in to the ranch, on this road that followed the contours of the hills, rising and falling to the easiest route originated years before by mule trains carrying charcoal to the plains below.

There was little daytime traffic, almost none in the evening. At the highest point before dipping into our valley, my sense of peace was abruptly shattered. A dozen bearded men, dressed in the manner of the peasant, all carrying semi-automatic arms, were blocking the road. It was a professional choice of site, a curve of road around the knuckle of the highest hill, which gave them the advantage of total surprise. An escaping turn was impossible.

Local gossip had reported a small group of insurgents forming in our mountains. Here before me was the proof, although all sorts of alternatives raced through my head: robbery, kidnapping, even mistake. With guns pointing to the ground, they stood to right and left and before my car. Quietly and courteously, the leader asked me out, and almost embarrassed, said my car was to be burned as protest against the elections. I might take anything I wanted from the car. They were neither detaining nor harming me, and regretted the necessity for destroying the property of a Yankee "so well-liked and respected" in the neighborhood. Unfortunately they must use *un destacado* to draw attention to their cause. The only American in the province, I suppose I was *well known*, though I didn't much like it.

The Buick station wagon, thoroughly doused inside with gasoline from jerry-cans they carried with them, flamed brightly for all the countryside to see. Momentarily mesmerized by the flames, I missed the men's silent disappearance into the dusk. One moment we were a group, the next I was alone with my ranch shopping in a pile beside me. I cached the ax handles, machetes, and other hardware well back from the road and started on the long walk home.

I could see the lights of our house across the stretch of valley at about the same altitude where I stood. For a bird, perhaps three miles. For me, closer to eight. I might have asked the loan of a horse at the first palm-thatched hut I passed, but after the emotional shock of my baptismal fire in the Revolution I was loathe to stir excitement at that hour and preferred the peace-restoring walk in the evening stillness. I needed to assess my feelings, why I felt no outrage at this act of piracy, no reaction of legitimate offense. An astonishment it had been, but in retrospect it seemed to have happened to someone else. I had been an observer, and as such, found myself sympathetic to these men, who in the only way they knew committed themselves to combatting the corrupt and often cruel Batista regime. That I had to lose my car for their ideals did not distress me as long as I shared those ideals.

The incident caused local excitement, but no interest from the newly elected government. A few days later, a strange message reached me through my foreman. It came from a man who claimed leadership of the provincial rebels, Franco Lemos, a truckdriver fallen from sight the previous spring. The message said none of his men were responsible for the burning of my car. If Lemos was telling the truth, and I believe he was, for what purpose would the Batista bully boys have done it? To discredit the growing influence of the Castro forces? An insignificant manner to accomplish that. And although I later came to know Lemos well, I never did discover the truth of it.

Toward the end of 1958, as rebel activity increased, army activity decreased until no longer viable. Sabotage and terrorism were widespread and no one seemed in control. Bombs were planted indiscriminately in movie theaters, department stores, and restaurants. Canefields were fired, banks robbed, and trains derailed. In spite of the instability of the government, the announcement January 1, 1959 that Batista had fled caught most by surprise, not the least of them Castro himself.

I participated in the general rejoicing throughout the island. I thought Castro's pronouncements from the Sierra Maestra indicated a new political maturity, a change from his anti-American, pro-communist convictions of student and Bogatá days. Those in the U.S. Embassy, who from the first had warned against Castro, assured me Cuba would be run into the Soviet corral like a docile bull, and there Castroted. Playing with words was one of the embassy pastimes during those first uncertain days.

For the next year there was not much I could report. Life changed but little, and I continued improving the ranch, naively trusting the Cubans' innate love of liberty to keep us free. I didn't yet understand that the communist discipline of a few fanatics would so easily overcome the indiscipline of six million Cubans with a small sense of social responsibility.

Never having been the object of social responsibility, the average Cuban could not in turn practice it, could not have the discipline that goes with laboring for the common good. (The exception to this I found in prison.) He may go about his own business and follow orders, but he does not initiate. Let *el patrón* do that.

Spanish feudal mentality still held in much of the countryside, especially on the large sugar and cattle *haciendas*. This mentality was worked indelibly into the natural texture of the people, making the Cuban more receptive and malleable to a changing social order. Castro's 26th of July Movement was the shuttle, the device to weave the essential element of this new cloth. Nationalism was the design. Once completed, the warp was found to be of different stuff. On one side, the national colors of red, white and blue, hammer and sickle on the other.

It was in keeping with the Maximo Weaver's manic character to shed those who might eclipse him in power or popularity. Camilo Cienfuegos, one of the Revolution's more respected and beloved *comandantes*, "disappeared" over Cuba in his small plane in October 1959. Che Guevara was abandoned to die in Bolivia without reinforcements for his guerrilla warfare. All the leaders of Castro's own 26th of July Movement were either killed or imprisoned. None would share the stage with this bearded prima donna. He would surround himself only with moons that would not outshine his sun.

From the remoteness of the Sierra Maestra, Castro had proclaimed a reasoned and well-thought-out agrarian reform. When published in May 1959, it washed quite a different color, stripping sugar mills of their cane fields, while assessing value at a fraction of their worth, no inheritance of agricultural lands (fatal to the peasants), prescribing crops and prices they could be sold for. Businesses were confiscated, and influential newspapers intervened, ending freedom of the press. The transparent mask of legality was discarded and properties were seized at random. Arbitrary decisions superseded laws, including Castro's own, and many enterprises passed to government control.

Cattle ranches, Cuban and American, were expropriated, very few in accordance with the law, allowing each rancher one hundred *caballerías*—3,330 acres.

Our five thousand acres, in my father-in-law's name and the sole Belgian property in Cuba, had so far remained inviolate. On the advice of a Cuban friend I kept low profile with INRA (Instituto Nacional de Reforma Agraria), the department responsible for taking over agricultural properties. His experience had proven the out-of-sight, out-of-mind axiom, and his property remained unexpropriated until the day he called on the INRA representative, who slapped his forehead and said, "*Coño*! I had forgotten all about you and your ranch. We'll intervene tomorrow." And they did.

In January 1961, not even the Belgian flag prevented the expropriation of one thousand acres of our ranch to the Revolution's voracious appetite. And so we joined the ranks of the semi-dispossessed to assess our reasons for staying or cutting our losses and getting out. Both Beatrice and I wanted to remain, but her third pregnancy, the breaking of relations between the United States and Cuba, and the deteriorating economic and political situation influenced our decision. She would return to Belgium with our two sons. I would remain to run the ranch as best I could under the Revolution's erratic new laws.

A year later, INRA took a second bite, everything but our house and garden. The Belgian Embassy objected strongly and six weeks later, the order was revoked.

For many months the plans for a United States invasion of Cuba had been an open secret. Only a question of where and when. Conceived under Eisenhower and implemented under Kennedy in an incredibly inept fashion, the invasion of April 17, 1961 took few by surprise. My wife and children had not yet left, and we learned of the landing at Playa Girón (the Bay of Pigs) through our own more-private invasion, the "taking" of our corrals at dawn by a full brigade. The "opposition" was twelve cows with their calves and the two milkers, all unarmed.

Like distant thunder interrupting the early-morning calm came the first indication of unusual traffic on our road. The labored rumble of heavy trucks gearing down to take the gentle foothills, followed by the harsh complaint of lower gears to meet the steeper slopes, until the head of a long, motorized column came into sight. Russian trucks loaded with soldiers, Czech anti-aircraft guns, a radio unit, all the baggage of an army on the move. Twenty trucks pulled into our corrals. Another ten continued, to set up roadblocks and check points further on. A young sergeant, in charge of settling into our corrals, bawled at the startled milkers.

"Hey, *chicos*, you're wasting time with those cows. The gringos are coming. They're going to cut off their tits and your balls if you don't haul ass out of here *pronto*."

This mighty army seen at such close quarters frightened both cows and milkers. Milk ceased to flow and my two men were only too eager to escape with half-filled buckets.

The soldiers set up a kitchen in a branding shed. In another, headquarters took shape with maps, radio, and one vintage Underwood typewriter. The Cuban army's interest in our corrals was tactical. Our ranch straddled the mountain range forming the spine of western Cuba. A gravel road, bisecting the ranch, linked highways east and west. Our corrals, fronting on this road, provided shelter, electricity and water. The swiftness and efficiency with which they settled in—closing the road, spreading patrols through the hills, establishing anti-aircraft posts—suggested anticipated plans for just such an invasion as was taking place one hundred and fifty miles to the east.

I was surprised at the army's apparent lack of interest in me and my workers. Had a beachhead been secured and the fighting become widespread there might well have been contingency plans for us, but it was not to be and we were virtually ignored. Our radio tuned to Florida, we remained glued to it that first day and night, hearing with joy the false optimistic reports.

"On this day, April 17, 1961, the Cuban Revolutionary Council (Anti-Castro CIA-backed Cuban exiles in Miami) announces a successful landing of military supplies and equipment in the Cochinos Bay area of Matanzas Province . . . Overcoming some armed resistance by Castro supporters, substantial amounts of food and ammunition reached elements of internal resistance engaged in active combat."

Later that day: "We predict that before dawn the island of Cuba will rise en masse in a coordinated wave of sabotage and rebellion to sweep communism from our country."

"On this day, April 18, 1961, peasants, workers and militia are joining the freedom front and aiding the rapidly expanding area already liberated by the Revolutionary Command."

Twenty-four hours later we were less sure of the landing's success, and by nightfall of the third day, knew of its complete failure. I was ashamed, stunned and angry at Castro's victory.

The Cuban army stayed with us a week, leaving an indescribable mess at the corrals, but with several hundred extra pounds on pigs I'd brought in to feed on the army's waste. Undoubtedly I was the only American to benefit from this ignominious defeat. It gave small pleasure.

My family's departure was accelerated, and the following month, with mixed emotions, I saw my wife and two sons—Antonio, four, and Michael, three—off to Belgium. They were to remain there for four years.

In June, my father-in-law suggested that I too leave Cuba, delegating responsibility for the ranch to some Cuban. I replied, "Not yet." My sister Faith was also concerned and forwarded a letter from a friend whose experience and opinion she considered apt. It said:

"I observed the takeover firsthand by the Chinese Reds in China. These same Chinese Reds are playing an important role in Cuba. When the Reds took over China, many businessmen stayed behind. Some stayed because they failed to understand the situation. Others stayed because of obligations to either their companies or their employees. Others stayed simply because of inertia. After the honeymoon of exuberance that at last there was an honest government, those who stayed behind found themselves hostage. Families or companies, anxious to get these hostages out, had to invest tremendous amounts of money before exit permits were granted. In your case the probabilities are that, if you remain, your family will have to pay large blackmail before you can leave. Although this may seem highly improbable to you, it certainly is important to think not only of yourself and your family, but what also those outside may have to do if communist history repeats itself in Cuba. It very well may."

It did. In retrospect I was only postponing history and the man in Washington was right.

Chapter 11

My family left in May 1961. In June, I was on a short visit with my sister Faith in Washington. I'd not been eighteen hours there before George Gallowhur's shadow once again crossed my path.

A buttoned-down, drip-dry, all-American man called to see me. Clothes and accent were Ivy League, his five-feet-ten appeared conditioned by tennis, and I would have bet two-to-one he drank martinis with a twist of lemon. I was off on the tennis, right about the martinis. Black leather briefcase and all, I invited him in.

His credentials seemed more the logical sequence of events leading to this meeting than a surprise. He was John Brightheim of the Central Intelligence Agency.

"Please sit down, Mr. Brightheim. How about some coffee? Good, just a minute while I ring for it. Now, what can I do for you?"

"If you're willing, quite a lot. We're getting an awfully mixed bag of information from the Cubans. We need confirmation by men like yourself. We'd want you to use a few people you can trust to help out on this. For instance, we need information on military movements, economic data on sugar cane and other crops, types of cargo loaded and off-loaded from ships, unusual construction sites, the Russian presence in the countryside, the counterrevolutionaries you know and your impressions of them. In fact, we want to know all you see and hear and feel."

Unconsciously I thought, Dear Lord, forgive U.S. our trespasses. Since the Monroe Doctrine of 1923, we'd been messing around in other countries' affairs, not always disinterestedly. Now, for the second time, here we were in Cuba, and I was a part of it.

"As you're undoubtedly aware, I was giving a rundown on local activities to an embassy attaché while he was there. You seem to want more detailed information."

"Yes, *much* more."

When he heard I knew many of the western diplomats, and sometimes went to their receptions, meeting the Foreign Minister, Raúl Roa, Che Guevara, and other bigs of the new society, he remarked, "We'd give a lot to get hold of Roa."

I topped his bid."Why not Castro?"

"You bring *him* in, and we'll give you his Swiss bank accounts."

He was looking for the dimensions of my capabilities as we talked, for more than an hour, dimensions of intelligence and the distance I would go. In the naive exuberance of youth, and intrigued at the chance to pluck a few hairs of Castro's beard, I was prepared to go the limit. He smiled like an indulgent uncle who'd heard such sentiment before.

"Then you agree to work for us, and you say you want no recompense?"

My response reached into memory—a carefree cattle cruise in the Bahamas that had started all of this, the beginning of things, never discernable to the eye.

"Yes, I want to do this, but I must have some training."

My reply was a pebble tossed into a pool of man waters where the ripples still persist.

Our second meeting the next day was across the Potomac in a Virginia "safe house" for the kindergarten course in writing cover letters with invisible messages between the lines. There were aspirin-like tablets in a Bayer bottle to dissolve in fresh milk for my reports, and other tablets to mix with iodine to develop Brightheim's between-the-lines instructions. Both could be harmlessly ingested. What I wrote as invisible, once developed, remained forever visible. Messages to me, once developed, remained two or three minutes before fading away—a safeguard for messages and agent alike in alien territory. And too, a pad of treated writing paper sensitive only to my ink.

My first report from Cuba in July concerned a spate of unusual activity—the chatter of low-flying helicopters violating the airspace of highflying hawks and buzzards, and an increase in Russian jeeps and trucks. We paid the military small heed unless they stopped for target practice on our pigs—too easily killed and roasted on the spot by soldiers tired of inferior rations. Pork on the black market at two dollars a pound was the mainstay of the ranch.

On one of these trafficky days, one of my *vaqueros* returned from riding fence to report a large group of armed men in our north section at a barn-size cave—source to a stream our cattle used. They'd told him to buzz off; I saddled a horse and rode for the pasture my man had been ordered away from. I didn't share the peasants' awe of a uniform, although I did for the soldier's casually carried gun with safety off, as apt to be pointed at one's head as the ground.

I found, not a heavily armed platoon as reported by my brave *vaquero*, but eight men in khaki, wielding nothing more lethal than surveying instruments. Realizing I wasn't one to be told to buzz off, they explained themselves in accented Spanish as a topographical team updating charts. As we talked, two men came from the cave conversing in what sounded like Russian to my untutored ear. They carried measuring tape, flash camera, and a device resembling a Geiger counter. One of them was John Polansky, the government geologist I'd met on Dave Gilbey's remote ranch in eastern Cuba.

The caves of this mountain range had always attracted geologists, spelunkers, extractors of rich deposits of bat guano, and even the old-fashioned medicine man, searching out the large *majá*, a harmless thick-bodied serpent peculiar to Cuba and prized by the peasants for the anti-rheumatic properties of its fat. But this was a first for the military, and I doubted the avowed purpose of map-making.

Polansky looked annoyed at seeing me, hesitated a step, then strode forward with hand outstretched. In his perfect English, "We meet again. You've caught me trespassing, I'm afraid."

I replied in Spanish with the customary Cuban greeting, a hint of cynicism in my voice. "My house is your house."

He remembered my name. "Well, Larry, you know, the law allocating mineral rights to landowners has been revoked. Now it's everything for the state. We're checking out old maps, and there's nothing better than these caves to give a reading on what's underground."

At the time, his story seemed convincing. In retrospect, it was evident the Russians were long curious about Cuba's substructure, sending in their own men for cursory investigations, laying the ground work throughout the island for the extensive subterranean installations done later.

Two months afterwards, I met Polansky once again at a Czech Embassy reception, a typical diplomatic cocktail crush, an extension of office hours for the various ambassadors and their aides, a chance to freeload for the others. To my amazement I saw Dave Gilbey chatting with the Czech Ambassador. A different man entirely from the rum-soaked plantation owner I'd met before. He wore a grey herringbone suit, white shirt and striped tie, but even from a distance had the air of frayed elegance about him. Polansky saw me first and left the lady he was talking to in mid-sentence to come and greet me. He looked hurried, or was it harried?

"Larry, what a surprise to see an American here."

"Good evening, John. What about our American friend over there?"

He looked distinctly uneasy now, and caught the elbow of a passing man to rattle off a sentence in a language I didn't understand. I did understand the tone of urgency, the command. With an arm firmly through mine, he turned me half-way around, away from Gilbey.

"Yes, looks a little like him. Come and help me make amends with the lady I was talking to. She must think me very rude to have left her so abruptly."

"John, if you don't mind, I'd like a word with Gilbey. I'll find you in a moment."

I turned out of Polansky's linking arm to face the corner where a moment before Dave Gilbey had been. Not unusual to lose a face in such a highballed crowd, but he was nowhere to be seen or found in the three reception rooms, or terrace and garden outside. I had not been wrong in recognizing the Spencer Tracy features and the familiar stance of a man with a wooden leg. He was not one to confuse so easily with another. I sought out my host, the Czech Ambassador, to say good evening, despite his coldness to me on other encounters. It was not he, but his wife, who had invited me. Acknowledging my gesture with the stock phrase, scarcely hiding his dislike, "How kind of you to come. Now, if you'll excuse me—"

Interrupting this brush-off, "Mr. Ambassador, wasn't that Dave Gilbey with you just now?"

Giving me each word as if set apart on ice, he looked me squarely in the eyes. "I know of no one by that name."

He turned away with a smile for someone else. I captured a daiquiri from the tray of a passing waiter and set off across the crowded room to cut and prune my way through the underbrush of Havana's new society to a friendly face I knew.

Only after I'd left the party could I focus on this enigma of Gilbey and Polansky. Why Polansky's agitation over my seeing Gilbey at a Soviet bloc reception, and his apparent order to have him disappear? Intrigued, I checked with the Italian Embassy. He'd said he was Italian, and therefore would be registered. The embassy had never heard of him. I did the same at the Swiss Embassy, now representing the United States. Dave Gilbey was on file, but nothing more. I sent off a report to Brightheim and forgot about it.

One stifling July day, struggling with the onerous task of ranch accounting, I heard a car climb our drive. It was a Russian jeep with two armed soldiers riding raggedy-doll in the back and two men in military uniform in front. At the wheel I recognized Comandante Dormitio Escalona, commander of our province. One year later, he'd be busted to lieutenant for being more addicted to rum and girls than the Revolution. I'd met him once before when one late afternoon, bleeding rum, he'd arrived with three young tarts in tow. With no by-your-leave, he said he'd come to use our swimming pool. Relieved his visit was not official, but visualizing our house an unofficial officers' club once Escalona's feet were wet, I churned out the first excuse that came to mind, an excuse he'd not lose face with before his scruffy little harem and so become my enemy.

"Glad to see you, Comandante. Awfully sorry, but the pool's off limits. The Belgian Ambassador's my guest this weekend. He's in conference there, doesn't even want me around. How about some coffee for you and your friends before you leave?"

He ran that through his sodden mind, sudden belligerency giving way to unhappy acceptance. In the mood for neither coffee nor further talk with me, he herded his disappointed quiffs back into the jeep, hauled a Bacardi bottle from under a seat to douse each squealing dyed-blond head with a stream of rum, took a swallow for himself, and ground the jeep into full gear ahead. I was glad to see him go. A mythical diplomat had made my day.

On this second visit, I'd gone to the front patio to see what Escalona wanted, once again afraid of trouble. He was sober that day and smiling. Nothing in that to ease my mind. His passenger was looking the other way, and I saw only his back as he got out and strode across the lawn towards the stone retaining wall, where he observed the long reach of valley far below. There was something familiar to his husky build, the shape of his head, and his purposeful stride. The totality was of great self-assurance. I felt invaded. At the wall he turned to Escalona, following close behind, and I recognized the co-author of the Cuban Revolution, a man who dangerously rivaled Castro in respect and popularity: the Argentinian, el Che, Ernesto Guevara.

Although pleased at the chance to meet el Che, I didn't believe this a social call—more likely a military interest in our one-thousand-foot-high ridge, dominating hundreds of square miles east and north.

He wore black parachute boots and clean olive-green fatigues without insignia, the same dress he wore in his office as president of the Banco Nacional. The habitual black beret was missing. Even without his notoriety, Guevara would impress. Shorter than I thought, about five-feet-nine, but solid, a football player's build. Protruding forehead, perhaps a distortion on another, added strength to a face framed by abundant, curly brown hair. A wispy beard lent an Asiatic look and an age greater than his thirty-four years. A golden flicker, a bit of sunlight in his wide-spaced, soft brown eyes, held much the same message as the broad mouth, creased in smile as we shook hands. His greeting was a strange one. "Don't be afraid, don't be afraid."

In reference to his once having headed INRA, the ministry that intervened farms and houses, I replied, "I am only afraid to offer the traditional Cuban greeting, *mi casa es su casa* (my house is your house). Otherwise you are welcome, *Comandante*. Please come in for some beer or coffee."

He said he didn't like to drink when working and accepted coffee. Escalona looked disappointed. Guevara's bodyguards, the two soldiers with light machine guns, relaxed enough about their job to sit with us for a *cafecito* on the porch, weapons at their feet. It was strange, the soldiers' lack of discipline, when Guevara had written a classic on guerrilla warfare—with discipline its strongest tenet.

The attitude of Cubans towards Guevara was typified by Ana, our black servant from Havana. She believed the Revolution would produce a messiah—in her mind, el Che. And now, here before her, was her hero. She was so ecstatic and confused she made the coffee with too much sugar. I suggested she sit with us but she didn't hear. She just stood there gazing at her idol with shining eyes, saying over and over, "el Che, el Che." He seemed unaffected by such passionate devotion and continued discussing local politics, which seemed to genuinely interest him. I took the opportunity to complain about the petty harassment one of my men had experienced the week before. While playing the usual evening game of dominoes on his front porch, a corporal from the small army post of San Andres had passed by on horseback and ordered the game suspended.

"Gambling is no longer permitted in Cuba."

Nothing less than the local *gendarmes* testing the strength of their uniforms on simple people too timid to stand up for their rights. Escalona laughed at my story. Guevara was incensed.

In just a few minutes I had formed an impression of Guevara as simultaneously gentleman and boy. Now I saw a Captain Bligh down to his last breadfruit. He spat out words like a royal command. "Escalona, get me the name of that corporal. He needs further instruction."

Justice was quick. Within days the corporal had disappeared and the national game of dominoes continued.

With Guevara I felt a mutual understanding and respect which could exist above our differing sociopolitical beliefs. In a friendly tug of words we agreed to disagree, while still seeing the other's point of view. To his question of why I paid my daily workers more than the government did (he'd done his homework on me), I explained I'd researched a peasant family's needs. He countered with, "The government gives free medical assistance to their workers."

"I had health insurance for my men until you chased the insurance companies out of the country."

And so we talked until his interest wavered to the beauty of the ever-changing shadows in the valleys below. I offered supper, with regrets that my wife was away in Belgium. He courteously declined, preferring, he said, to eat and sleep with his men in the field. After a final coffee, he thanked me for the visit with a twinkle in his eye, "Even if you did not have enough confidence to offer me your house." As had Ana, I too fell under the man's charm.

Following el Che's visit, and to comply with Brightheim's request for information on maritime traffic, I went to call on Pedro Fuentes from whom I'd bought my first pigs. His frail father and robust mother lived adjoiningly, and the two houses leaned on each other as the old often do. A war of parental genes had been maternally won, with a solid Basque physique passed on to the son. When wanting to tease, there was enough muscle in Pedro to lift his mother off the ground, pound on pound, mound on mound of too many carbohydrates.

Pedro knew more about pigs that he did of his own children. He must have had several hundred pigs and knew every last one of them as individuals. To me, pigs are just bacon and ham, as similar, one to the other, as twin frying pans. He loved those Duroc Jerseys and undoubtedly had the best in Cuba, providing money enough to buy a commercial-sized gas refrigerator for his wife. In reality, it was to assure a constant supply of cold beer for himself and friends. I was one of these, although it was more a mutual appreciation of beer than pigs that made me so.

Pedro lived on an elevation above the deep water port of Mariel, thirty-five miles west of Havana, where strategic material, too sensitive for the docks of the capital, was loaded or off-loaded. Having lost land and a son to the Revolution, he proved an avid recruit. I provided high power binoculars, sent through an embassy, and cautionary advice. In return, I received fortnightly accounts with the names and nationalities of all ships and, when possible, the nature of the cargo. As Pedro had never learned to write, the reports were laboriously blocked out by his wife, often misspelled and sometimes illegible. I insisted on the ships' names, but could only suppose the rendering of the Slavic was correct. He creased his papers into tight little squares, as if each fold gave more security to the reports he was so proud of. He left these with his brother, proprietor of the bar Tocayo, on the road to Havana where I stopped for beer or coffee.

Whenever a sensitive cargo was to be handled, always a Soviet ship, the Cuban stevedores were exchanged for Russians, alerting my friend to something special. Cuban propensity for exaggeration—big is better—is surpassed by few other nationalities, and gave me endless trouble teaching Pedro the value of accuracy. We knew the length of docks and so could judge the size of ships, and thus the rough dimensions of enormous crates lifted from Russian holds could be ascertained when viewed dangling from a crane. For smaller crates, a truck or stevedore gave comparative measure.

But I needed a double check. Fortunately, the family-oriented Cubans count their cousins by the hundreds, and my friend, ignorant of my intent, produced Juan Soto, living and working in the port of Mariel. Provided with binoculars and a miniature Minox camera, this second man confirmed, or confused, Pedro's figures. Juan, too, left his information at the bar Tocayo, inserted in a new package of cigarettes—four extracted to make room for the missive, more when there was film, and resealed with glue. This was a trick that appealed immensely to Juan's sense of the dramatic.

Occasionally a crate would break open, giving the lie to the letters "agricultural equipment," stenciled in both Russian and Spanish. I'd hear of the wing of a plane, a tapered fuselage (either plane or missile to untutored eye), or a jet engine nacelle (always a missile to my two stalwarts).

It was strange, that these "agricultural" shipments were always destined for San Antonio de los Baños, southwest of Havana, the site of an American airbase during World War II. Between there and the port of Mariel, a mechanic in a roadside garage, a farmer at his cultivation, and others of my recruiting along the route, all reported the same destination. U.S. Air Force reconnaissance showed the metamorphosis of "agricultural equipment" into the latest models of the Russian air arm, MIG 19s, and Illyshun troop carriers.

Another maritime intelligence source was a fisherman. I had known Tonto before the Revolution at the north coast village of Puerta Esperanza, where each week I haggled with him over fish for my family and *vaqueros*. An acquaintance more tactile than verbal,

61

he was more a back friend, a shoulder slapper, than conversational. The sea had made him so. He was thin and gangly, and stooped, a bent sapling in the wind, hardy enough for the ocean life.

Under the Revolution, Tonto had become incensed at being forced into a fishing cooperative, losing both income and independence. As partial compensation to his outraged soul, he provided information on a small Russian base at Malas Aguas, just west of Puerta Esperanza. It was unapproachable by land—high chain-link fence, search lights, and patrolling German Shepherds with machine-gun-toting handlers. But from the water a fisherman might spy. Tonto received binoculars and instructions from me. He used the binoculars, ignored my instructions, and paid the ultimate price.

His first reports indicated nothing more interesting than a weather station—the daily flight of one balloon, followed with a telescope by its launchers. A month later, a new planting of pines, fifty yards inland, turned yellow. In two months, the needles had gone and so had the camouflage intended to hide a small ground-to-air missile, hunkered on its launching ramp. The wrong tree in the wrong soil. Had the Russians only asked a Cuban . . . .

Tonto had always lived free, and it was not for him to be told when and where he might fish. His brown disgust with the Revolution turned black, and his thoughts turned to sailing his boat and family to the north. But first, revenge, and that meant fishing for the Russian secret at Malas Aguas.

I'd told him to observe from a distance, to use the binoculars from under a tarpolin covering the bow of his small open boat. He had nodded wisely, slapped my back, and paid not the slightest heed. Later he'd said, "If only I could get a little closer." That should have warned me. It didn't, and cost Tonto his life.

Tonto's oldest son, Tomás, had fished with his father since reaching fisherman's maturity, age twelve. He was then fifteen. And though ocean discipline had instilled blind obedience to his father, he thought it strange to weigh anchor under sail at ten one evening. No engine this night, not even a moon to bring fish to the surface. One hundred yards off Malas Aguas' beach and the Russian base, Tonto let down his anchor. Without further explanation, he told his son to await him until the rising of the moon. Tomás remembered the next three sentences to repeat to his mother.

"If God is willing I will be back with you. If I am not, you must return home as quietly as we came. May God be with us all."

Tonto slipped over the side of the boat in his shorts and Tomás never saw his father again. The boy stared his eyes into oblivion watching the lights of the base. He prayed and thought of taking the boat closer in. Discipline kept him where he was, silent, immobile, for half an hour, he thought. There were shouts, then long bursts of gun fire, and finally search lights converging on the missile launcher. Tomás said he heard his father cry out.

It was his mother who told me this. She finished her story with the Cuban *comandante* coming to question her and forcing the identification of her husband's mutilated body. Not at all concerned with the woman's plight, he had been furious with the Russians for killing Tonto. How could G-2 interrogate a dead fisherman?

Tonto had turned up an intelligence prize of good value. What more had there been to gain by invading the base? A fine man had gone, leaving only my poor thanks for his widow. I felt morally responsible and sick at heart for a future the family would never enjoy.

And then sex finally reared its ugly head. Actually the head wasn't all that bad. It was the body that was wrong: all bellied, thighed and buttocked with excessive flab from too many years of rice and beans. It made the lady indigestible. This came about through interaction with a mining engineer at Cuba's Matahambre copper mine. To flesh out an overall graph of the country's faltering economy, he reported production, labor troubles, and minor sabotage. And he left his monthly analysis with his widowed sister-in-law in Havana for me to recover. As the lady was more intent on being picked up than the letter for which I'd come, recovery was hazardous. This self-styled *femme fatale* was as fatal as a jelly doughnut. Since I had never been trained in such exigencies, I changed the letter drop.

Then there was a citrus-vegetable farmer who trucked his produce to the capital. He brought back occasional news of interest: the murder one night of three Russians in their stalled jeep near Havana's old central market, the hunting down by German Shepherd dogs and killing of two Czechs (defectors from an experimental hydroponic farm), and the Russians storing quantities of metal canisters in sealed mountain caverns (lethal gas for bacteriological warfare?). While many such facts were difficult to check, these were all confirmed.

I tried to weed out idle gossip or pure fiction before sending my reports to Brightheim, but there was always the fear of deleting some part of the whole necessary to the final analysis. I suppose the end result was messages overlarded with trifles, but the advice had been, "better a full ear of gossip than the dreamings of a blind man."

Thirty-five miles west of Havana on the north coast lay a sisal farm near San Cristóbal—sisal, that spiked, hard-leafed plant yielding the durable white fiber used in cordage. It belonged to Angelo Portuondo until expropriated by the Revolution. Enormous caves, called los Portales, surfaced on the farm's plateau. At a half-mile radius around these caves the army built a high chain-link fence and posted signs that shouted "Military Base—Off Limits." As usual for such an installation, there were stilted guard towers with machine guns and search lights, leashed German Shepherds on their rounds, and a perimeter road for patrolling jeeps, all the measures for high security.

But even high security can be penetrated. This time by my recruit of greatest value, Roberto Bravo, foreman of a heavy-equipment crew. One of his bulldozer operators reported building a road on this off-limit base and leveling a site "the size of two baseball fields." An aficionado of the sport, he described everything quite accurately in baseball terms. (His wife's miniskirt was "so small it wouldn't cover homeplate.") From later work he deduced a missile site, and I so reported. And I imagined my handler in Washington striking his all-American brow and saying, "Oh no, not another missile from Lunt."

By January 1961, the United States was orbiting SAMOS, Satellite And Missile Observation System. It was for the U.S. Air Force to follow up missile site reports with high altitude photography. In the following months this San Cristóbal military zone was repeatedly photographed until finally confirmed for what it was, a Soviet intermediate range ballistic missile site.

Following the October 1962 crisis, the offensive arms supposedly were removed. But due to the proximity of what later came to be recognized as a military cave complex honeycombing Cuba's limestone substructure, it is quite feasible that missiles remained, and still remain, cached and cared for, ready for future blackmail.

Who ever heard of a dry spy, one that didn't drink? I never had until Roberto Bravo joined my stable of recruits. And this man, whose bulldozer operator had unwittingly revealed an atomic hornet's nest, was a man for whom drinking was not his vice, but chain-smoking long, black cigars was. I asked him once how his wife withstood the perpetual smoke screen of his acrid tobacco.

"*Hombre!* It was my woman who started me on cigars. Mountain born and raised near you, and from her father's patch she rolled her own at six. Makes more smoke than I do. Our house stinks like a burned-out tobacco barn. Guess it's not such a bad thing though." After a moment's pause, "We don't have any cockroaches."

For a heavy-equipment man he had a surprisingly light handshake. Like the eyes, a clue to character. I didn't think much about it although I should have. It was Roberto who betrayed me in the end. It was his Budweiser draft-horse build that made me think him strong throughout. His brown eyes looked straight at you, and that too had given me confidence.

Roberto and his men had worked on many military camps and could often produce an engineering map of the installation, location and size, and from the number of barracks its estimated personnel. And from the type of construction, it could be deduced whether built for Cubans or the Russians. With high security fences and cement block construction, the camp was for the Russians, East Germans or Czechs. For Cuban soldiers, it was the minimum of expense and comfort. There were wood or canvas huts, no security fences, no outside showers, and no toilets, and let them wash their clothes where they could. With this information we could evaluate fairly accurately the number of foreign personnel.

There were other contacts in Havana, also, each useful in their way. Tony Barletta worked alternate days in the cafeteria and room service of the Capri Hotel, used exclusively for communist bloc technicians and their wives. Tony's Latin eyes and swarthy good looks brought him heavy tips from the Slavic ladies crying "room service" when their husbands were away.

"Larry, *qué Dios me ayude.* With all that room service, and I mean service!, I have nothing left for my wife. She wants me to see a doctor! Why should I have to screw all those communist bitches just because their husbands have no balls?"

"Tony, listen. Just tell them you have syphilis or something. They'll leave you alone "

"Sure, and I'll lose my job." With strong white teeth showing in a grin, "Anyway, some of them aren't so bad."

His reports on the blond wife of one of the Czechs, "a sexual turnstyle through which all the employees had to pass," were more colorful and interesting than transcripts of technical data left lying around. Perhaps Washington found it of some value to add another nymphomaniac to their lists.

Another recruit was José Puig in his raunchy and paunchy early fifties with a questing eye and three times married, a realtor in the days when Cubans could buy and sell property as they pleased. His interests ran from women to cockfighting, and with his own flocks of both he had gained and lost as many fights with the one as with the other. He knew everybody the length and breadth of the island and should have been the intelligence gatherer summa cum laude. But he was completely unreliable. Aroused by a few rums and the needs of Uncle Sam, he could bring tears to your eyes with his patriotic fervor—until a pretty girl passed by. I maintained contact more for what he could ferret out for the ranch in the shrinking market than for his un-intelligence reports.

José, with friends in ministries and armed forces, could verify many reports on missile sites, the Russian submarine base at Cienfuegos, defections from Fidel's inner circle, and which minister's wife was sleeping around. He proved to be an encyclopedia of the most diverse information, while at the same time uncovering a supply of barbed wire for the ranch. Although he cost me a brewery of rum, he was worth it.

And then there was Guillermo Gómez, still there, cultivating his garden and a safe submissiveness to make life more tolerable for one who was caught and talked. He talked of everybody and everything he knew, and of much he did not know. He voided his poor soul of its light baggage to escape prison only to find himself incarcerated in something worse—a life sentence in the solitary confinement of his conscience.

What is the prototype of a man who will not break? Can the carpenter always choose a flawless piece of wood to work? Isn't there the chance of some unseen internal weakness hidden under a fine strong-grained exterior? The tree's branch has left a knot, comely to the eye, fiber weakening. A thunderbolt has scarred the bark, superficially or to the roots. One can only tell by peeling back the bark. And so it is with men. We live behind a normal facade, carrying the normal weight of a normal life until called upon to bear an unaccustomed strain. Only then are the fibers, moral, spiritual and physical found whole or wanting. When the bark is peeled back in interrogation it can then be seen how deep the scar, how sound the fibers.

Physically, Guillermo was a veritable oak, standing strong and straight with nary a flaw. A good natured six-feet-two with wide-spaced eyes, bracketed by the wrinkles of a lot of smiles—a slow-to-anger guy. Blunt work-calloused fingers could pluck a guitar with strange gentleness. He was as handsome as a god, the weak link in anyone's chain.

I had first known him as an honest and good mechanic with his own four-horsepower garage in what had once been the living room of a derelict ground-floor apartment—a gas pump before the door. To one side, a closet opening into the street where for three *centavos* his wife sold *cafecitos*. Unlike most Latins, Guillermo was monogamous—well, almost—devoted to his wife and work, saving together for the purchase of a real garage.

The three-story building where Guillermo lived and worked was condemned in 1960. His garage gone, he accepted work as driver-mechanic with INRA, chauffering the top dogs on their inter-provincial trips and retaining in his memory much of their gripes and gossip. He turned in valuable information from visiting military installations and eavesdropping on back-seat talk. It was Guillermo who alerted me to the vast radar web being woven over the island and the amount of Russian burrowing underneath. It was he who made me aware of how well the Russians were prepared below ground before showing their hand above.

Not all my contacts were recruited. Some came to volunteer information because I was the only American around, ergo I was CIA, the *bête noire* of Fidel, the great white hope of the anti-Castros. There was the case of a navy captain, a friend of a friend, asking me to broker with the British Embassy his defection to the Bahamas with ship and crew. There were incendiaries of factories and other acts of sabotage, the pecadillos of certain luminaries of the "new society," all of this and more to be winnowed from the chaff that blew my way.

The time arrived when Brightheim deemed that the quality of our work warranted lines of communication more secure than the increasingly erratic Cuban post. A radio transmitter-receiver and code book were made available in an embassy for my reports. As Cuba had not yet perfected a system for localizing clandestine transmitters, I passed my coded messages and received instructions once a week, unconcerned for my embassy hosts.

Early 1962, a strange voice from Washington briefed me on my first airdrop, scheduled for our ranch to coincide with a waning moon and an urgent need for counterrevolutionary arms. I alerted the man for whom this manna from heaven would fall, and made arrangements to meet at the ranch corrals on the designated night.

The idea of receiving one's first airdrop in enemy territory at night is thrilling—the mechanics of it, quite different. D-day, late afternoon, I readied the packsaddle used for salting cattle and corralled my horse. Half an hour of hard swimming in the pool smoothed the edge of nervousness. More to pass time, I ate a supper not really wanted, then tried to lose myself in a book—a useless strategy of turning pages without content. Deciding my horse better company than a worried imagination, I went early to the corrals for animal consolation. I carried two flashlights and a thermos of strong coffee fortified with rum. Right on time at ten thirty, a jeep drove up. For the arms of a woman or a revolution this Cuban would forever be on time. We left the jeep out of sight in the branding shed, and horse-in-tow, took off into the hills. A twenty-minute walk and we came to a mile-long plateau between two peaks, navigation landmarks for the drop. I'd prepared dry logs to light as beacon. Too early to kindle the fire. The drop was for eleven thirty. Twenty-five minutes to go.

Bruno Álvarez, my companion of the night, I knew but slightly. He was the foreman of a small neighboring ranch still privately owned. Half a foot shorter than I, dark-faced, stubbly chin, hard-eyed above thinly smiling mouth, he was curt of speech but an ace with an ornery cow. I liked him and had to assume he was trusted or he'd not have been in on the drop.

I uncorked the thermos, and we drank to each other and the mission. We talked cattle, and I lit the fire. The flames seemed to signal to the whole province our work and made my friend nervous. He drew back into the shadows and complained when I added more wood.

While anxiously awaiting the noise of a small plane at one thousand feet in the dark of night, every shadow hides a man of G-2, and the sound of a lone vehicle on the public road through the ranch is the army come to investigate. When the uncertain drone of an engine in the sky becomes a shadow reality to the eye, the plane is off course, too far east of the higher peak. The small fire has not been seen. The whole thing is a fiasco. I throw on more branches. But as we lose sight of that black trace in the quarter-moon sky, we hear it banking west and turning, coming into view again—for all the world to see, it seems—this time on course and lower still. It has seen our fire and in acknowledgement cuts its engine twice, leaving in its wake a small white puff. Continuing low, maybe five hundred feet, the plane and its telltale drone disappear to the north. The parachute drifts silently down three hundred yards off.

I am concerned with extinguishing the fire and hiding it with earth. My companion, more eager to retrieve the drop. We each do our job simultaneously and meet at the white spread in the grass. There were light arms, ammunition, six bundles of false *pesos,* and the nylon parachute as dress material for Bruno's wife and half a dozen friends. Christmas in May. Back at the corrals we emptied the thermos and clasped hands. I bid him Godspeed and my part was done. His, only beginning.

Mid-1962, Brightheim asked me to Washington to discuss airdrops and other generalities. We were both concerned with growing Cuban security and my becoming too bright a color in a fading tapestry. With the American exodus from Cuba almost total, a six-foot, fair-haired Anglo-Saxon in his jeep was too conspicuous. I was more and more taken for a Czech, but with the unpopularity of Soviet bloc natives throughout the island, this was of little help in passing unobtrusively.

My apartment telephone had recently been bugged, a distinct lowering of volume in the receiver five to ten seconds after lifting it. The CDR (Comité de Defensa de la Revolución), with their eyes and ears in every village and city block, at the fork of every country road, was becoming better organized. They had come to both my ranch and my Havana apartment to catalogue my furniture—and spy out what they could. Each time I left Cuba to see my family, the return visa was made more difficult. My jeep was illegally requisitioned for three weeks by a local chieftain before the Belgian Embassy forced its return. Attempts were made to lure away my workers. I ceased keeping money in a checking account to thwart the government's inquisitiveness over each deposit and withdrawal. And only later under interrogation did I know that all this time G-2 was photographing every weekend guest, who left a car in our nearest village for the rough nine kilometers into the ranch in a rented jeep. I had become persona non grata.

With such negative signs, Brightheim decided to phase me out of running the group I'd enlisted throughout the countryside, turning them over to Roberto Bravo, one of whose men was a former radio operator in Batista's air force. He'd receive a radio and Roberto would be in business on his own. For the time being, Brightheim asked that I maintain contact with my Havana recruits and take a final airdrop, the most bizarre of the many I'd received.

This drop was not the kind of female pick up I'd once practiced. It was Ana-María Lima, the *enamorada* of the guerrilla leader Cara Linda, until switching affection and sides to the province commander, Dormitio Escalona. There was more elegance to being bedded under a roof by a *comandante* with fringe benefits than tumbling under the stars with a guerrilla and a million mosquitoes. Under Escalona's influence she informed on a tryst with Cara Linda, almost succeeding in causing his death.

Following this debacle, her family had migrated to Miami, taking Ana-María along. Conscience for her first love made for unhappiness, deciding her return to Cuba and Cara Linda. The CIA learned her request for a Cuban visa had been denied and offered a round trip and lovely reward if she'd play Macbeth to the province commander. She agreed and was given the poison to play out her role.

I asked Brightheim the obvious question of why the girl was not to be delivered by boat instead of by air and got some four-letter words in reply. Seemed G-2 had infiltrated our coastal contacts, making clandestine landings unsafe until new sources were organized. And so, our ranch, one hill over from an aunt of Ana-María, seemed to Brightheim the perfect location. To me, there seemed no perfect location for dropping a Cuban girl into the night.

Bruno Álvarez, my first drop companion, was with me again. We greeted each other more warmly this time with an *abrazo*. A shot each of the ritual coffee with rum and we were off for the plateau. This night of no moon, the drone of the plane (unseen till directly above) homed right in on our fire. The same puff of white in the sky, the same diminishing hum to the north, and then to our horror, the screech of a cat in heat, long and loud enough to be heard in Havana. As the chute drifted down we could hear Ave Marias mixed with vile invective, then shrill keening lament. It was unearthly to hear this din from the sky with only a parachute in our eye. I wished I were somewhere else and set to killing the fire. Reluctantly, Bruno loped off to the drop. The sound of a punctured tire—a loud ooooph—a moment's blessed silence, then the cry of a wounded animal. I heard a sharp thwack, then again. In mid-crescendo the wail stopped, and I thought he'd strangled the wench. He said later he'd been tempted, but had only slapped hard on both cheeks. I'd heard he was good with ornery cows.

We untangled the girl from the chute, walked her a few steps for hurt, and decided her fit to take to the horse. The few sobs left to her turned to hiccoughs after a drag on my coffee. The unholy caterwauling from the skies had triggered some dogs off to the west, probably my foreman's, but we couldn't be sure, and we worried our way to the corrals. My last drop was over and done with, mission accomplished. I wanted no more heaven-sent girls.

Ana-María was delivered to her aunt. Escalona continued in excellent health pursuing rum and girls to the exclusion of the Revolution until busted in rank. Bruno Álvarez lives on in Cuba, a silent mole in a silent majority, one of the many unsung heros in the Cuban resistance.

71

Chapter 12

With CIA work cut in half, I now spent more time maintaining the ranch on diminishing supplies. A constant need was horseshoes. If I could provide scrap iron, the local smithy could knock out my needs. Though I knew every junk yard in two provinces, so did everyone else. Scavenging was a national game. Government corruption and thievery were rampant, supplying the black market with many necessities. By improvising, saving, and doing without, we got by. Horses had their horseshoes, the jeep its renovated spare parts and patched tires, and the refrigerator cooled with pieces cannibalized from another. The country stumbled along from sheer momentum of the pre-Castro boom days. And then came October 1962 and the missile crisis.

To my surprise, once again I was left alone as the crisis unfolded. I lived by my radio and got what satisfaction I could at hearing the San Cristóbal site proven out for what it was with low level aerial photos. Our work was not in vain.

The crisis passed. Kennedy pledged the unwarranted "no invasion," and Cuba settled more securely into the communist camp. The supposed courage and wisdom of Kennedy before this

Soviet threat was best summarized by Nixon: "The United States pulled defeat out of the jaws of victory."

For the second time I appraised the situation, debating whether to cut my losses and leave or remain and keep the ranch going. For all the same reasons of January the year before, I stayed on.

A love affair with the land is hard to explain. And there were the loyal men and their families who worked for me. Beatrice and I were close to these simple folk, felt responsible for their welfare. And too, there was the unrealistic feeling that "I'll be damned if I'll let the commies take over," coupled with my belief the Belgian flag would protect us.

Chapter 13

In March 1963, I met el Maximo Leader. Weekending in a friend's house at the beach resort of Varadero, I was walking the shore before breakfast, the new day for sole company. A few hundred yards from where I was staying, one of the more opulent vacation homes was rumored to have been confiscated for Castro when the owners fled. Separating the lawn of this house from the beach was a low, stone wall on which half a dozen men dressed in army fatigues and light machine guns were perched. With great attention they watched my slow shell-picking progress—in bathing trunks, not much of a threat, but still they were alert to my approach, raising their guns to my knees when fifty yards off. Forgetting the shells, I studied with more interest the uniformed group with the soldiers. Two men stood tall above the other five men and one woman. I recognized her first from the media coverage she'd had. Celia Sánchez, Fidel's paramour of the mountains. One of the taller men was Dr. René Vallejo, Fidel's personal physician and constant companion. The Titan, facing away, was Castro himself. From back or front, from any angle, there's no mistaking the man. The Devil broke the mold after forming him.

Vallejo said something to Castro, got a nod, and called out, *"Buenos días, compañero."*

To all who used the communist *compañero* with me—people I gave lifts to on the road and others thinking me Czech—I replied, *"Compañero no, amigo sí."* I replied in the same way to Vallejo, adding a *"buenos días, señor."*

Castro turned, showing his teeth in a grin, and beckoned me forward, perhaps intrigued at my unorthodox greeting. No hands were extended across the two yards of sand separating CIA agent in shorts from communist dictator in fatigues. His frenzied ego was in his pocket out of sight, a smile on his face.

"So you don't like to be called *compañero*. Who are you?"

"Buenos días, Comandante. I'm an American, Larry Lunt, ranching in Pinar del Río."

"Ah yes, that Belgian property. I've heard about it."

His prodigious memory was famous. Even this brief encounter and our conversation on pasture clearing was filed away in his head. Two years later, after I was arrested and the Swiss Ambassador first brought up my case, Castro said to him, "Ah, that American on the beach who tried to sell me on picks for clearing pastures."

I'd long ago prejudged the man bad, so could find little good. Sensuous lips seemed obscene. A beard with a moth-eaten hole to one side of the mouth disguised a weak chin. Despite a sense of banked fires, there was no warmth to the eyes, none of the compassion I'd seen in el Che's. Perhaps Americans didn't rate a warm spark. Women fell hard for him. Whether the romantic fantasy of fame or chemical combustion, I don't know. And although there was rugged authority in the face, there was good eating and drinking in the paunch. His Mack truck frame could carry it though. He still looked tough. True, I was fascinated by the man's magnetism, but the moral gap bothered me, the political and humanistic gap too.

The cruelty inherent in Spanish history lies latent in many Latins. The man at the bottom of the pecking order, who has suffered all his life from those above, will most likely show no leniency should he himself rise a grade or two. And so it was with Castro. He had suffered the stigma of illegitimacy and would have his pounds of flesh. Who else but Castro cried for "more Robespierres in Cuba"? And the incredible disparity between his own "gentleman's imprisonment" under Batista after attempting to overthrow him and the abattoir conditions of the Castro prisons! There's little greatness to a man who harbors hates and grudges.

From the missile crisis of October 1962 to my arrest in May 1965, life assumed an uneasy rhythm. My use to the CIA was diminishing, maintaining the ranch required the art of wizardry, and family life was Atlantic commuting. After much hesitation, Beatrice and I decided she and the children would return to Cuba. They came in January 1965 with Miss Caroline Ittensohn, nurse to my wife, now to our sons, a much-loved member of the family. There were few ills she could not treat, and living remote from medical aid, we and our peasant neighbors often were grateful to this Swiss woman, whose fortitude in the months ahead stood us all in good stead.

My family's return was a joyous reunion, shared in by the men and their families who worked for us, tangible evidence we were still with them. In this new-found happiness of family life I discounted my own precarious position. To all intents and purpose, life was back to normal and I made reservations to fly to the States for my parents' fiftieth wedding anniversary.

LEAVE ME MY SPIRIT

Chapter 14

In Santa Fe, New Mexico, a golden wedding anniversary. In Havana, Cuba, another arrest among hundreds each day. To me, life-shattering. And then, life-saving with the miracle of God coming into my soul and cell.

The interview following my baptism by tears was unique. I felt strangely calm, out of reach of my three inquisitors. I thought them baffled by my new attitude, that our roles had been exchanged, and they, not I, were on the defensive. This was the last interview with three.

My first interrogator of the vile tongue, The Man, returned to plague me. At our second round he handed me a neatly typed document for my signature—a general acknowledgement, nothing precise, of subverting the stability of the state as a CIA agent. The details, true and invented, would be filled in later. To the right of my typed name at the end of this single-page confession was the name Jorge Denis Rivero, 1st Lieutenant of the Department of Investigations, G-2. The Man now had an identity.

The paper lay before me on the desk, a cheap Chinese ballpoint pen to one side—a delaying tactic of the mind to note the origin of pen. Right on cue came the memory of the CIA lesson on interrogation. Never sign a confession. Admit if you must, but never sign. I slid the paper back across the desk and shook my head. Staring at me hard, without a word, he pushed it back at me. I shook my head again.

In a surprisingly reasoned voice, "Larry, you're alone and forgotten by your wife and children. They're ashamed of you. They don't want to see you again. They've left Cuba. Sign this paper and you'll be out of here sooner than you think to follow them."

In my heart I knew he lied. He didn't know my wife. Anger replaced passivity. I reached for the offending document and very slowly tore it down the middle, replacing it on the desk. He seemed not to notice and buzzed for a guard to take me away. Menacingly quiet, he said, "I'll see you tomorrow."

Tomorrow and tomorrow, I saw him on many tomorrows.

Perhaps it was my curiosity that prevented the development of the Stockholm Syndrome, that love-hate relationship between prisoner and his keeper. I don't know what the necessary ingredients are for this Freudian fruit salad, but in my case the chemistry was wrong and I neither loved nor hated him. In retrospect, I guess I pitied him, although in the beginning there was a mixture of awe and grudging respect for this man who held the whip. It was that strange detached curiosity that finally reduced him to an ordinary person. I learned months later from his younger brother, a fellow prisoner for a time, that he had sold haberdashery in Havana's elegant department store, El Encanto, and that he was married with two children. The Italian-cut suit he alternated with his tailored uniform indicated more affection for *la dolce vita* than the austerity of communism. That he could be cruel, and even delight in it, I didn't doubt. His small effeminate mouth, carved into a permanent sneer, gave credit to this supposition.

The interviews continued, always in Spanish, lasting hours or minutes, at any moment of the day or night, many or only one, or none, in a twenty-four-hour period, every day, or not for several days. No uniformity to this life, no respite from *them*, from the confining cell, from myself.

My cell remained bare, no mattress or any part of my "shopping list" appeared, not even a bar of soap, nothing. Knowing now that *sí* meant *no*, I was learning not to ask. I was learning to accept my grey cement walls, my grey tiled floor, my grey de-pressing ceiling. To combat this dreariness, this suffocation, I formed a rough schedule for my waking hours.

After bread and watered milk were passed through the judas window, the empty cup returned, I focused my mind on infinity and dozed until a diffused light filtered in, marking time for prayer. I sat lotus-fashion facing the outside wall to pray and meditate. During these periods of concentration I began *to think* for the first time in my life. How many of us have been without a visual or auditory object to act as catalyst for thought? It is difficult, often impossible, to find the time and place and necessary silence for *thinking*. I had the solitude and the silence. I would *think*, make something worthwhile from this loss of freedom. My curiosity was still alive, not only for what went on around me, but for the new direction of my mind.

In compensation for confinement, my ill-used memory began to function as never before. Phrase by phrase a prayer took shape in my mind. I added, discarded, cut and polished, tasting each word before setting it in place. After weeks of meditative memorizing I had an interweaving of thoughts, intentions and entreaties in a single flowing narrative that satisfied both soul and ear. That I was capable of performing these mental gymnastics stupefied me. Undoubtedly it was the absolute lack of visual distraction, the silence, the aloneness, and a spiritual serenity quite new and foreign to me. With access to a watch months later, I found the finished prayer took four to five minutes to recite. Since then I could never duplicate this feat without memory's worst enemy, pen and paper. Ralph Waldo Emerson wrote, "His notebooks impair his memory; his libraries overload his wit." On being freed, I made the mistake of neglecting this prayer over many nights for a shorter, more intense thanksgiving. On turning to my standby once again, I found it gone, and now only fragments return, triggered by my subconscious to meet some need.

In this newly discovered occupational therapy of *thinking*, I debated with myself, arguing first one side and then the other, from abortion to communism vs. democracy, believing vs. atheism. I composed short stories, revising, improving. I recalled music and lyrics from my youth. In slow motion I reran each day—images of my life: adding water to my father's rain gauge to upset his calculations, taking fifty cents from my mother's change purse and being miserable for a week, my first bicycle, first girl, first kiss, an unending feast of memories. Each forgotten memory detoured me so far that I relegated this exercise to Sundays as a form of relaxation and schedule change. Often the lunch tray surprised me, still sitting before the wall.

And so I reflected on what I had lost and to what poor advantage most of us put our external freedom. Compensation manifested itself little by little in a growing awareness of an inner freedom. Viktor Frank writes of his imprisonment in *Man's Search For Meaning*, "The ability to choose one's attitude in any set of circumstances, to choose one's own way. It was this spiritual liberty that gradually gave purpose and meaning to my life."

With a growing preoccupation for this spiritual liberty, I resented interruptions. Aside from interrogations, lunch and supper, there was the sometimes daily bucket of soapy water to clean the cell. Unless fortunate enough to be among the first, the water was almost too dirty to use. From the rag that came with it I tore off a corner, my first acquisition, to keep for later cleaning when water ran in the pipe. Each morning I took my small square of rag to clean just one of the ten-inch-square floor tiles. In two weeks, with elbow grease and the dedication of one who has plenty of time I had the floor cleaner than myself or uniform. Even the slop-bucket guard noticed and gave a nod of approval. No idle conversation here. Guards talked only to give an order.

If cleanliness is next to godliness, my filthy uniform and unwashed body placed me far from God. Water ran from the shower in proportion to my cooperation. As I was uncooperative, it ran in spurts half a dozen times a day, enough to satisfy my thirst. Lacking toothpaste and brush bothered me more than lack of soap. And so I invented. The hem of my undershorts made do for polishing teeth. I discovered fingernails could be kept short by rubbing them back and forth on the angle of the cement louvres. I went naked in the cell to beat the heat of May. Even so my uniform and body took on a rancid smell from the sweat of interrogations. At first repelling me, I became accustomed to my smell and hoped it bothered my interrogator.

Breakfast, lunch and supper were the only invariables. The sweet, hot milk and hard roll at breakfast only opened appetite and left me hungry. A piece of bread can be a lot if eaten at once. Broken in two, half saved for a mid-morning snack, it's very little. I tried both ways and decided the animal pleasure of instant gratification was greater than that of self-discipline. I reasoned that discipline, to be effective, must be optional, and eliminated my "coffee break." The compartmented aluminum lunch tray offered watery soup in one section, a handful of maggoty corn meal mush in another, and bread. The remaining sections were hungrily empty. Squeamish or not, I ate the mush to the last maggot and wished for more. Supper's soup was thicker, accompanied by bread with either rice or macaroni. There was never meat, vegetables or fruit—a subsistence-only diet.

Immediately after lunch I lay on the floor with feet raised against the wall, a position more thought- than sleep-provoking. An hour's exercise, more meditation, and pacing the cell brought the afternoon to the supper tray. With my stomach still crying more, and the empty tray returned, I continued my walk till evening fell, interrupting it for another period of prayer and meditation. During the day I never used the bed. I saved it for the night, making of it a small luxury, although there was little difference between the hardness of pine board and cement floor.

Once a week, the unsympathetic face of a doctor appeared at the judas window dispensing aspirin and other placebos. Chronic constipation might have been alleviated with a diet including fruit, but G-2 preferred prescribing placebos. In the hall outside each door was a shelf for prescribed medicines. Later, when my wife could bring American vitamins, I had my supply there. Within twenty-four hours they were substituted for some Cuban variety, stolen by the doctor or a guard—common practice where good medicines were in short supply.

The walls of my cell were covered with the graffiti of the desperate souls preceding me there. Beneath the crossed Cuban and American flags I found the Lord's Prayer in Spanish. With time I etched in the English words. In another corner, legible only by the morning light, was a poem I translated in my mind into English. If the Lord's Prayer affected me profoundly, so too did this verse expressing something of every caged man's anguish and longing. I wished the two men who had so laboriously worked these words into the walls of that bare cell had some way of knowing the moral support their work gave. Here is the verse as I memorized it in English.

> Now I'll not be there
> When the trade winds push my sail
> Towards a dying sun.
> And when the net is raised,
> Full of silver and gold
> Of a thousand startled eyes,
> Now I'll not be there,
> In the blue more blue,
> In the green more green,
> Under the fugitive cloud.
> Now it will not be mine, the star
> Shining beyond my sadness.
> Now I'll be illusion of wing,
> Wish of sun, envy of moon.
> And on returning, at the break of a wave,
> In the contour of the embrace,
> At the profile of a kiss, I'll not be there.

Toward the end of my second week in G-2, I was still being uncooperative and Denis was becoming impatient.

"*Coño su madre*, Larry! When are you going to brighten up? You don't realize how much we can help you. Hey, you listening?"

"Sure I'm listening, but I can't tell you things I don't know."

"Things you don't know! *Coño!*" Cunt in English, an indispensable part of Denis's vocabulary.

"A little confirmation on what we know and everything'll go easier for you. You think I can't have you shot, hey? Stand up!"

I stood.

"Sit down."

I sat.

"You see? I tell you to stand and you stand. I tell you to sit and you sit. I can just as easily tell you to get lost, to get shot, and BAM!, you are just another dead gringo."

There was nothing to reply and my unperturbed silence infuriated him.

"*Coño, Americano*! You think you can get out of here through all your influential friends. You'll learn, you'll learn."

84

Sweating in frustration and anger, with a rising inflection in his voice, almost a roar, "There's not an embassy or royal family in the world that can help you here. No one! Only me! Understand? Now get your stinking gringo ass out of here. You need a bath."

A blunder on Denis's part, my first hint that I was not forgotten and that family and friends were working on my behalf. My morale soared and more than ever strengthened my resolve.

As quickly as I fell asleep the door clanged open and that sound of iron on iron dragged me back to consciousness. Another marathon of interrogations. The following days and nights were a blur of sleeplessness and exhaustion. I must have eaten. I vaguely remember endless interviews, refusing to sign a second typewritten confession, refusing offers of a mattress, clean uniform, soap, towel and all the other simple amenities of life. Even water!

One morning the sound of water running with unaccustomed force awoke me. In an instant I was under its refreshing cleansing stream, and not caring a damn what the guards might do, letting the water run on my uniform bunched at my feet. If they wanted to take me out they'd either have to provide another or wait till mine had dried. It dried.

And then the miracle occurred. A guard slammed open the judas window. Without a word he shoved through a towel, soap, toothbrush and paste. I couldn't make the simple move to take them from his hands. He dropped them on the floor. I hung the small, green towel on the supporting chain of the upper bunk and arranged the pink soap, red and white tube of toothpaste, and pink-plastic toothbrush along the edge. I was a small child with his Christmas gifts displayed. The colors made the cell almost cheerful. Once again the judas window flew open to give a clean uniform, taking my filthy one in return. I couldn't remotely guess the reason for this change in treatment.

It was but the swing of the pendulum from nothing to much, from rotten bad to good. But the pendulum swing is irrevocable and soon swings back. To blackmail this time with the introduction of an old lady into my cloistered life. Mary McKay, a widow of seventy-six was living out her life in Havana—mornings of charity and afternoons of bridge, a harmless enough existence. We lunched together each week in her Spanish-colonial house. I brought country produce for herself and her charity cases, food difficult or impossible to come by in the cities. We had become good friends and enjoyed our lunches, quite innocent of any counter-revolutionary activities more serious than cursing Castro.

On being taken to my first interrogation with clean uniform and soap-bathed body I could not believe my eyes at seeing this old lady sitting on a bench in the corridor with head low, body shaking in silent tears. Without breaking stride I passed close enough to touch her hair and say, "God bless you, Mary," when my reaction should have been to stop and take her in my arms. The guard behind said nothing, so what had prevented me? Shock? Believing her a mirage? Cowardice? Later I was ashamed I had not offered this good friend greater support. She never raised her head. I wonder if she felt my touch, or had I touched her at all?

Confused by this appearance, I sat opposite another facet of Denis's many-faceted character, quiet self-assuredness. Today, no bluster, no shouting or waving of arms, no jumping up and down. Sometimes I wondered what the real Denis was like and thought perhaps he himself no longer knew, the original lost through multiple projections into so many roles. Today he was all concern for saving Mary. But only I could save her.

"Sit down, Larry. How you feeling? O.K.? You look better. You *smell* better."

With undisguised cynicism, "I'm sorry if my smell offended you."

"Careful, Larry, careful! A little respect or you go back to an empty cell. Now, you saw Mary out there, didn't you? Well, my friend, her future is in your hands. Understood? In your hands! When you come clean on your espionage ring—and I mean clean—Mary McKay will go free. It's just as simple as that."

Suddenly I exploded with an anger I'd not felt at any outrage against myself. No words could convey my feelings, but unconsciously the most derogatory tumbled out—a dumb reaction to their blackmail I was incapable of stemming. Realizing my mood was negative to his needs, Denis yanked the door open, yelling for the guard.

"Take this man back to his cell."

I never saw Mary McKay again. I could not sleep that night, and the next morning felt drugged and depressed when taken for another round with Denis. I expected the worst, but Mary was not mentioned. Instead a new screw was turned.

"Who taught you the trick of dotting the *i*?"

Denis could not have told me more plainly that Roberto Bravo had been arrested, the construction foreman, whose bulldozer man had first uncovered the San Cristóbal missile base. My mind went racing back two months to a Sunday afternoon in March. Roberto appeared at the ranch, something he had never done before. The change in him during the year I'd not seen him was shocking—thinner, older, painfully reserved and nervous. His radioman had been arrested and he wanted the CIA to know. Strangely, I thought, he'd asked how I would accomplish it. I hadn't replied. A waiting silence, then, with eyes on the ground, he'd reminded me of our arrangement if one were arrested and forced to write the other. Our sign was the dotting of the *i* in his *nom de guerre*, Luis. Otherwise it would go undotted.

Many months later, Roberto and I met in prison. In tears he told me he'd been arrested ten days before coming to the ranch. Said he'd been tortured, though wouldn't say just how, and forced to bare his soul. Six days under interrogation and released, obviously on a leash to lay all sorts of trails for his handlers to follow. Unwittingly, or wittingly, he'd tugged G-2 along behind him, sniffing at all the lamp posts and trees where agents meet, cocking a leg here and there to establish territory, as he did with me. For his cooperation he was rearrested to serve thirteen years of a twenty-year sentence.

To talk or not to talk, the constant question I had to live with. It's a dangerous game admitting to truths and half-truths while holding others hidden, and more important still, remembering all I'd said before. Memory is the prisoner's only aid, while the interrogator has his hidden tape recorder.

With the peculiar psychology of interrogation under stress, when part of the truth is forced out, there comes a time when you long to tell it all, to shuck off the unbearable burden of that remaining truth. With chronic weariness there's a tendency to rationalize capitulation as only logical. It is against this flabby thinking one must constantly be on guard.

As in poker, you try to deduce the others' cards to play your own accordingly. I laid out my truths sparingly, sparring for a hint of what the other knew. Holding a winning hand, Denis was generous with his cards so that little by little I admitted my relationship with Roberto until he seemed to believe I had complimented what he knew already.

"Why couldn't you have told me this before? It would have saved us both a lot of time. Doesn't an intelligent man like you realize that cooperation is your only salvation?"

"O.K., for two weeks you've been saying you never heard of Roberto Bravo. Now you say you not only knew him, but recruited him for the CIA."

"No, I never mentioned the CIA. I said he volunteered information and—"

"Ya, ya, I know all that. What else you going to tell me? That you never knew Cara Linda? *Coño, Americano!* Stop insulting my intelligence."

The relationship between this guerrilla of the hills and myself might well be supposition on their part. (Never confirm the enemy's supposition, said my CIA instructor on behavior under interrogation.) Wearily, I thought, could a simple admission to once having met hurt either Cara Linda or myself? But how about the fallout from this confession? Who put me in touch? How and where did we meet? There was Lino and his jeep, and that old couple with their son, all heroic in their way. I remembered sitting in their hut that night, Lino introducing them as *mi familia*, signifying closeness, confidence. No, this freely given confidence could not so easily be betrayed.

To my denial once again of knowing Cara Linda I sensed a blandness in Denis's insistence, as if he didn't really care. He terminated the interview with a shrug.

"Be seeing you, *Americano*. Go get some sleep."

Denis recalled me in less time than it took to twice pace my cell. Returning, I found myself face to face with Lino, Denis standing to one side observing with ill-disguised delight.

Lino was unable to meet my eye, I could feel the fear and shame in his lowered head. Denis didn't say a word, just prodded the pathetic man. As if a switch were touched, a dull, lifeless, halting voice recounted all too accurately the story of that night four years before, a full confession seeking an absolution never granted. When the spring unwound and the record stopped, a second prod reactivated the switch to play the other side. This time the story of the rebel, Chicho Suárez, hidden on our ranch and for whom my foreman, one *vaquero,* and gardener were imprisoned. He finished in a rush, relieved to be through, briefly raised the eyes of a beaten man, and collapsed in tears. As he was led away I silently wished him God's help in his misery.

Left alone with Denis, I tried to gather scattered thoughts, on the defensive once again. But it was their job to dig for what they wanted, not mine to volunteer. I had no intent to help when not betrayed into it by some weaker link. I was fast learning that few chains of secrecy can long endure the stress and strain of silent, unacknowledged work. First Roberto, and then Lino. How many more to come?

G-2's compelling tools for inducing mental and physical fatigue, uncertainty of mind, mushy thinking and weakened resolve, were constant tests of character, of never relaxing one's guard. And so the more compelling of my jumbled thoughts led me to prolong this post-mortem on my Cara Linda meeting, to keep the interrogations on this track as long as possible, away from as yet untouched topics. I dreaded the next swing of the pendulum.

LEAVE ME MY SPIRIT

Chapter 15

At my next interrogation Denis threw the Russian punch, thirty-six photographs prepared on a heavy sheet of cardboard under Plexiglas. I remember the exact number because I put myself to counting them again and again, six to a side, to keep my eye off the one photograph I recognized at the bottom right-hand corner: a Russian technician I had met at the swimming pool of the Czech Embassy in the summer of 1963. I had been invited by the wife of the ambassador, as warm and friendly toward me as her husband was cold and hostile. We had first met at a British Embassy dinner party where my hostess had warned that the lady from Czechoslovakia collected men by nationalities and her American shelf was bare.

The following week at her pool, I found myself the only westerner among three Czech women and one man, a Russian. After one daiquiri the Russian maneuvered me apart, a plain man of about forty, slightly built. What struck me most were the fine hands of a pianist and the intelligent face with soft brown eyes, whose melancholy only a smile could efface. He didn't smile much.

Our hostess had laughingly introduced him as Raúl. "You could never pronounce his name in Russian and Raúl is not far from it."

"Olga has told me of you," he said in Spanish. "He says you are friends with many western embassies. I envy you your freedom. When I'm alone the only places not off-limits are this embassy and my own." With one of his rare smiles focused on the Czech ambassadress, "The Czechs are one of the few good chaperones permitted a Russian. You know, you may not believe me, but I sincerely admire your country and the American way of life, your freedom of expression, and specifically the free exchange of technical data between western nations. I am an electrical engineer and in Russia we are far behind the west."

With this thin end of the wedge into his country's shortcomings, he drove it deeper still.

"I deplore the years of oppressive governments that have robbed us of will or capacity to independent thinking. Educated people like myself, we are so often at odds with our government for its uncompromising stand on Marxism. That's nothing but a closed philosophic system, a pseudo-science. No one even believes in it anymore."

This Russian's eyes had opened to see the communist leaders lying brazenly in the face of truth as an act of moral and political domination. The intellectuals were forced to accept the lie, knowing it as such. Raúl condensed his soul-searching into two sentences.

"If I dissent in my heart, I must dissent with my hands. If not, I am a silent accomplice to the Soviet lie."

Strong words from a Russian technician working abroad. I wanted to believe in the sincerity of this man. The anguish in his voice mirrored his doubts as well as profound love for his country. But what did he want from me? Was this a trick to have me introduce a Russian mole to American soil? A scene staged by G-2 to see what role I would play? I showed my understanding of his dilemma and asked him nothing. It was for him to tell me what he wanted.

"Thank you for having listened to me. I wanted to meet you. Now I shall decide what I must do. Perhaps Olga will invite us both again one day."

That was all. I never saw or heard from Raúl again, and on next crossing paths with the Czech Ambassador and his wife, received from him the expected glacial eye, but to my surprise, from her as well. In fact, I imagined pure loathing in her look—in retrospect, perhaps it was fright.

I thought it a mistake on Denis's part to have displayed so many photographs. It made my deception the easier. I had misjudged their technique. After idle questions about various of the men and women shown, I was dismissed and not called for two days. A time to brood. On returning, I was shown a smaller board with only twelve photographs, all men, four across and three down, in the lower right hand corner, Raúl again.

The board was placed vertically on the desk leaning against the wall, the pictures at the level of my chest. There was no hiding my expression by bending over. My only idea was to avoid the slightest emotion as Denis watched my eyes go from left to right and back again. It took all my willpower to look at the pictures in their logical sequence, as one reads a book.

"The other day you said you knew no one among the pictures. You've had time to remember. Tell me who you recognize today. There's one or two I'm sure you know."

Always in the plural, always ask for more than you expect to get. To play the game, I studied each face with time-consuming care, even the one I did know, Raúl, in the bottom right hand corner. Denis became impatient.

"*Coño, Americano*, you're wasting my time. Do I have to confront you with your friends? As I did with Roberto, with Lino? How about this one?"

And he jabbed his finger first at one and then another, finally coming to rest on Raúl. Once again I shook my head.

"Maybe the photos aren't clear enough. Here are some more."

From his briefcase he drew out about a dozen loose photographs, the size of playing cards, pasted on cardboard, and threw them on the desk face down.

"Turn them over!"

He watched me carefully as I reversed each card. Raúl was there, and also a face so badly beaten it could have been him or almost anyone at all. I didn't have to hide my emotion at that one, it was too sickening. The actor in Denis registered surprise at its inclusion.

"*Coño!* How the hell did that one get in there? Well, it shows that a little cooperation can prevent such unnecessary misunderstandings."

Was he referring to me or the Russian? Then, picking up the handful of pictures, he discarded the mutilated face, like an unwanted joker. As if dealing cards, he threw the others on the desk one by one face up. It became more difficult to mask my feelings, to throw off this stage fright as if a thousand eyes were on me. Silently he dealt the deck, never releasing me from his gaze. Silently he retrieved his cards, lightly shuffled and dealt again. A different sequence at each shuffle. Anticipating "the" card and trying too hard not to show it, overreacting, was a dead giveaway to Denis.

I knew the purpose of the game and the stakes. To stay in the game meant rejecting all cards, and so I did till Denis's patience gave way. He slammed down the whole bunch, withholding the Russian till last to land face up on the top of the pile. When I raised my eyes to his he was forced to shift his scowl to the cards lying before him on the desk. Like a dog, he was incapable of sustaining eye-to-eye confrontation. For the moment I had won to gain the premium of respite in my cell.

The next day, pictures again, harmless ones of our weekend guests as they garaged their cars in our nearest town. Denis's interest was not in these, but in those G-2 had not photographed. I finally realized he had his list from our ranch guest book. None there to apologize for.

"Why so many western diplomats?" he wanted to know. "Didn't you know any from the east?"

"Yes, some of them, but they never came to the ranch."

"What eastern embassies were you invited to?"

"I've been several times in the Japanese Embassy."

"No, I mean the communist countries."

"Can't recall ever being invited to any of the Soviet bloc receptions."

He didn't accept this, and with threats of firing squads and years of solitary confinement he tried every trick, without ever mentioning Czechoslovakia, to have me admit to Raúl and the Czech connection. He never did succeed in this.

Chapter 16

Accustomed to the uneasy rhythm of my existence in G-2, I began to long for a healing glimpse of nature: a tree, a wave breaking on a beach, a cloud, a bird soaring in the sky. "I .called to the Lord from my narrow prison and He answered me in the freedom of space," and my mind was free to seek out these things. Kneeling before my wall, it was so easy to escape that I wondered why all people everywhere did not more often bend their knee to evade their personal prisons. Under no physical restraint, so many are psychologically captive. Imprisonment I had discovered as a state of mind, and like that song of the twenties, "If I Had The Wings of An Angel, Over These Prison Walls I Would Fly," those freedom-giving wings were there for the asking.

Later, when I was able to compare experiences with other prisoners, there seemed to be two classes of men who instinctively sought God's help: the intellectual, and the humbler man in tune with nature, both sensitive to the needs of others. Although having suffered physical and mental pain, the harm done to their inner selves was less than to those of a more brute nature. Those more physical souls, lacking nobility of spirit, formed a protective shell of insensitivity or apathy to dim reality. They burrowed into the oblivion of self-pity or the make-believe world of fantasy, voluntarily accepting their unfreedom. Some cannot bear too much reality and there was much too much of it in G-2.

If it is as Paul the Apostle says in his epistles to the Hebrews that "Faith is the substance of things hoped for, the evidence of things unseen," then my new faith was bearing substantial evidence of my hopes. Hope—for strength to withstand interrogations of mind and body, hope—for spiritual enlightenment and serenity of spirit, hope—for my family's well-being and our coming together again. The evidence of things unseen was my God-given spirit.

This temporary slacking off of pressure and the now-familiar atmosphere of G-2 permitted less egocentric reflections. With respite from constant interrogations and more time to tend to the housekeeping of cell and soul, I tacked on a supplement to my daily prayers asking for the sight and feel of my wife.

My wife, children and the indomitable Swiss nurse, Nene, had been held incommunicado within the limits of house and garden from May 7 until May 16—nine long days and nights. About five the morning following my arrest, Beatrice had been awakened by the frenzied barking of our young German shepherd. The house was surrounded by rifle-toting soldiers. About forty of them stood on the slopes above, below and to either side of the house. A wax-faced youth in his early twenties called to Beatrice to muzzle the dog or have him shot. As the besieged—two women, three children under eight, and a German shepherd pup—gave no sign of counterattack, the youth and an older man in civilian clothes circled the swimming pool to where Beatrice and Nene were waiting on the porch, the boys mercifully still asleep. The men said a house search had been ordered. "The authorization?" asked my wife. Only conspiratorial grins in reply, but the civilian did show identification: Domingo Gonzáles Moro, Lieutenant of G-2. A thumb jerked over his shoulder at the soldiers indicated the authorization. Search warrants were a luxury only democracies could afford.

The soldiers were dead tired, unshaven and dirty. Those not delegated to search had dropped asleep on porch furniture, pool-side mattresses and lawn. The children were much intrigued by this unexpected invasion of "guests" with their weekend baggage of arms and ammunition. As the"guests" behaved correctly without incident, both women encouraged the boys in their innocent beliefs.

The room-by-room search lasted all morning. The two men in charge said I had left the country, and as they were sure Beatrice was not involved with my counterrevolutionary activities, she could disclose without fear my cache of documents, arms, money and radio. By noon, they seemed unhappy with the quantity and quality of their assembled loot: a Kodak movie camera and projector with a dozen family films, our guest book signed by anyone who had ever visited the ranch, family albums, my Air Force records, a twenty-two pistol, and the prize, my wife's miniature Minox camera. Disappointing for G-2 as the film would show no more than family photos. For the invaders it had been an unsatisfactory occupation of enemy territory with no incriminating booty upon which to hang a man.

Five soldiers remained to see that my family stayed within the confines of the garden. They slept on our porch and ate at my foreman's house four hundred yards below.

My two men, who had cared for our counterrevolutionary refugees in the mountains, were arrested at three that morning, their houses turned upside down. Cleto, our gardener, who lived off the ranch, was taken as he rode his mare into our corrals for the morning milking. Pepe, the yard boy, who had ridden in to the ranch to work, was sent packing and not arrested. High in their hills, my family became as isolated in their house as I in my cell.

My foreman's house on the road below could be clearly seen from our own where Beatrice awaited the Norwegian Ambassador and his wife for the weekend. Saturday morning, Beatrice and Nene watched from our lawn as the Norwegians arrived at our gate below, only to be turned away by the soldiers. Not even a message was allowed. The two women watched in anguish as the Norwegians drove off. If an ambassador were refused contact with them . . . .

Monday, Pepe was allowed to return to work, and for the first time since early Friday morning, Beatrice could get news of our three jailed employees and their families. The charges were aiding and abetting counterrevolutionaries. At no small risk to himself, Pepe had brought a cleaned chicken, refusing payment. In the following week, many of our more humble neighbors opened their hearts to send small gifts of provender through Pepe. Their show of solidarity was heartwarming to Beatrice and Nene.

The days were long for these women, under house arrest, without telephone or outside moral support, an uncertain future, and three small children to care for. The boys amused themselves in the garden and small spring-fed fountain in the patio. They were aware only of a bothersome restriction, one of those unreasonable adult laws, limiting their radius of action, cutting them off from their beloved horses and rides over the hills. The soldiers occasionally fired off short bursts of their guns to entertain themselves and the boys, providing spent Russian cartridges for games only to be imagined by seven-year-olds. Their natural exuberance carried them through each day until nightfall and exhaustion took them, and then they slept like the healthy puppies they were. For the women, tired from a day of chores in house and garden, worried constantly by their dark thoughts, nightfall brought restless sleep, disturbed by the soldiers outside. The boys slowly absorbed the surrounding stress, and soon avoided the soldiers. Intuitively, they shared the animal instinct of our dog, who had shunned these interlopers from the start.

On May 16th, André Adam, Belgian Chargé d'Affaires, and Charles Monnier, First Secretary of the Swiss Embassy, in charge of American affairs, were allowed to visit. They brought letters from family and friends and assurances that the Cuban government had no charges against my wife. The two women's spirits lifted with a tranquility they had not known these nine days of isolation. The Swiss were ignorant of my charges and assumed the worst would be expulsion from Cuba and expropriation of the ranch. Even this did not dampen the women's relief at touching a solid base once more. The garden was still their boundary, but there was contact with the outside world and for the moment that was enough.

The following week brought another visit from André Adam and Emil Stadelhoffer, the Swiss Ambassador, and a less pleasant few hours with a captain from G-2 trying to intimidate Beatrice into an admission of knowledge about my underground activities. There were several of these interrogations, always at night. During this second week the guards were withdrawn and Beatrice given the run of the ranch. She was able at last to visit our three *vaqueros* (who had not been arrested), to exchange moral support with their families, and in anticipation of expulsion from Cuba, slip them supplies from our imported stock of soap and other scarce household necessities. Told she could remove nothing from the house, Beatrice was determined to give as much as possible to these good people before losing it to the Cuban government. The game was discovered and after only four days of semi-freedom, a counter order relegated my family to the confines of the garden once more.

The Belgian Ambassador, Marcel Rymenans, and his wife received permission to come one day. They brought the news that the Swiss Ambassador was to see me June 14th, and expected to have my family's house arrest lifted a week afterwards. On June 22nd, Beatrice could finally pack Nene and the three boys into her car for Havana. On June 25th, she saw me in G-2 for the first time. Forty-seven days of quarantine, a long ordeal for these two women, but not yet over.

LEAVE ME MY SPIRIT

Chapter 17

Thirty-nine days after my arrest on June 14, the monotonous routine was shattered. I was taken to the G-2 barber shop, a mirrorless cubicle, where with cold water and heavy hand, my six weeks of beard was grubbed off and an indifferent shearing done. Neither barber nor guard spoke a word.

Returned to 59, I thought the guard mistaken in cells. A pillow and new mattress lay on one bunk, a mattress stuffed with rags to a good two-inch thickness. The orange, green and blue stripes of the ticking gave off a festive air, complementing the tube of toothpaste, toothbrush and much-diminished soap. And then, wonder of wonders, as if these new-found riches were not enough, the judas window opened to spew forth a sheet, pillowcase and clean uniform. With enormous pleasure I made up my bed, recalling the proverb, "He who makes his own bed must lie in it," and threw myself down naked, revelling in the sensuous feeling of clean sheet against skin, the fresh laundry smell, and a sense of well-being not experienced in weeks. But where were the thorns to this new bed of roses?

With real excitement I made my next trip an hour later to hear Denis, in new role of big brother, announce a visit that afternoon from the Swiss Ambassador. The new luxuries and subsequent visits would depend on my comportment. Conversation would be in Spanish, and any mention of my interrogation was taboo.

Nervous, worried, and hopeful, I was taken down to the ground floor along narrow corridors to one of the small visitors' rooms. There was a comfortable couch, three easy chairs, and a coffee table with artificial flowers. There were no windows. As at a formal party of another era, my escorting guard announced me, "*Señor Teniente*, 1256 here." Denis was there, acting host to the Swiss Ambassador and his First Secretary, and accompanied by a man from Protocol.

My delight at seeing the ambassador was momentarily eclipsed by astonishment over the man from Protocol, my friend from the Foreign Ministry, José Luis Gallo. After his first lightning glance, he looked away without recognition. I understood. Had I foreseen our next encounter, I would have been even more astonished.

This first touch with a familiar world brought a lump to my throat and I dared not speak till I had gained control. Finally, I could talk of what interested me the most, my wife and children. And then the charges against me, of the interventions on my behalf of both the American and Belgian governments, and through telegrams to Castro, of the personal interest shown by the Queen Mother Elisabeth, grandmother to King Baudouin of Belgium. The Queen Mother had been a close friend of my wife's grandmother, and her very real concern came close to tipping the scales in my favor before she died in November of that year. And so I understood why Denis had shouted that no embassies or royal family were going to gain my freedom. Perhaps not, but this interest was profoundly heartening and my morale soared.

A glance at Denis showed an unhappy face. His man was slipping away from him, all his good work at undermining morale, hours that could be called days spent breaking this man down. G-2 must have fought hard to prevent this visit, far too early from their point of view with so much ground yet to uncover. But pressure from two foreign governments had convinced the Foreign Ministry that after six weeks of incommunicado, Cuba had to present this man as alive and reasonably healthy. The two Ministries, Foreign and Interior, seldom agreed, and when in conflict, only Castro could decide the issue. I was to be a bone of contention between the two Ministries for many months, and my wife was to suffer the cruel disappointment of decisions taken by one, rescinded by the other.

The twenty minutes allotted for the visit were enough to reassure me on my family's account and to know that everything possible was being done to free me. A most heartwarming end to weeks of isolation. My faith was substantiated. Here was truly "the substance of things hoped for, the evidence of things unseen."

Back in my cell I had so much to consider, a veritable smorgasbord of thoughts. For some time I had been on a diet rich in the protein of self-discovery, appropriate to the monastic life of solitary confinement, when all of a sudden this was balanced by the leaven of rediscovering values of family and country. Heady food for thought that kept me further from sleep than any threats by Denis ever had. Even the luxury of a soft bed palled before the spiritual nourishment from those twenty minutes of visit. I finally slept, dreaming of promises to see my wife the following week.

Twelve afternoons later I was again treated to shave, haircut and clean uniform, and back to my cell to wait. Never had time passed so slowly. I showered, brushed my teeth, straightened an already immaculate bunk and paced the cell. I said a prayer and cursed my interrogator, a Christian incompatability that bothered me not at all. With that morning-after taste in my mouth, I brushed my teeth again and paced the cell. After an eternity the door swung open. Clicking and whistling our way, my guard headed me for the party.

If the previous week's encounter had upset me emotionally, it was as nothing compared to having my wife in my arms. Each ignorant of what the other had suffered in the last seven weeks, together we took courage and strength from the touch of our hands and the message in eyes. She found me tired, white, and very thin. I found her beautiful, warm, and tremendously understanding, although bewildered by all that had happened and much worried.

I beseeched her to leave Cuba. For the moment, she refused, saying her aunt Marie-Thérèse was coming from Belgium, Marie-Thérèse Ullens de Schooten, a second mother to us both, a woman of strength and wisdom, generous to the needs of others. I hoped she would be allowed to see me. I did not want to see my sons in G-2. At four, six and seven, I thought them too young to understand, and feared their reaction at seeing a man under such conditions they could not recognize as father. I would not see my sons for four years.

Thereafter, Wednesday afternoons, for twenty minutes or half an hour, depending on Denis's mood, Beatrice came, accompanied by either the Belgian or Swiss Ambassador. She was allowed to bring soap and toothpaste, but not a book or magazine. Conversation and reading family letters aloud to me had to be in Spanish. At diplomatic insistence, Beatrice could bring me something to eat each week. At my first "picnic," I consumed an entire apple pie and cheese without a sign of belly protest. The weekly snack became a liter of very sweet tea and either peanut butter, jelly sandwiches or a pie. Never did such simple food taste so delicious! This, plus vitamins she could leave with me, made a substantial difference in my life and did away with an annoying dizziness.

These brief interludes with my wife became the focus of my existence. But each privilege or tangible possession given to a prisoner only makes him more vulnerable to his captors. Something of value may be withdrawn at will, a further inducement to cooperation. It is dangerous to acquire too many privileges or possessions, but I didn't know this then and was eager to stockpile as much as I could. In those early days it was pathetically little. Relatively, it was a fortune.

The day after Beatrice's first visit, Denis said he thought me cynical on replying to her queries of my health and treatment. He warned again that visits were a privilege and depended on my attitude.

"Beatrice is a most attractive woman. Doesn't it bother you that she shares a house in Havana with your friend, that Dutchman, Paul Redeker? He's a bachelor, isn't he?"

Paul had been generous enough to put his house at my family's disposal each week they came from the ranch to see me.

"It doesn't bother me at all. On the contrary, I'm most grateful to him."

As I didn't take the bait, Denis rummaged in his briefcase and produced a photograph taken from a distance with a telescopic lens of Beatrice standing beside her Opel station wagon before Paul's house. Paul was smiling with an arm around her shoulder, a natural gesture for an Anglo-Saxon, but too intimate for a Latin.

"Well now, what do you think of that? Do you still trust your friend with Beatrice?"

I smiled and said, "That's an excellent picture of them both. You know, Lieutenant, that among sophisticated societies it's quite customary for friends to embrace without the sexual connotations imagined by you Latins."

"*Coño, Americano!* Smart bastard! Keep talking like that and you won't have visits with your wife or anyone."

In my newness to the game, that first visit so fresh in mind, I backtracked in haste, falling all over myself to assure no intended insult. He had me floundering and drove home his advantage.

As the interrogator's tactics change to suit the occasion, so too can the prisoner's, depending on his morale, courage and state of confidence. A good interrogator recognizes this and strikes when the prisoner's frame of mind is favorable to exploitation, easing up when not, probing always for the soft spot, getting to know his man's strengths and weaknesses. An interrogator worthy of his job must have something of the psychologist in him to correctly evaluate his "patient," or he loses him along the way. The bulldozer method of threats and cajoling is not enough without character insight.

I believe G-2 assigned the wrong man to me. Denis may have understood his fellow Cubans, but he didn't have an inkling of what makes an Anglo-Saxon tick. This put him at a disadvantage with me, which even his string-pulling puppeteers in the upstairs office (the officers who evaluated interrogations) could not quite dispel. Perhaps they, also, were too pathologically caught up in their inquisitions to assess an American's character correctly. They goofed with Denis and it was to my advantage.

As all interviews were in Spanish, this provided a useful linguistic hedge to hide behind, claiming uncertainty in the language when I needed time for reflection. This annoyed Denis and damaged not at all my supposed superiority complex to pretend this stupidity in his tongue. The prisoner too must get to know his interrogator's strengths and weaknesses to play them as he can. On one of my better days I baited Denis into rage. He criticized my imperfect Spanish after eight years in Cuba. I replied that my vocabulary was superior to his, that I didn't punctuate my every sentence with "*coño*." I don't know why I antagonized him. It never paid off, but one had to find one's pleasures in G-2 where one could. And, as I said, it was one of my better days.

Interrogations took a new tack, touching on the defection in 1960 of a small Cuban vessel to British territorial waters in the Bahamas. My only part had been as broker between the ship's captain and a British diplomat, assuring the captain of a reserved welcome and asylum for himself and crew if they left the ship undamaged for return to Cuba.

The captain was caught returning clandestinely to rescue his family. In G-2 I didn't know this. Only later did I run into him as fellow prisoner in la Cabaña, waiting four years for trial. He told me then that he had foolishly carried his address book back to Cuba with my name inside.

Despite Denis's insistence on my part in the ship's defection, I failed to see how he could implicate me. I admitted to a casual acquaintance with the captain, denying any knowledge of the plot. Denis eventually tired of involving me and let it drop.

On meeting this naval officer later in la Cabaña, he told me he had said nothing of my part in the affair. He shared his modest supply of chocolate, milk and crackers with me, as well as the few books he had. After a fortnight of close companionship, we were walking in the patio together when the loudspeaker called him to the gate. I went with him to a soldier from the Director's office.

"Are you Alfonso Torrado Farías?"

"I am."

"Prepare yourself to leave."

"Where?"

The reply was hunched shoulders, the inevitable refusal to inform the prisoner of any move. The gate swung open as Alfonso turned to shake my hand. Changing his mind, he gave me instead an *abrazo* of *adiós* and said very slowly, as if immensely tired, "It's my trial. This is goodbye, Larry, I'm sure. Please get word to my wife. Tell her I tried to get freedom for all of us. That God may bless her."

At first I didn't understand until the infinite sadness in his eyes told me all. He knew he was going to be shot. He followed the guard away without once glancing back.

That night at nine fifteen we heard the fusilade in the moat outside.

Chapter 18

During my fourth month in G-2, I was taken to a small soundproofed room furnished with a chair and table, no handle on the inside of the door. Denis gave me a dozen sheets of paper, two pencils and all the time I needed to write out my counter-revolutionary activities from day one.

"If you need more pencils or paper, bang on the door," he said. "Paper and pencils will be accounted for when you finish."

It was a novel experience to have writing materials in hand. Instead of cataloguing my sins I began a letter to my wife, printing as small and clearly as I could. I would have to justify the missing half sheet, but that would just have to take care of itself. Here is what I wrote:

"I have never before been so alone and yet felt so close to you. God having come into my life in such a wondrous fashion explains this impact. He has improved my perspective of life and shown where true values lie. With days, weeks, months to think, to come out of the clouds where you said I so often dwelled, I know now I put too much emphasis on our ranch, not enough on wife and children. In keeping together the ranch, I lost sight of family. Can you ever forgive me for involving you in the unhappiness and unpleasantness of my debt to Cuba? How I wish that I alone might pay for this. But God bless you for standing by me so courageously. You can never know what this has meant. It is something that shall stay with me as long as I live. I cannot simply say thank you. That conveys nothing. Through the years I can only show my gratitude for what you mean to me, the admiration I have for you, how I love you and all that you are to me. You are those three fine boys, nine years of much pride and happiness in my life, all the sweetness, strength and goodness I ever wanted in a wife, so much a part of me and so much more I cannot put into words. So desperately I want you to know, to be comforted and strengthened by your husband's love, as each week I am comforted and strengthened by your courage, patience, cheerfulness and loveliness. I pray you love as I do and that this will keep us together always, making a strong and good home for our children to mature in. I don't know what lies ahead, but if I have your love, trust and encouragement I have the strength to make our future a happy and good one. God puts the rough with the smooth to make life more meaningful. We are having the rough, but I pray the smooth is not so very far ahead. I bless God for you, Antonio, Michael and Larry and pray to be worthy of your love, respect and trust through the years ahead. I cherish you, my darling, as I do my freedom and the thought of our life together. God bless and keep you and our sons well and free from all harm."

When Denis returned he took the unused papers without counting them. The palm of my hand was burning from the small wad of paper I held. Once again palmed in my hand at the next visit, I slipped the letter to my wife, unnoticed.

For almost three weeks I saw Denis only on his Wednesday afternoon chaperone duty. I didn't dare believe the interrogations were over. Were they settling for the tip of the iceberg? I cautioned myself against more surprises.

Chapter 19

Since the end of July, I had the great joy of seeing Beatrice's Aunt Marie-Thérèse at each visit. She was a breath of fresh air and we all breathed deeply. Her first question was to ask if I were doing exercises. She suggested another to fortify my back, lately giving me more pain than Denis. It was a swimming exercise, lying flat on the floor. Wishing to demonstrate its intricacies, she hiked her elegant skirt above her knees and dropped to the dirty carpet to kick and stretch in the swimmer's crawl. More than Marie-Thérèse's petticoat was on view and my intrepid interrogator would have put his eyes in his pocket had he known how. Afterwards, he sneered to the embassy chauffeur that this hysterical woman could not see a man without rolling at his feet.

The Swiss and Belgian Ambassadors, together with the Queen Mother Elisabeth through Marie-Thérèse, worked hard through June and July to have me expelled from the country without trial, and were encouraged in this by Raúl Roa, Cuba's Foreign Minister. The Swiss Ambassador had talked twice with Castro about my case and been led to believe expulsion was plausible.

On the morning of August 11, Roa told the Belgian Ambassador that, as a special gesture to Belgium, the Cuban government was agreeing to release me that afternoon into his charge until I could be deported on the weekly British flight to Nassau. My family would accompany me, and I must agree to no publicity, or the fate of other Americans in Cuban jails would be in jeopardy. The ranch would be sacrificed. In my family's joyful expectation of bringing me back to the embassy with them that afternoon, champagne had been put on ice and a telephone call reserved that evening to my mother and father in New Mexico. Despite the ambassador's optimism, some intuition made Beatrice follow the weekly ritual of preparing my picnic.

Arriving at G-2, the ambassador handed Denis the authorization for my release, signed by the Foreign Minister himself. Without even glancing at it, he said, "The Ministry of the Interior will handle its own affairs. The American's interrogations are not yet over. With new charges to be investigated, he cannot be freed."

Strong medicine for Beatrice, who had all she could do to compose herself before the guard announced 1256. For me, the visit went off as happily as all others, and I failed to sense the frustration and deep disappointment. To spare me the knowledge of how close I had come to freedom, Beatrice, Marie-Thérèse and the ambassador were superb actors.

That night, the champagne was taken off ice unopened and the call to my parents cancelled. When the ambassador spoke to Roa a few days later at an official reception, Roa's normal eloquence failed him, and his reply was the Latin shrug with hands outstretched, palms up, as if to say, "What can I do? I'm only the Foreign Minister."

Who can know what went on behind the scenes at the Foreign and Interior Ministries over *el caso* Lunt? Whatever the truth, the screw, momentarily having slipped its thread, was tightened once more. Three months in G-2 had accustomed me to mercurial changes. I expected nothing else. It had become a way of life.

The interviews began again, a medley of charges and half charges, a potpourri of doubts and suppositions touching the Russian, Raúl, and an unsuccessful attempt to link me with a counterrevolutionary group jailed the year before, captained by Ramón Grau, nephew of a former president. Then, circling round but never clinching, Denis hinted at collusion with Roa's son, Raulito, and his attractive Italian wife.

I knew them both, their scorn for Castro, and their lifestyle which had been quite incompatible with the supposed austerity of the Revolution. From Raulito I heard the joke: "Why does the whole country suffer for the sake of one loco? Because it's difficult to get the loco certified when he happens to be the director of the asylum." Raulito had failed dismally as the Revolution's first ambassador to Brazil. Less his fault than the fault of an inexperienced government pushing a brash, arrogant and untried youngster into too deep water. His early retirement from the diplomatic corps solved that embarrassment. Later, his attachment to *la dolce vita* landed him in a disciplinary camp for the strayed revolutionary sheep. If Denis were methodically going through my address book and had reached the R's with the young Roas, I was relieved the alphabet was almost at an end.

The alphabet was not at an end. From R for Roa, Denis doubled back to O for Oswald, Lee Harvey Oswald, the alleged assassin of President Kennedy. No Oswalds figured in my address book. The illogical reasoning in connecting Oswald to me was more complicated, more worthy of some banana republic police force than a Soviet-trained intelligence service. How, when and where had we met? Had I known him in Cuba under another name? How often had he stayed at the ranch? Why did the Americans think Cuba would want to kill President Kennedy? Had I known the President well? No, I had never met him. But if I knew Jackie (this from an address book of my bachelor days), and one of his closest advisors and wife (from my current address book), then I must have known Kennedy. Insinuations continued without real conviction until without warning, "How often and where did you meet your Russian friend Raúl?"

There. G-2 had finally named the man. Heretofore incognito, hidden among a number of photographs—and, I thought, forgotten. But though Raúl had become an entity, G-2 was still loathe to name the embassy and this encouraged me to bluff it out. I could never understand their reticence to name the Czech Embassy, but it worked to my advantage and I denied Raúl more emphatically than the biblical three.

If their intention were to mix in a few well-known names with the one of real concern, the script for these interrogations was freshman written. The only positive thing for G-2 was the blocking of my freedom and the furthering of time to dig at their leisure.

The law of compensation now came into effect. My physical freedom blocked, I was presented with the means to broaden my spiritual freedom. The unexpected gift is the best, and that which I received at the end of August was as unexpected as finding a desert spring to slake a raging thirst. From the first I had been refused all reading material, so that when Beatrice said the Papal Nuncio, Monsignor Zacchi, had received permission to send a Spanish bible, I could not believe it would ever reach me. I underestimated the influence of Rome. That same evening, the judas window flipped open and in the uncertain light, unseen hands held out an object I took for a box until I felt its texture and realized a miracle had occurred. The bible did not glow and illuminate the cell as one of the old masters might have painted, but it was manna to the soul, and felt strong and good to touch. In the darkness I could make out no words, but was comforted in simply holding it and went to sleep a happier man, looking forward to the morning light and this treasure that would transform my solitary days. I had it only a few weeks before it was taken from me, but during that time it was a godsend.

Unable to push hard on the Raúl question, Denis was losing form and often seemed bored with our talks, only going through the motion of inquisitor to justify my being held. What I couldn't know was the constant struggle between the Foreign and Interior Ministries, the former influenced by the broader perspective of Cuba's international image, the latter more by a narrower police-state mentality, often psychopathic in its bent. A regime of terror cannot behave otherwise, but must allow its security apparatus an influence out of proportion to its need. And so, in my case, as the Foreign Minister labored to declare me persona non grata, the Interior Minister insisted on a tough trial. Roa finally agreed, if, I could leave Cuba directly afterwards as a gesture of friendship to the Belgians—something that interested the Interior Ministry not at all. Temporarily, they acquiesced.

The uneasy pact quickly came unstuck. A mass exodus of Cuban nationals, unexpectedly allowed to leave the summer and fall of 1965, provoked unrest throughout the island, unnerving the government, and causing a general call to arms and the suspension of all trials.

And even more fatal to my case, an anti-Belgian sentiment emerged in the government. Cuba was backing the Congolese, fighting for their independence in the Belgian Congo, later to become Zaire. This was enough to dissuade Roa from backing my expulsion. A third letter from the Queen Mother Elisabeth beseeching clemency, and the redoubled efforts of the Belgian and Swiss Ambassadors, were to no avail.

The day finally arrived that I had been both praying for and dreading. From the first, Beatrice knew I wanted her to leave Cuba. Our ranch and home definitely confiscated, she, Nene and our sons had been living in Havana on the generosity of our Dutch friend, Paul Redeker. It was time to put the two older boys in school. Beatrice and Marie-Thérèse could accomplish nothing more by staying on. They decided to leave without telling me beforehand, saving all of us a painful and senseless scene. My intuition had prepared me for this. No explanation was necessary when I walked into the visit the second week of September to find only Marcel and Marima Rymenans, the kind Belgian Ambassador and his wife. A hard blow, even though desired and urged. Until that moment I had not realized how much I counted on my wife's moral support.

Two weeks after Beatrice's departure I was awakened one night and told to gather my belongings. My belongings—a toothbrush, a tube of toothpaste, half a bar of soap, a towel. On the ground floor I found eight other prisoners as white and emaciated as myself. Herded outside, my spirits soared, like a young colt released from winter stabling into spring pasture. I breathed deeply of the cool night air and instinctively threw my eyes upwards to the star-filled sky. A spiritual romp in the pastures of the infinite. There was only this brief moment of respite before being ordered into the Russian paddy wagon with its four locked cages. Nine of us packed into a cage designed for six. An appropriate introduction to what was to be many months of a sardine-like existence. While speeding through Havana's deserted streets, a police car before and another behind, we stretched our eyes for a glimpse of something familiar, but could see nothing through the small window of the door. Twenty minutes brought us to our destination, a forbidden mountain of stone in the darkness. One of the men whispered, "la Cabaña."

Chapter 20

La Cabaña: feminine in Spanish but masculine in every way, solid and strong, domineering, and cruel. One of Cuba's oldest and most feared prisons. Spanish-built in the mid-eighteenth century on the heights above Havana Harbor, of immense coral blocks with twelve-foot-thick walls, and moats thirty-feet deep and forty-feet wide. It never lacked for tenants from its first days under tyrannical Spanish rule on through each succeeding Cuban president, and now, under Castro, it was packed even tighter with unhappy Cubans and others from around the world.

One can be intrigued by, indifferent to, or frightened by the unknown. Because of my inherited make-up I have usually been intrigued and often sought it out. Not this time. To find myself at one thirty in the morning before the enormous gates of la Cabaña was not what I liked after five months in G-2.

The nine of us were admitted through a postern gate by two bored and sleepy guards. Once our G-2 uniforms were exchanged for the political prisoners' khaki with a large *P* on the back of the shirt, we were led down a stone passageway into a "holding pen." An airless, fecal-urine smelling high-arched dungeon, fifteen feet to a side. It was customary to hold new prisoners here for hours, and also those awaiting transfers or interviews. It served, too, as an overflow for the punishment cells. There was no water, and only a four-inch drainage hole in one corner to relieve oneself in, the reason for both the stink and nickname for this underground cesspool, "*la cisterna*." The walls, as high as a man could reach, were covered with the same graffiti as in G-2.

For the first time, we nine prisoners could talk among ourselves. But although the Cubans were friendly, I sensed a reserve at finding themselves with a Yankee, a common enough experience in my last few years. Most Cubans considered any American still in their country as communist and therefore to be mistrusted. I would have to prove myself.

Seven of them were representative of Cuba's educated twenty- to thirty-year olds, driven into ill-prepared counterrevolutionary activities through their violent opposition to the shotgun marriage between their country and Russia. They had the will and courage to fight, but no solid organization. One by one these small groups of valiant men and women fell before the more-disciplined and better-organized communists. Cuba's prisons were overflowing with groups like this. United, they might have moved mountains. Individually, they were helpless.

The eighth man, Tomás Estrada, belonged to no group. In his early fifties, he was big of belly and heart, a Santa Claus face with jolly blue eyes behind thick lenses, one glass splintered by an "over friendly" interrogator. His small publishing house had been confiscated without compensation. In legitimate anger Estrada had written Castro an all too frank critique of his policies. The response had been quick, energetic and typical of all totalitarian states. Late one evening a police car called to escort him to G-2 for a "talk." The talk lasted six weeks under the constant threat of psychiatric treatment. Many months later at his trial the prosecutor sought twenty years for "defamation of the state." In a "humanitarian gesture" the judge condemned him to twelve. This man, in prison for the courage of his convictions, was to die there eleven years later for lack of medical assistance, a simple case of unattended asthma weakening his heart.

Finally released from "holding" and its sewage stench, we were marched in pairs through underground passageways to an interior gate giving into Patio Two where, off and on, we were all to spend so many years. The pre-dawn darkness softened the stark, hostile, fifteen-foot confining walls, and led the eyes upward to the great free space of the sky. We passed dimly lit, grilled caverns, giving no hint of the human beings filed away inside like so many useless statistics in their four- and five-tiered bunks. At Gallery 13, one of our escorting guards unlocked the grill with a huge brass key and motioned us in without a word. Impatiently, he pushed us through and slammed the gate on our heels and returned to his interrupted sleep.

The weak bulb at the entrance and another at the far end showed us little, but our eyes, by now accustomed to the dark, could pick out the vague outline of one of la Cabaña's many galleries—galleries of stone and broken cement, a hundred-and-twenty-feet long, twenty-feet wide, with low vaulted ceilings pressing down from above. Both extremities were heavily barred, with one end opening into the high-walled cement patio, a Dutch oven nine months of the year, the other end opening into the thirty-foot-deep moat, stagnant air until the winter northerlies tumbled in, making frigid wind tunnels of each gallery. Two hundred and fifty men, sometimes more, were jammed into these two-century-old *casernas*, originally ammunition dumps. Despite three ceiling-ventilation grates there was little movement of air in the center of these packed galleries.

From one end to the other, we could see only solid rows of four- and five-tiered bunks with a narrow passageway down the middle. Each two tiers, side by side, one tight against the other, formed a block making a double bed effect of the two contiguous bunks. There was the space of a thin yard between blocks: truly communal living.

Gradually we could see that not only was every bunk inhabited, the broken-cement floor, too, was covered with sleeping forms, filling the central passageway, spaces between blocks of bunks, under the bunks, everywhere, and anywhere. From the ceiling and each bunk hung uniforms, towels, pails, burlap sacks with personal belongings, and foodstuffs sent by the families. There was little space to move in, and we competed for this space with cockroaches, bedbugs, mice, and rats, all of them healthier and fatter than us. At first glance, it seemed impossible that nine more men could squeeze in. But squeeze we did, and we squeezed again when still more arrived.

Like strange horses introduced into an unknown corral, we stood with uncertainty by the gate. From one of the nearest bunks came a drowsy but friendly, "Welcome to your home. How many of you? Okay, *momentico*."

The *momentico* endured as long as it took to waken the gallery chief, the prisoner elected every two months to this thankless task. In the dim light of the sixty-watt bulb, he noted down our names, lamenting about the scarcity of bunks and sleeping space on the floor, but prophesizing an improvement in conditions soon. Wishful thinking, the prisoner's strong suit when all else fails, was the substitute for reasoning. We were tired novices, eager to accept the prophecy of better things to come. We would learn in our own way and time to evaluate for ourselves each set of circumstances, and not to lean lazily on others' unsubstantiated opinions. For the present, we wanted sleep. Where, we didn't care.

The familiar, metallic ring of iron on iron erased the events of the night, bringing several bewildering minutes before I realized where I was. It was dawn outside the open gate, and men carried in burlap sacks of bread, a twenty-five-gallon container of hot, sweetened milk, and a smaller container of watered coffee. I had fallen asleep on the floor, leaning against the wall, and awoke to a forest of legs before me, lining up for breakfast. Having no aluminum cup to collect my ration of *café con leche*, I felt in no hurry to face this new life. I remained where I was, accepting the stares of my new companions who were curious to see the new arrivals, and in particular, the *gringo*, a comparative freak in this zoo.

A familiar voice called my name and startled me into wakefulness.

"Hey, Larry! Over here. It's Julio."

And there, before me, were Julio, my foreman, Mongo, the *vaquero*, and Cleto, our gardener. I knew through Beatrice they had preceded me to la Cabaña by three months from their prison in Pinar del Río, but I hadn't expected we would be together. I learned then that Gallery 13 was for those awaiting trial. We were to be tried together, so they had had to wait for me.

As I took each in my arms in the Latin *abrazo*, I saw tears in their eyes and felt them in mine. The loyalty and friendship shown by these good men were to cause them much trouble, but they never wavered or let me down. They took me in hand, found an extra cup for breakfast, and a spoon for lunch and supper. I refused the offer of one of their bunks, but, to be together, did accept a redistribution of sleeping space on the floor beneath them.

"But, Larry, you are *el patrón*. We cannot sleep on bunks while you sleep on the floor. What would *la señora* Beatrice say?"

"Julio, I was *el patrón*. That's finished. Here we are all the same. I give you thanks, but it will go better if we remain as brothers. Loan me a blanket if you can. And I'm sure Beatrice would say it was good for me."

I was automatically at the bottom of the list for sleeping space, but as men were tried and moved out I would eventually get a bunk. For the moment, I was more concerned with getting a mattress. Those first months, there were never enough to go around, and I counted myself fortunate in having a worn blanket between myself and the filthy floor. The patched and crumbling cement was kept as clean as possible with daily sweeping, but the rationed water was hardly enough for sanitary needs, let alone washing clothes or floor. A five-hundred-gallon tank at each gallery's door, filled daily, translated into less than two gallons per person. Showers in the patio were turned on two or three times a week and rationed to ten minutes per gallery. Even fresh air was rationed, so that the old and sick, particularly the asthma cases, were given preferential locations near the gate into the patio or the window into the moat. Everything was rationed here except the good humor of the prisoners and the bad humor of the guards.

As I was indoctrinated into the life of la Cabaña by my three friends, I was struck by the disciplined acceptance of this most unnatural environment, a veritable beehive in constant movement and sound. With such a compact mass, every action had to be mindful of one's neighbor, remembering he was before and behind, to either side and above and below. A careless gesture, knocking a cup of precious water from someone's hand, could cause a riot. One soon learned to carefully control every start and stop, turn and climb, a kind of close-formation flying discipline. Courtesy normally practiced at yards was brought down to inches. Instinctively, one even took into consideration the location of one's nearest neighbor before a fart.

119

If a plant cannot live according to its nature, it dies. Not so a man. He adjusts. I would learn this in due time, but for the moment, I was appalled at how we had to live. I felt vacuum-packed by the stagnant gloom of insufficient light and air, and weighed down by the compactness of a life without privacy, the forced intimacy of living in too narrow quarters under such unsanitary conditions.

For more than two hundred and fifty men there were two urinals, made from old pails attached to the wall, with rubber hoses which led into the floor drainage pipes we defecated into. These could only be flushed with water left over from the rare washing of clothes.

When diarrhea struck, it struck en masse, and with such primitive toilet facilities, the result was the same as when a heavy rain backed up the sewage to flood the floor. Small wonder that cockroaches thrived and were only outnumbered by the foul-smelling bloodsuckers: bedbugs—competing for the prisoners' attention and curses with the large sewage rats: fat, healthy and aggressive. We used to say, "a prison without cockroaches, bedbugs, rats and stool pigeons is like a home without children."

In compensation for all of this, I rediscovered the joy of companionship and the truth of a shared misery, making of it the less. There were times later when I would long for the solitude of cell 59 in G-2, but for the moment I was content in the novelty of finding myself with people I knew, sharing experiences and family news. And too, presenting thoughts and hopes to receptive ears rather than an echoing wall returning question for question. A greater relief than all of these together was the end to the interrogations, with a backspin to every question. I dared not believe this final, as I would always be at their beck and call as long as I remained in prison, in Cuba.

Denis's questions had ceased, but I had a thousand new ones to answer for Julio, Mongo and Cleto, and they for me. We agreed that of first importance was to arrange for my twenty-five-pound *jaba*, the food parcel. I telegraphed the Belgian Embassy asking for powdered milk, chocolate, sugar, and crackers to augment our slim diet of watery soup with a sometimes sweet potato and hard roll for lunch, a small portion of rice or macaroni and roll for supper, with an occasional fish head or tripe.

These fortnightly *jabas* represented a considerable sacrifice for the Cuban families with food so hard to obtain and ration books not always honored. Families could not put into the *jabas* whatever fell to hand. To make prison life more frustrating, many products were forbidden. Although abundant on the market, toothpaste was one of these, and so we brushed our teeth with Russian, yellow laundry soap. To show the petty stupidity of prison regulations, talcum powder and deodorant were allowed. Medicines and vitamins were not. We had to rely on prison medicines, if they were available. Clothes that families might send in *jabas* were white undershorts, one white sweater, one towel, and bath clogs of wood or rubber. Living in shorts made from old uniforms simplified our clothing needs, except in winter.

It was as difficult to deliver the *jabas* as it was to assemble them. For the wives of my three men it meant leaving at two A.M. to walk six miles into Consolación del Norte, their brothers accompanying them on horseback to carry the packages. The first bus of the day got them into Havana by seven in time to catch another to la Cabaña for the eight-o'clock two-hour visit, a visit separated by two wire-mesh fences.

Twice a month, dressed in their best and with smiles on their faces, if not in their hearts, they dedicated a day to caring for their men—twice a month, with only one of these a visit. For those who lived nearer, they still had to leave their homes at dawn to cope with the erratic bus service, carrying the twenty-five-pound *jaba* containing many items they themselves might have used, but proudly sacrificed for their men.

These *jabas* were usually well-washed sugar sacks, colorfully transformed with bits of ribbon and old dress material, woven into a pattern among the strands of jute. There was pride in making something gay and distinctive of these sacks, and they formed colorful splashes in our otherwise drab galleries. There was pride, too, in carrying them to la Cabaña, or whatever prison of the dozens throughout the island, to be remarked in public as a true patriot with a political prisoner in the family. There were times when some over-zealous militia would signal them out to practice the authorized delinquency of publicly searching their *jabas* for contraband. But this outrage, too, they bore with dignity, while the shame of it rebounded on the militia.

These women carried no anti-Castro slogans though they might as well have. Their faded sugar sacks, resurrected with striking love, spoke out against the police state more poignantly than any written word, and commanded the respect of all who crossed them on their pilgrimage. Strangers helped them on and off the buses, offered seats, and exchanged smiles in recognition of shared sentiment. With their badges of dignified resistance, they were the only anti-government symbols permitted in all of Cuba.

While the families began their preparations for the monthly visit days ahead, the prisoners had only to bathe and dress and walk the fifty yards to the "corrals," as we called the visit shed. But the prisoner would not let it be so simple. Each made of his visit day something equivalent to a national holiday. If he were in a study group, all studies were suspended for three days: the first to prepare, the second for the visit, and the third to recover. Preparations were as much an excuse to break routine as to appear clean and well-pressed before the family. Latin vanity played an important part and no debutante before her first ball paid more attention to bathing and dressing than did my brawny, hairy-chested friends in prison.

Starch, like toothpaste, was not allowed us. Yet there wasn't a uniform that was not so stiff as to deflect a bayonet thrust. It came from bread bought with cigarettes from prisoners in the kitchen. Old bread soaked overnight in water and strained through a T-shirt leaves a starchy syrup that serves admirably for a heavy pudding or stiffening clothes. And although forbidden, most prisoners altered shirts and pants. The addition of a monogrammed shirt pocket to hold a white handkerchief was all the rage. No attention to detail was too much. Even the shoes, unseen by the families, were shined to mirror brightness. Woe betide the man who inadvertently stepped on another's new shine or laid a dirty hand on a uniform ready for the family party.

But clothes were no better cared for than the body. It was as if the entire gallery was off to a dance. From economies made days before, there was plenty of water for bathing, perhaps all of three gallons per man. The Gillette blade was brought out from its hiding place for an extra-close shave that would never be felt through two separating fences. The knowledge was enough. Then, a blizzard of talcum powder from face to toe with enough falling on the floor to discourage the scrounging cockroaches. Next came the stick deodorant, that good three-in-one Cuban brand, largely alcohol and a better fuel than deodorant—an excellent substitute for Sterno to heat milk, or as a perpetual flame before a picture of some saint. It was also mixed with black shoe polish by those alarmed at grey hairs. Before a small square of mirror, using the deodorant stick as brush, they dabbed at the polish and then at the offending sign of years. With patience, they managed to look like clowns, but their vanity was satisfied. As long as there were separating fences, the ruse went undiscovered.

The day before and the day itself were festive with an undercurrent of jitters. These pre-visit nerves on both sides of the dividing fence were something that no amount of years could change. While anticipating the next visit, one was exhausted and relieved when the day was over. The day of recovery was the most peaceful day of the month with everyone either sleeping off the hangover of nerves or quietly discussing what significance the latest news could possible have for political prisoners.

These monthly visits gave meaning and perspective to the years, maintained morale, and established that necessary line of continuity between past, and present, and the future—where hope lay. Hope was with the *bolas*, the rumors so prolific from friends of friends in some ministry, reports on a general amnesty, or prisoner exchange, or that Fidel had cancer. We ate them all and cried for more. Although much of this was government disinformation, we survived the disappointments with a sense of humor and floated our own disinformation campaign. Our homemade rumors returned in better shape than when released, always embroidered to the point of foolishness.

The families brought more than idle gossip. They brought love and understanding and two hours of freedom. Some brought their troubles to be solved or discussed although prison put the man at the margin of decisions. Inevitably, some women stopped coming, sending legal papers for the husband's signature demanding divorce on grounds of desertion. The government sanctioned and simplified these divorces as further means to break morale. A few divorces were instigated magnanimously by the man himself to free the woman from sterile years of grasswidowhood. These men's anxiety of the early prison years had died, together with their hope of freedom. They lived in resignation, their mainspring unwound, the winding key lost. In them could be seen the dependence we all had on wives, mothers, and other women close to our hearts. Cut them from your life and much of your raison d'être goes up in smoke.

The steadfastness of most Cuban wives was magnificent, although there were the inevitable infidelities. Some husbands, incapable of wearing horns in good grace, vowed terrible things against their wives. Others shrugged and blamed God. *Es el deseo de Dios.* Still others accepted it, blaming no one. Raúl was one of these, married to a Mexican. With six years in prison, his wife living in Mexico the last three of these, he received her letter announcing a pregnancy. She asked Raúl's advice on naming the child. He replied that their first child must carry his or her name, and explained to his friends with a wink that the gestation period of Mexican women was often three years.

Visits were held in a long, narrow shed built against the outer wall of our patio. Down the center ran two wire-mesh fences separating family and prisoner by one meter. It took one ingenious prisoner and his visiting brother just a few minutes to enlarge the mesh and to bridge the gap with a hollow-ended cane. Toothpaste, coffee and other prohibited luxuries passed through to the inside, and prison letters passed to the outside. The idea caught fire and the guards caught on. Soon, it was effectively stopped by guards patrolling this no-man's land between the fences.

Clever smuggling ideas were of short duration, either copied to death or spoiled by informers. Smuggling in and out of prison was one of the prisoners' major occupations and therapy. The more repressive the system, the more smuggling was practiced. It was as much a challenge to beat the system as material gain.

The contraband business was not easy. One was constantly up against the guards, and even more, the detested *chivatos*, the stool pigeons. Among this subspecies the lower echelon was the easiest to recognize, those who reported the more tangible misdemeanors— writing and receiving clandestine letters, dealing in the black market of cigarettes and medicines, food from the kitchen, all the visible activities. These *chivatos* were usually the least educated, the delinquents, the homosexuals, those with nothing to lose of a self-esteem they'd never had. They were easily sucked in by the government's promises of special privileges and early release, seldom honored. It was not the obvious *chivato* that presented the problem as much as the supposed friend offering a hand with the foot out to trip. These were the educated, able to infiltrate any cultural level, interested in the intangibles of prison life—what certain men were thinking, trying to influence their thoughts through mutual studies and reading. Some cooperated with the authorities because of honest convictions, others for selfish motives, and still others because of government blackmail against themselves or their families. In time, most gave themselves away. They walked among us as moral lepers, tolerated, but not accepted.

As depraved as the *chivatos* were, so were our guards. In those early days of la Cabaña there were no white guards, only blacks and mulattos. Generally the blacks did not exceed their authority, while the mulattos often looked for trouble, inventing rules to fit their mood. And strangely enough, they were crueler and more unreasonable toward the black prisoners. And there were also the favored few who escaped the guards' machetes, looped around their wrists with leather thongs, the despised *chivatos* among them. The rest of us carried the scars of bruises from blows with the flat of the blade, or with only a flick of the wrist, ugly red slashes from the cutting edge.

While filing outside for lunch and supper, for morning and evening head count, we were continually urged faster by the two machete-wielding guards at the door. During our daily hour in the sun, the guards would swagger among us, "knighting" one here, another there, for imagined infringements of nonexisting regulations. These guards cut a wide swath in the patio and many prisoners renounced their chance at a little sun and fresh air rather than play target to these sadistic children.

Machetes really came into their own at the monthly *requisas*, the great searches when all eighteen hundred prisoners of la Cabaña were swacked into the patio to be massed at one end while platoons of soldiers ransacked galleries and our few possessions. It was carte blanche to blood machetes, throw everything to the floor, and steal Gillette razor blades or whatever else they wanted from our belongings. The half-day operation under the tropical sun in the enclosed patio was torture. We were forbidden to sit or have water. Body against body, we were compressed into an ever-tightening man-swarm, the unfortunates of our perimeter getting the rifle butts and the cut of machetes which crowded them inwards. Many fainted from the heat and the stink. Only the other compressed, sweating bodies held them upright.

Machete wounds, at least, rated prompt attention in the small prisoner-staffed dispensary, by doctors who had been caught up in counterrevolutionary movements. Illnesses of graver consequence might simmer for days before a guard would permit medical treatment. Not that there was much that could be done. The dispensary was less well-stocked than one's own medicine cabinet at home; it was more white paint and 150-watt bulbs than anything else.

That we depended on the guards to receive medical attention was incredible enough. Even more incredible was that, living as we did, we had so few epidemics. There were outbreaks of diarrhea, lasting three or four days, efficiently corked by a medicine brought around in buckets. Flu, of a week's duration, was more democratic and laid low the guards as well. And generally, there were few ailments we could not cope with ourselves. Animals, caged in our condition, would have sickened and died in weeks, while we survived for years. But those with ulcers, heart problems, asthma and other chronic illnesses suffered cruelly from such confinement, without adequate diet or medical care. The worst of them were sent to the prison hospital of el Principe in Havana where living conditions were no better. At least there, there were the proper medicines and professional care—if the authorities wished to give them.

Although we could receive no medicine from outside, one thing the families sent in all *jabas* proved the most versatile of all. *El limón*, the wonderful Cuban lime that grows wild throughout the island. Cubans prefer to take their *limón* with rum in a daiquiri, but those days were long past and *el limón* had become a more serious affair. Heroic with a fever, devastating with a cold, it did well as disinfectant for cuts, controlled athlete's foot, acted forcefully with equal impartiality on constipation or diarrhea, could put the majority of deodorant manufacturers out of business, stopped dandruff, and disciplined the hair. It was almost as valuable tender on the prison black market as cigarettes. Thanks to *el limón* and smuggled aspirin, we coped with the day-to-day physical ailments ourselves.

As in all sciences, there were differences of opinion in our do-it-yourself medical practice. There were those who wouldn't have prescribed *el limón* for diarrhea to their worst enemy. This school favored charcoaled starch, or burned bread. Bruce Catton remarked in *Mr. Lincoln's Army* that "at times the hard tack was toasted on the end of a stick. If it charred, as it generally did, it was believed good for weak bowels." In our case, there wasn't always so much food that we could afford to burn our bread.

One of the more persistent bothers was athlete's foot, with the cure disputed between *el limón* and the aspirin schools. I tried them both and found that a quarter tablet of aspirin pulverized and held between the toes with a small wad of toilet paper will not only clear up the fungus most efficiently, but if left too long, will eat its way to the bone. I've never since dared take one of these time bombs for a headache, although my medical friends assure me the effect on the stomach is less devastating than between the toes.

But the miraculous *limón* could not overcome a broken bone or appendicitis. These were tangible disorders that even the prison authorities could not ignore, forcing them to pack the patient off in the paddy wagon to el Principe. Nor could *el limón* cure a nervous breakdown, an intangible disorder that the authorities had neither the intelligence nor the will to cope with. The majority of these "slipped cogs" were young and well developed, broken under excessive physical mistreatment. They could only count on the kindness and understanding of their fellow prisoners, inadequately trying to shield them from the harsh reality of their surroundings. Mental problems only became tangible in the official eye on turning violent. And then they were trucked off to the mental hospital of Mazora for electric shock and a return to the disturbing and clamorous rawness of la Cabaña. No better for their "treatment," they were still often obsessed with things of the past, still frozen in time.

It was the military in charge of Cuba's prisons who determined if a prisoner's condition warranted hospitalization. And in those early days of the Revolution, from the top administrator on down, the only qualification for getting hired into a prison job was to be a dedicated revolutionary, the ability to be repressive. Revolutionary enthusiasm proved a poor substitute for administrative experience. Later, administrative posts were filled by men and women with at least one year of studying the penal system in Russia, and medical decisions were relegated to the doctors where they belonged.

The worst hell of la Cabaña was the night sound of the firing squad at work in the moat, less than one hundred yards away. In the fall of 1965, six years into the Revolution, the senseless massacre continued. Sometimes only two or three, but often more. It began at nine fifteen, fifteen minutes after lights out. First, the explosion of six rifles firing as one, seconds later, the single "pop" of the *coup de grâce*. It was a profoundly impressionable sound, all the more so when the empty beds that night were in my own gallery—for men without benefit of trial. After the shots, subdued mutterings, curses, and prayers broke the tense silence of the darkened gallery, like the ocean breaking on a pebbly beach. In less than two minutes there was another sound, small and insignificant, caught only by my ears straining against their will: the tap-tap-tap of nailing the coffin lid shut. More than the *coup de grâce*, this distant tapping signified the end of another life. One by one the condemned were shot. Only after a silence of many minutes was I sure no more would die those nights, that I might say a final prayer for them before an uneasy sleep. For those whose deaths we heard, a minute of silence was held the following evening and, though forbidden, prayers were said by Protestants and Catholics alike.

Chapter 21

Each man was compelled to suffer his imprisonment in a multitude of ways. The communists are never content to deprive a man or woman solely of their liberty, but must constantly be degrading, demoralizing, and destroying their prisoner. Nobody insisted that you like or even believe in the system. It was sufficient that you fear and submit to it, that you metamorphose as another mindless sheep to swell the flock. To reduce a person to the quality of sheep, he cannot be left alone to live his life in his own small world. He must be herded here, and there, and back again, learning discipline, and losing something of himself along the way. Shuffle the prisoner periodically from gallery to gallery, breaking up his nucleus of friends. Unexpectedly send in a gang of soldiers to ransack the prisoners' possessions, and confiscate books and magazines just received. Ration their water, food, and light. Sow mutual recrimination, and practice collective responsibility: punish an entire gallery for the misdemeanor of one. Let every day bring uncertainty, unpleasantness. Wear the stone down with constant drops of water.

And by drops was how we received our water. Rationed at less than two gallons a day per man, it became a black market item for bathing and washing clothes. From the prisoner in charge of filling each gallery's tank, a bucket of water cost two cigarettes in cold weather and four in the heat of summer. When the showers ran in the patio, it was forbidden to take out a pail for collecting extra water. I tried sneaking a pail empty out and full in with three friends to shield me. I lost my pail and gained an open machete wound on the back.

The scarcity of water was disciplinary. There were pipes which ran from la Cabaña's huge central cistern to the cement laundry tubs in the patio and also inside all of the sixteen galleries, each with beautiful brass spigots that turned on only air. In our materialistic society, it is an act of faith to turn a tap. One is only surprised and unhappy if no water flows. In Castro's Cuba one is surprised and happy if it does. Like everything else in a communist country, one learns to take nothing for granted, not to assume that because there's a tap in the wall that there must also be water.

Electric light was in short supply as well. Cuba's dependence on Chinese light bulbs at this period of the Revolution was not illuminating. With relations tense between the two countries, Cuba curtailed its purchases and economized on its stock. I wondered who in the future would light Cuba's darkness.

From the ten sockets hanging from the twenty-foot-high ceiling, we had five low-wattage bulbs to light a distance of thirty-five meters. Of such poor quality, they lasted no more than two to three weeks, burning out with a spectacular display of fireworks. Each new bulb rated its own sweepstake as to date and hour of demise, stakes paid in cigarettes or crackers.

Prison mood was in inverse proportion to the weather. Sun and blue skies were unsettling, while rain and clouds brought peace. With a lovely day seen through the bars the talk was louder, penetrating, and more incessant. There was more restlessness. Disagreements were closer to the surface. Rain and gloom softened the feeling of confinement, mellowing us into more amenable moods, constant chatter often fading into peaceful murmur, less raucous playing of checkers and chess (normally sedentary games limited by the rules to two players, but in Cuba, played by as many as can gather round to kibitz).

October, and November, cool freshness blown from the north brought cruel but happy memories of Rocky Mountain autumns, the magnificence of the turning aspens, and the first snows on the highest peaks. For the moment, my Rocky Mountains were the limestone walls of the immense moat, seen through heavy iron bars at the north end of our gallery. There was real beauty and interest in this living rock. Lichen, orange- and green- and gray-colored, much of it in a patina of age that only centuries could achieve. From the crevices grew small, yellow flowers, ferns, and other plants, providing the hunting ground for the bayota families inhabiting the wall.

These lizards, five inches when mature, wore their dragon tail perpetually curled above their back, and their inflatable, bright-crimson air sack under their chin, a bagpipe inaudible to us. They became quite tame, coming through the bars to accept moths and flies from our hands, even climbing our bare legs in search of more. It became our sport to kill insects for these engaging little beasts, and as word got around the lizard world, the more timid chameleons came as well.

Fifteen feet below, the grass-covered floor of the moat was a veritable farm yard of chickens, turkeys, ducks, guinea fowl, and goats, all belonging to the soldiers. These, the rats, and the stray cats were our wildlife. The tamer cats completed daily scavenging circuits through the galleries, and we envied them their contempt for bars. Fifteen feet above our window was the top of the moat and the frustrating blue sky with free, soaring gulls.

La Cabaña was not rated maximum security for nothing. Rifle-carrying guards patrolled the far side of the moat twenty-four hours a day. Over our heads were four machine-gun emplacements placed to fire directly into the patio. There had been cases of prisoners sawing through the window grates and escaping into the moat, but they had soon been recaptured, then to spend months in solitary confinement for their effort. The only successful escapes from la Cabaña were made after the visitors' dividing fence had been removed, allowing prisoners and their families to intermingle. On two occasions, prisoners had used the toilets in the visit shed to change into civilian clothes brought by the family and had been able to walk out to the limited freedom of the street, and eventual recapture.

Among the cross section of society which we political prisoners represented, it was often the sugar-mill owner who organized a school and taught the unlettered peasant to read and write. The peasant, who had never owned a watch, taught the man whose Rolex had been taken from him how to know the hour from the sun's shadow in the patio. And often the simplistic reasoning of the peasant moderated the educated man's intellectual superiority.

Said the peasant, "You tell me you had property and expensive ulcers, that you have lost everything. I never had property or even inexpensive ulcers. You lost your property, but still have your ulcers. Therefore you have not lost everything. You say you were self-reliant. I never had enough to be self-reliant, so I am God-reliant. You say you have lost everything. I have lost nothing. I am still the man I was."

Depending on the books we could get from our families, many of us studied on our own, with others, or gave lessons on what we knew. I gave a geography class from old *National Geographic* maps to a group of peasants. I had first to teach that the great expanse of blue was ocean, not land, and that Miami and New York were not the only settled regions in my country. I helped another group with English. The eagerness to learn was touching, and their unreserved enthusiasm at triumphing over irregular verbs and repeating geographical facts was most rewarding—although I was not always as sure of the facts as my pupils gave me credit for.

I attended a bible class, as did many others coming late in life to an interest in religion. Bibles were in short supply. Despite Castro's talk of religious freedom, they were denied us, as were books on yoga—its self-discipline incompatible with communist dogma. Those few with bibles, usually smuggled in by guards, carried them under their uniform to avoid a sudden gallery search. One man reasoned differently, leaving his bible on his bunk with a small seashell lying on it. Anyone might borrow this bible as long as it was returned with the seashell in place. The owner trusted God to protect His book. In the event God was off on other business when a search took place, the shell was substitute, commanding respect from the superstitious black soldiers with its mysterious power in their African-based religion.

Although forbidden to hold religious services, every gallery had its nightly Catholic rosary and Sunday morning patio. The Baptists held services in alternate galleries. The Catholics were never bothered in their devotions, while our Protestant ministers were unnecessarily harassed, and for celebrating Christmas and Easter, they were transferred to other prisons. From the tolerance accorded the Catholics, it was evident that even Castro yielded to the influence of Rome. Unlike the Catholics' Papal Nuncio, the Baptists had no ambassador to represent them.

The most set upon of all were the Seventh Day Adventists. Their refusal to honor the nation's flag, their self-discipline, and faith in God alone were in direct conflict with all that communism stood for. They were hounded from their temples, denied jobs, schooling, and housing, and jailed by the hundreds. They stood their abuse with admirable stoicism, indicative of their total faith in God. Of all the Seventh Day Adventists with me in prison, I never knew one to bend before the humiliations heaped upon them. They were a valiant lot.

On the margin of all religions, and persecuted by none, were the spiritualists, trusted in all stratas of revolutionary society, from Castro down. One of Castro's closest confidants, and personal physician, was René Cirilo Vallejo, a medium with his own spiritualist center near Manzanillo, an open adherent to the Afro-Cuban religion Lukumi.

Of all religious celebrations in the west, Christmas headed the list. Castro had abolished Christmas in favor of July 26, his arbitrary date for Revolutionary Cuba's national day. He said, "Christmas is a bourgeois custom inherited from a decadent society. Cubans must form their own customs." But a communist decree cannot so easily eliminate a two-thousand-year-old birthday embedded in the heart and soul of man.

Despite our scarcities in prison, there were great efforts to mark the 25th of December as a special day—small alters to the Virgin Mary with candles of deodorant, cardboard cutouts of pine trees and Santa Clauses festooned with cotton wool and mercurochrome, and bracelets of colored paper cut from magazines. For my contribution I made mobiles from dip sticks and used hypodermic injection ampules filled with colored medicines from the dispensary, seashells from a pile of sand in the patio, and birds cut from the silver paper of chocolate bars. These hung above the door catching sunlight to throw elusive colors into the dreariness of our gallery. But the art of mobiles was unknown to the guards and within twenty-four hours they'd torn them down. The other decorations were tolerated until the 26th when they too were destroyed, the cutouts of the Virgin Mary trampled on the floor.

On my first Christmas in prison there seemed little "peace on earth, good will to all men," except that which we practiced among ourselves. But "Hark, the Herald Angels Sing," and by God they did. They sang in our hearts and we sang with them. The familiar carols, sung Christmas Eve in Spanish, had special meanings of depth and strength, even to the guards who gathered outside our iron bars to listen.

We sang carols, the old Cuban *paso doble*, tangos, the monotonous but popular *punto guajiro*, and then the popular songs of the day. Finally, the music of hand-to-pail and spoon-on-cup in pure African beat dominated diminishing voices.

No white can coax rhythm from an upended pail as can a black. Rhythm is as much a part of the black as the air he breathes—the natural flow of related coordination between brain and muscle, activated by sight or sound into a music of its own. Given the most basic materials, small stones from a river bed, sticks of dry wood from the forest floor, bleached bones of some long dead animal, pebbles inside a wild gourd, given any two objects that struck together produce sound, and a black will return to you a rhythm.

Axiomatic it is that a pail becomes a drum, and bottom up between the knees, it is as good a percussion instrument as the man who plays it. Sticks of wood razor-bladed into drum sticks were favored by some, while the purists used only fingers and the flat of the hand. By either method, the humble pail rose to artistic heights for which it was never intended. And many a man looked high and low for his missing pail, once full of hoarded water, only to find it between the knees of some friend, full of sound, and entertaining a group of aficionados.

A week later, New Year's Eve was another night of music and declaiming poems. At midnight, the harbor below erupted with ships' whistles, sirens, and the deep-throated hoots of the larger vessels. A new year emerged, full of hope for a prisoner exchange, never to materialize, and full of hope for a better life for the Cuban people, only to get progressively worse. What a blessing that man cannot foresee the future, for how many of us could have supported the years ahead, given a clear vision of them at the dawning of 1966?

Chapter 22

Imprisoned, eight months. Without recourse to a lawyer, without a trial. Only in January was I allowed to see the Cuban lawyer assigned me by the Swiss, caretakers for American interests, a matter of form alone, when no lawyer anywhere could influence the predetermined sentence.

Raúl Carro was a small, unsympathetic man. Everything about him was brown: shoes, suit, tie, hair. A sense of humor would have helped us both, but that too, was brown. I suspected his life was as colorless as well. At our first visit he told me in his cold, impersonal manner that my trial could come at any time, and to expect the government's request for the maximum sentence of thirty years. At our second visit, he would answer nothing but legal questions, and in a manner more appropriate for a judge than a friendly counsel. Had he only told me of the immense amount of work on my behalf outside of Cuba, it would have eased a pre-trial stint of solitary confinement and interrogation in G-2 (although the end result would have been the same).

There were many who worked for my release. Three weeks after my arrest, my sister, Faith, had established contact with a Cuban,

Señora Berta de los Heros, who had been influential in the release of prisoners from the Bay of Pigs fiasco. And she still had an open line to Castro. It was hoped she might interest him in my exchange for badly needed medicines. For reasons of their own, the U.S. State Department pulled the plug on this one.

Also, James Donovan, a New York lawyer who had been pivotal in the release of prisoners from the Bay of Pigs invasion, had agreed to help. His usefulness was soon destroyed by the publication of *The Invisible Government* by David Wise, which disclosed the hand of the CIA in his prisoner negotiations. Anything which even remotely smelled of CIA was anathema to Castro, and he wanted nothing to do with Donovan.

Friends in Mexico asked the Foreign Minister, Antonio Carrillo Flores, to sound out the Cubans on my worth in merchandise or dollars. Anticipating this at my first visit in G-2 with Beatrice, I had said I wanted no part of being bartered. Apparently I was unconvincing, as my family never gave up on trying to buy my freedom. They considered a man with vision cut in two by iron bars incapable of reasoning clearly. They would not understand I could never live with a clear conscience had the communists fattened off my family, and that I preferred years of prison to being ransomed.

Before the Mexican Foreign Minister could act on the ransom proposal, it was put on hold to see the results of intercession by three distinguished Belgians: the Queen Mother Elisabeth, the Foreign Minister, Paul Henri Spaak, and the Christian-Democratic Senator, Raymond Sheyven. Scheyven had traveled often to Cuba and much admired Castro. The Cuban Foreign Minister, Raúl Roa, had been impressed and was favorably inclined to negotiate my release, but conflict of interests between the repressive hard-liner Ramire Valdés, Minister of the Interior, and himself, prevented this.

In Belgium, another strong champion of my cause was Beatrice's aunt, Marie-Thérèse Ullens. Before arriving in Cuba in July 1965, she had been advised to see Celia Sánchez, Castro's paramour of the Sierra Maestra, and still influential. The wife of Che Guevara, said to have been another of Castro's castoff mistresses, was also recommended as worth seeing. Discussing the best way to contact these women with the British Ambassador, Adam Watson, she was told, "Neither of these women can help you. Castro's real mistress is power."

There were Cuban prisoners in foreign countries, but none that Castro wanted to exchange me for. It was suggested "to go out and get one," as the Russians do when in need of barter. Impounding works of art which had been confiscated in Cuba and sent for sale in Europe, was considered. But attempts to impound Cuban shipping ran into court orders adverse to this. Multinationals were approached through their presidents and chairmen to tighten Cuba's blockade. Their general attitude was pragmatic and brutally summed up by one: "Let this albatross rot around the neck of Kennedy's successor."

And so it went, with one avenue after another explored, all dead-ending. But not for lack of imagination or initiative.

Completely unaware of all that was going on behind the scenes, I was awakened by a soldier in the pre-dawn cold of February 1st and marched through the silent prison to the administration office. Even the guards were huddled—asleep at their posts. Complaining of the hour and the cold, they too were awakened and unlocked the great iron doors to let us through. The snappy, clear air off the ocean was heady breathing after the oppressive, stale heat of the gallery: one of the positive moments in a life too full of negatives.

The lieutenant on duty was sufficiently awake to verify that I and the order-of-transfer were one and the same, that the prison seal functioned better if inked, and that, *Coño su madre!*—his Russian ball-point pen wouldn't write. Instinctively I reached for my own, thought better of it, and scratched my head instead. Does the fish help bait the hook?

Bureaucracy satisfied, I was hustled out to the paddy wagon to be locked into one of the four cages. Unable to catch a glimpse of my destination from the order of transfer, I guessed G-2. Where else? The purpose worried me. Why now, just before my trial? G-2 it was and as I emptied my pockets of the ball-point pen, a couple of broken pencils, and a nail clipper, I thought, *What poor pickings compared to the rich booty of nine months ago.* And down the long, shoulder-wide, low-ceilinged passage to the narrow stairs I went—it was as claustrophobic and sinister as my first walk here had been. On the second floor, I changed my uniform for G-2's one-piece jumper. I was put on the same floor, different cell. It was not as terrifying as the night of my arrest, but still darkly depressing. There was no mattress, and in my inexperience, I had brought no

137

toothbrush, towel or soap. Back in square one, a little wiser in prison ways, but not enough.

I was taken to G-2 on February 1st and returned to la Cabaña February 11th. What transpired in between is lost to me. It was not customary to return a prisoner to G-2 immediately before his trial, even a foreigner. It was suggested later that I had been drugged to elicit a last act of contrition. A psychiatrist fellow-prisoner offered another supposition. My mind had simply rejected a particularly unpleasant ten days, relegating whatever it was to total eclipse. I wish I knew.

My world came into focus once more on returning to la Cabaña, and the reassurance of running with the herd again dispelled the maverick feeling of going it alone. My friends in prison had alerted the Swiss and Belgian embassies to my transfer through messages to visitors, and they had made their official inquiries. It was comforting to know of their interest in my welfare, not just from one embassy, but from two. There were foreigners in la Cabaña who had not even one embassy interested in their welfare—two Greeks, among them.

I returned to new excitement and speculation on prisoner exchange, based on the acceleration of clearing the growing backlog of tribunals. During my short hibernation in G-2, the courts had been busy churning out their grade-B judicial scripts. Those of us still untried could expect our trials at any moment.

Among political prisoners there was a certain pride in having a heavier sentence than another, a childish "I'm more of a tiger than you are." At the expiration of a thirty-year sentence, I would be seventy-two. I'd let the others play tiger. Usually the sentences handed down were half of what the prosecuting attorney requested—"a humanitarian gesture." Balls! A tragi-comedy that fooled no one. For myself, short of the firing squad, I anticipated Castro's maximum, thirty years at forced labor.

I had been notified February 12th that my trial would be held on the 16th, time for alerting both Swiss and Belgian embassies. Knowing my lawyer could say little, and that his presence was all part of the charade, an empty gesture, I lay long awake those three pre-trial nights reviewing all that touched on the accusations against me, storing mental notes to use, and realizing the futility of standing up for myself. So I decided on another tack. Attack!

Few prisoners, innocent or guilty, availed themselves of legal aid, either speaking for themselves or refusing to speak at all. If I took advantage of my right to speak in court, it was only to release the pent-up outrage of all I had lived, seen, and heard in the five months I had been pigpenned in la Cabaña. There was nothing new to what I had endured. The world had seen it a million times before, and would see it all again. But it was new to me, and to my companions. To accept it in silence, unprotestingly, seemed a cowardly denial of all I believed in, of the very reason I was there. My family would later call my speaking out an obstinate, naive tenacity. Had I not talked, I would have called it a sterilization of spirit.

I knew about the tribunals. I had heard the story a hundred times from those already tried. But still I sought out Chino, a sensible man of large proportions, heart included—of gentle nature until aroused by some injustice done himself or friend. Spanish ancestry, with a sortie into the orient at some forgotten time, accounted for his nickname. Two months before, Chino had gone to his trial in despair, prepared for the firing squad, and had returned elated with thirty years. I felt like a small boy before a dental appointment seeking reassurance that it wouldn't hurt, but I wanted the story of the trial one more time.

"*Bueno*, Larry," said Chino, "I hear you're thinking of going on the stage. You better damn well put on a good show, or you'll get your applause in the moat like I almost did."

"Chino, cut it out. I'm in no mood for jokes. I'm not worried about the firing squad. It's the number of years they're going to hand me, the number of years I'm going to have to look at your stupid face."

"*Hombre!* They can't give you more than thirty *añitos*. You'd look ridiculous sitting on a cloud with a halo and pair of wings. And anyway, *amigo*, when your time comes it's down below with me."

"You may be right about the *añitos*, but all the same, like you said, the first thing I'm going to do when I walk into court is count the chairs."

In la Cabaña's makeshift courtroom there were five chairs for five judges when a verdict of the firing squad was being deliberated, three chairs for all other cases. I was not expecting the firing squad, but I would count the chairs.

We had been up before dawn, nervously busy at the pre-trial ritual of bathing, powdering, and perfuming. Then we dressed carefully in shoes and cardboard-stiff uniforms that would have done credit to any Marine. No need for begging today. Shoe polish was gladly proffered as was scarce deodorant and hair oil. The man with threadbare underwear was loaned new shorts and T-shirt, though none but he would know. It was a preoccupation with appearances that was as much to absorb apprehension as to communicate spirit and morale to the families across the courtroom.

At seven, a guard with typewritten list called us out, our names for once correctly spelled. There were twelve of us: myself, the three men from my ranch, and eight other Cubans from another case. We knew each other well. On this day of judgement we felt as one, and yet isolated, each off on his own tangent of thoughts, a feeling of unity mixed with remoteness.

Leaving the patio, there were shouts of good luck, and obscene messages for the judge, and not a few for Fidel Castro himself.

"Tell the judge to stand up when he pisses."

"Tell the judge I shit all over him, and his mother too if he ever had one."

"Tell the judge I've still got the clap his wife gave me."

"Ask Fidel why he doesn't have a birth certificate."

"Tell Fidel if he has the balls he can come up here and kiss my ass."

"Tell Fidel to buy a new skirt for his fairy brother."

Tell the judge, tell Fidel—it made everyone feel great to shout this dirt in front of the guards. After all, we political prisoners were the only ones in Cuba who could shout like this. We had nothing to lose. There was nothing more they could take away from us.

We formed in twos to be marched across the patio to the applause of sixteen galleries, men who had gone through this farce months or years before. It was a moving experience to be the focus of this spontaneous show of solidarity.

We passed through two sets of twenty-foot-high iron gates, a fifteen-yard no man's land in between where we were frisked, superficially or thoroughly, depending on the guard. Awaiting us beyond was our escort of eight bored soldiers, smoking and leaning on the muzzles of their old Garand rifles. The corporal in charge tried to march us in step over the two hundred yards to a small drill ground on the battlements. He could form us and drive us, but not force us into step nor threaten with bayonet. Not this day of public display.

We waited on the drill ground in the warm February sun for almost an hour, a welcome defrosting from the cold and humid gallery, while our escort eyed us from under a tree. There was little conversation, each guarding his own thoughts, each suffering the stagefright of an "opening night" performance. Despite my nervousness, I could not but appreciate the beauty of the day, the view of Havana across the sparkling bay below, the rusty Spanish cannons still in position, each with its pyramid of shot neatly stacked, the two-century-old walls lichened a soft grey, green and pink, the graceful wrought-iron lamps of gas jutting from niches in the coral wall.

Nine o'clock drew near, and a bark from the corporal unslouched the soldiers from under their tree. Another bark instructed us to form into twos and move off, this time the "keep in step" omitted. We went down the wide tunnel, through solid rock, from the heights of la Cabaña to the very edge of Havana Harbor, to the low stone building, a storehouse in the days of Spanish rule, now fitted out with the bare necessities of a court.

The ambassadors of Switzerland and Belgium stood by their car. The small, Swiss flag on the right fender was a pretty sight for all to see. While their presence could not change the trial's outcome, it worked wonders for my morale. I raised a hand to them in gratitude and greeting, and got smiles in return. From the corporal, verbal machete slashes.

"*Coño su madre, Americano,* I told you no talking with the public. You wanna spend those thirty years you're gonna get in solitary? I can arrange it!"

His narrow, hatchet face with green eyes too close together was convincing.

I looked for friends from the American and British press: George Arfeld of UPI, Tim Crocker of AP, and Robin Doyle of Reuters. I knew they'd requested passes, and naturally they'd been turned down, although the Cuban press was there in force.

Near the entrance was a crowd of relatives, waiting to be admitted. A few of the women shyly waved handkerchiefs at their men, but none dared speak across the distance.

Julio, Mongo, Cleto, and I were separated from our eight companions and marched inside. As one, our heads swung to the head of the room to count the judges' chairs. Three! None had

141

expected five, but still— Prodded forward, we were parked on wooden benches at the front of the long, narrow room, facing the tribunal. To our right sat desks for the prosecuting attorney and court secretary. To our left, a desk for the defense, if the prisoner had one. There was no Cuban flag, no banner of the Revolution's 26th of July, not even revolutionary slogans on the walls. The whitewashed room was strictly functional with no pretense at being anything but what it was, a small stage for Castro's long-running, smash hits.

Back of us sat the public, with a sanitary zone of fifteen feet in between. Two guards stood behind us, and one sat on either side. As we instinctively turned to watch the families enter, we were told, "Eyes front and keep 'em there." From the corner of my eye I saw the two ambassadors isolated in a corner.

Carro, the lawyer for the four of us, took his seat at the desk for the defense. A young mulatto woman, dressed in army uniform of shirt and skirt of different washings, made a pretense at dusting desks and shuffling chairs from one position to another and back again. The ballet of her rump in a skirt too small was a welcome distraction. Later she sat behind the prosecuting attorney taking notes and gossiping with another mulatto woman, who seemed to have no function whatsoever.

A corporal called us to our feet as the three judges and the prosecuting attorney filed in. The president of the tribunal was white and middle-aged, his two assistants black in their early thirties, all in uniform without ties or rank. Shoes unshined, uniforms unpressed. Altogether not a very impressive forum for a court of justice, but adequate as sounding board for "guilty."

The corporal read the charges. My three men were accused of collaborating to hide and protect counterrevolutionaries. I had the additional charge of espionage, illegal dollar exchange, selling black market pigs, and providing money for counterrevolutionaries. Corroborated by others, I admitted to it all.

I was called first to the stand, or more literally, to the wooden chair before the judges. I was allowed to sit for my trial. When the others' turns came, the chair was removed and they stood. A hollow courtesy to me because of diplomatic presence?

Without reference to speaking only the truth, the whole truth, and nothing but the truth, so help me God, my trial began.

"Do you plead guilty?"

"I do."

142

The prosecuting attorney then spoke quietly, in detail, reviewing each charge. He looked like any successful lawyer in well-pressed suit and tie, in his thirties, with an intelligent face that under different circumstances might have encouraged confidences. He showed photographs of equipment I had either introduced into the country (myself or through an embassy), or been responsible for, and asked me to identify them. A miniature Japanese camera, binoculars, map projector, a device for measuring distances up to ten miles, and other items. I denied responsibility for blown-up pictures of plastic explosives, a snorkeling gun with poison-tipped spears (so said the caption in bold letters) to attempt the life of Castro while practicing his favorite sport of underwater fishing, electronic gadgets of vague use, and other figments of their imagination. Following the interrogation, the tribunal president asked if I wished to make a statement. On replying that I did, I saw my lawyer drop his face into his hands.

I had smuggled out a pencil stub on the advice of a friend, and used it to write notes on the palm of one hand during the prosecuting attorney's long-winded speech. On noticing this, one of the black judges surfaced from his boredom to nudge his colleague and whisper in his ear. The other raised outraged eyes to mine, considered a moment, and gave an eloquent gesture of his chin towards the ambassadors. The two only glared, hoping, I suppose, to intimidate the gringo from further notes. I scribbled on.

When I rose to speak I was told to sit. Standing, I might have spoken better, but I sat. Checking the notes on my hand, I began by denying the more flagrant of the prosecuting attorney's bombastic lies, concocted to spice his dish of scrambled propaganda. None showed the slightest interest in my denials. I denied corrupting the peasants of San Andrés with anti-Castro tirades, enslaving my workers, and other untruths larding their case. Against undocumented charges, I denied proselytizing any Russians for the CIA, much less even knowing one.

I didn't need my notes to express my thoughts on Cuban justice, considered carefully through three days and nights. With my sentence a foregone conclusion, how could a few words of truth harm me? I talked of my appreciation for the Cuban people, of my initial enthusiasm for the Revolution eroded by the gradual disillusion that came with Castro's betrayal of all he pretended in la

143

Sierra Maestra. I talked of my disgust over the conversion of Cuba into a police state—the judges exchanged nervous glances here—of the inequality of sentences when equal years were meted out to a saboteur as to one whose only crime was trying to leave his country, and others imprisoned on no evidence whatever. Why should a simple peasant like Cleto, our gardener, receive ten years for providing food to a counterrevolutionary hiding on our ranch when others, who had supplied arms to this same man, were jailed for only two months? I talked of the sadistic treatment in la Cabaña, of "justice" dispensed by machetes, and the work of the firing squad at night. "Firing squad" was too much for *el compañero Presidente de la Tribuna.* Half rising from his chair, he brusquely shouted, "Enough! Enough! It's we who make the charges here, not you. Your time is up."

I had more to say, but condensed it in one final barb.

"I have little faith in Cuban justice for myself, but hope you will treat these three men with me to the justice they deserve."

Their outrage was glorious. The president clasped his hands on the desk before him and threw his eyes to the ceiling, clicking his tongue rapidly as if summoning some revolutionary minion. The two blacks on either side rolled their eyes and slumped lower in their chairs, then turned on cue to their boss, as if seeking a clue to putting the script back together.

The president dropped his eyes from the ceiling, looked quickly at the two ambassadors, and enunciating each word with venom, spat, "That is enough, I tell you! You can retire yourself to the bench. Now! This minute!—Next prisoner!"

In the intensity of my emotion while talking I had forgotten all else. My mind was clear with little need of the notes on my hand. I saw and felt only the three judges, ten paces before me. My eyes never left theirs, first one, then another, and back again to the first. They in turn responded with their full attention, an almost physical contact in which I felt their contempt and outraged egos. Only the presence of western diplomats kept them from silencing me long before. It must have been painful for them to play their part.

None of my three men wished to speak, and were rushed through their charges with small interest. More of a chorus to the principal song.

Carro, lawyer for the defense, was then called. While he talked, one judge yawned, one picked his nose, and the third was lost in contemplation of the prisoners' families. The prosecutor studied his shoes and the court secretary nodded on the edge of sleep, no longer fulfilling the empty formula of recording the trial. The comedy continued with Carro asking clemency for the three Cubans.

"They gave shelter to a friend and neighbor, not knowing what he had done against the Revolution. Julio, Mongo, and Cleto are not counterrevolutionaries. They are patriotic, God-fear—"

He stopped, realizing that God was not an acceptable plea before this atheist tribunal.

"They are patriots," he repeated. "They have children dependent on them. Their wives—"

Carro was talking to the hearts of men who had no hearts, and asking understanding of a court that had no understanding, a court with no ears to hear, a voice that could only say "guilty." He went on.

"And for Lawrence Lunt I ask clemency too, to demonstrate the strength, humanitarianism and goodwill of the Cuban Revolutionary Government towards all nationalities. Let this man return to his country to be evidence of the Revolution's high moral ethics."

There was more, but I hardly listened. Carrying little animation or conviction, it was an uninspired defense, but he had been actor in these farces before and knew the futility of his job. When he finished, the president registered surprise. Surprise at the brevity of the defense, or that he had dared to defend at all? The court was declared in recess and the room emptied of all but ourselves and guards.

Fifteen minutes later, the court reconvened, and the prosecuting attorney launched into a desk-thumping brawling justification of Cuba's right to treat her enemies as she saw fit, shooting them if necessary, without need to apologize. How could an *Americano* exhort justice from a country rebuilding a new peace-loving society from the ravages of imperialism when exhibiting his hate and fear by working against it as an agent of the CIA? An *imperialista*, whose only idea was to exploit the people and land of Cuba with his cattle ranch! What right had an *Americano* to talk of firing squads when trained by his government in two wars to kill, maim and destroy? How could an *Americano* discuss justice when he had flown in a night-fighter squadron bombing and strafing hospitals, schools, innocent women, and children? (Our planes had never carried bombs, and he was breaking my heart with his list of atrocities.)

It waś his conviction that had I been captured by the North Koreans I would have been shot. I deserved the death sentence, but as the Cuban government was humane he would ask only thirty years at forced labor. There was more of his broken record of communist propaganda, but finally he wound down his spirited attack to return triumphantly to his desk. Everyone on the stage had played his part. I hoped the show was over.

It wasn't. From the back of the room appeared the state's witness, my interrogator from G-2, Jorge Denis Rivero. He had done his homework well and without notes went over in detail each charge against me, reiterating with relish my war record, inventing economic rape of the countryside where I ranched, and for good measure, fabricating untruths of my personal life. When not occupied subverting the authority of the state, I was subverting the morals of diplomats' wives. The bacchanals at 464 San Lazaro were legend in all of Havana for their depravity. And on the ranch I was seldom sober enough to sit a horse. A grade-B script unacceptable for even the morning TV serials.

A summing up by the president, and the trial was over. Two hours and thirty-five minutes of judicial burlesque with a verdict in hours or days. It would be twelve days before I knew mine.

Unknown to me, my family was counting on the promise of Raúl Roa, the Foreign Minister, to release me after my trial. Now they were worried over my attitude in court, feeling that in ten minutes I had undone their months of behind-the-scenes work. But a Cuban friend, active in the counterrevolution outside of Cuba, said to my family, "Larry's behavior at his trial was an inspiration to all Cubans. I wish we had many Larrys."

Another comment on my behavior at the trial came from a family friend in the CIA, "Larry is one of nature's noblemen belonging in the Civil War leading a cavalry charge."

The most pragmatic comment came from Adam Watson, the British ambassador in Havana, who had followed my arrest and subsequent trial with friendly interest. He said to my sister Faith in Washington, "Your brother's behavior in court was gallant but foolhardy, very prejudicial to his interests, infuriating the Cubans with his remarks on machetes and firing squads."

He thought a good deal of time should lapse before attempting first aid on my case. The Swiss and Belgians agreed.

According to revolutionary law the verdict is given orally to the defense lawyer, or family, with two weeks to appeal. If no appeal, the written verdict is given at the end of that time. On February 28th, my lawyer was called to el Palacio de Justicia to hear the sentence: thirty years for me, fifteen for my foreman, ten for the other two, all at forced labor. As I had pleaded guilty, and to draw no more attention to my case, no appeal was made. My value to the Cubans had already been inflated by too much international interest.

Thus, after five months of solitary confinement in G-2 and four of convalescence in la Cabaña, I was judged, convicted and declared qualified to participate in the Cuban Penal System of Rehabilitation, *el Plan de Reeducación*.

From an official bulletin: "The progressive regime of political prisoners, *El Plan de Reeducación*, is humanitarian and disinterested, divided up in phases of reeducation, rehabilitation and re-integration into society. Each phase represents an easing of prison discipline corresponding to the individual's attitude during this modification of his conduct and customs. Only through *el Plan* can a prisoner achieve freedom."

El Plan was copied, like much else in the Cuban Revolution, from the Russians and designed to brainwash through political seminars and schooling. The dominant theory of the early Revolutionary years was that forced labor and study were the basic method of reeducation with political, cultural, and recreational activities serving as stimuli. But forced labor was the stick without the carrot, while studying was nothing more than pure formality, satisfying an obligation rather than a process of learning.

I refused *el Plan* to join the passive majority known as *los plantados*, the planted ones, or those who would not budge.

In order to swell the percentage of prisoners opting for *el Plan*, the Russian-trained *reeducadores* worked incessantly selling their product among us in short interviews two or three times a month, or more often if the subject seemed receptive. And when particularly interested in an individual, they were not above blackmailing him into *el Plan* through false accusations, pressure on the family, threatening the wife with loss of a much needed job, or refusing the children participation in vacation camps or higher education—any means to an end.

These *reeducadores* were quick to recognize the difference between *un duro* and *un limón*, the former hard to crack, the second more easily squeezed. Once *un limón* agreed to rehabilitation, he was sent into agriculture or to on-the-job training in construction, where the caliber of his work was often superior to civilians'. And the reason was simple: prisoners in *el Plan* were promised the freedom of civilian status, and so worked hard to attain it, while those already having civilian status found it lacking, and so worked less.

Time passed with the days seeming longer than the weeks. The present was all uphill from morning to night, from Monday to Sunday, and then suddenly it was Monday again, and the week just past had flown downhill leaving one wondering at the passage of time. As none had a watch, our timepiece was breakfast, lunch, supper, and the sun's shadow in the patio. Our calendar was the monthly visit. We lived for each day alone, letting tomorrow take care of itself.

Tomorrow belonged to the spiritualists, foretelling the future with enough hazy latitude to satisfy the dreamers gathered around. Jorge Delgado was a spiritualist in my gallery. Fifty-two, appearing seventy, with an old man's stoop shortening his already short body, he had an unhealthy pallor with age-blotched skin adding to the impression of great years. An uneducated, quiet fellow, he was at the tail end of every queue, at the head of all spiritualists for veracity.

Jorge had many spirits to call upon. In April, his most reliable, a Congolese chief of the last century, foretold a great movement south in mid-May. To the south lay the Isle of Pines—Cuba's largest concentration camp, built in 1923 as a model prison to hold three thousand men. In 1966, it held four times that.

As April eased into May, the Congolese chief came through more clearly, reiterating his prediction and specifying some "half a thousand" in the transfer. Giving substance to this ethereal message was an unusual amount of office paper shuffling about and a moratorium on interviews by *los reeducadores*. Even the more skeptical among us began to take an interest in this Congolese chief.

By mid-May, we milk-toast converts returned to scoffing at Jorge and his spirits. But then, in the early evening of May 21st, a platoon of soldiers invaded our patio. Word ran from one gallery to another, *requisa*, the dreaded search. But long lists of names were handed to each gallery chief with orders to pack, and we realized it was not a *requisa*, but a sizeable transfer. Jorge and his friend from the Congo had been right. From eighteen hundred men in la Cabaña, six hundred were chosen, I among them. A jump from the frying pan into the fire, but I didn't know that then. If this move were really south to the Isle of Pines, I reasoned there'd be more space to suffer in. That in itself seemed good to me.

Assembled in the patio, we were forced down long lines of soldiers to be checked from head to toe, our meager baggage emptied at our feet for closer inspection. Some older prisoners, wise in prison ways, escaped this by pretending they'd been searched already, stumbling down the line with clothes unbuttoned, dropping and picking up belongings as they went. In this confusion, there was no opportunity to bid farewell to friends over the shouting of guards and prisoners, for all the world like bawling cattle, branded "P," being worked over in corrals. With the roster complete, we yawned the rest of the night through, packed tight against each other in the no man's land between the two gates. Before dawn, bread was passed out. Then, as the sun rose, we were formed on the battlements and marched to busses a quarter mile away. The only time I had seen this view had been my day in court. I hoped that now it was for the last time.

Usually prisoner transfer was in Russian paddy wagons. Today, we had the luxury of busses. Dependable British Leyland busses, not the Czech, whose motors were forever giving out in the tropical heat. Security wanted no mechanical failures on this trip. Our good fortune was the misfortune of the Havana populace from whom these busses came. The already serious transportation problems throughout Cuba were aggravated each time vehicles were needed for some mass movement. Sometimes they were needed to move prisoners, more often to move civilians from a factory or residential block "voluntarily" attending a political rally or "spontaneously" going to Rancho Boyeros Airport to greet some arriving dignitary.

Just a year since I had lost my freedom. Excepting my trial day, I'd had no chance to gorge the eye on healing glimpses of distant views. Now, vicariously, I felt part of normal life again, seeing houses and their clotheslines as bright with colored laundry as their gardens were with flowers, small towns alive with movement of the free, men and women working in the fields, a dog chasing a cat, children on bicycles and playing games, young bucks Sunday-dressed romancing their *novias* on front porches. All this unfolded itself through the windows as, in convoy with twenty other busses and a swarm of police cars, we drove south to the small fishing port of Batabano. Batabano, home to the car ferries that crossed to the Isle of Pines.

At the end of the long cement pier were half a hundred soldiers cradling automatic arms and another ten soldiers walking our lines with German Shepherds pulling taut their leashes and eyeing us in hungry challenge. One hundred yards off either side of the pier were trim coast guard cutters with manned fifty-caliber machine guns at bow and stern.

In the fourth bus to arrive, I was among the first to board. I realized the dark and airless car deck would be my lot when I heard the man before me complain of asthma to the officer-in-charge. He was directed to the deck above. I too wheezed "asthma,"and was pointed in the same direction.

Although the night was cold with blown spray, there was air from the sea and the sky above, while those below-deck spent a miserable night in seasickness and stifling heat, urinating, defecating, and vomiting where they lay. Once settled, none were allowed to move. Provisions were what each man carried with him. Not much more than crackers from his *jaba* and water from his liter plastic bottle, always kept full. The guards, spaced at intervals along the rail, shivered in shirts or light jackets, while we only had our one allotted blanket. In the bow and stern and on the raised bridle amidship were soldiers with submachine guns.

Our two-hundred-foot double-deck boat had too long served the Isle of Pines from Cuba. Betrayed in life by her too long living it, her motive power was zero. Without spare parts, the engines provided no more than the energy necessary for lights, winches, and steering. Like an old lady unable to walk, she had her companion, a small tug, to tow her back and forth. This old ferry had never been designed to carry six hundred passengers, and no maritime law would have permitted such overloading. There were no life preservers visible, and if there were any auxiliary lifeboats or rafts, I didn't see them. For an emergency, there was only the tug at the end of her leash, and the two small escorting cutters. Both decks were crammed, making the ferry dangerously top-heavy. Mercifully, the seventy-five-mile crossing between Batabano and the Isle of Pines is on shallow and protected waters. We made it in fourteen hours.

To see the rising of the sun, there is no place lovelier, nor more void of distraction for the eye, than the ocean. An empty stage with no supporting scenery to turn the senses from the principal performer around which we all revolve. To those long kept from this, it seemed a wondrous thing, a remembrance of man's insignificance on earth, making petty and unimportant our present plight—petty and unimportant to those of us with eyes to see and feel the magnificence of this dawn, this beginning of another day, another life in another prison.

Following the sun over the horizon came the low hills of the Isle of Pines and presently the island itself, the romantic setting for Robert Louis Stevenson's *Treasure Island*. To us there was little romance in an island whose agricultural economy functioned almost exclusively on slave labor—political prisoners and student brigades shipped in "voluntarily" from Cuba. Nor was there anything romantic about our future "home," the huge grey beehives of el Presidio which we saw half a mile inland as our boat paralleled the north coast, heading for the mouth of a shallow estuary. Three quarters of a mile upstream lay Nueva Gerona, capital of the island. Making big with small toots, the tug pulled us into the back yard of this little town before casting off the tow. Momentum carried the ferry broadside to the dock and our voyage was over.

We were rostered off the ferry and repacked into open Russian trucks to wait. Prison was always wait or hurry, with nothing leisurely in between. The sun was well up and our uniforms were soaked in the stench of old sweat. Our water bottles were empty, and our stomachs as well. In thirty-six hours, we had eaten only the bread of yesterday morning. And without water, it was impossible to eat our supply of dry crackers. Pleas for water were met with uncaring shrugs, or *sí, sí, momentico*—the prison affirmative to indicate the negative. With the patience of necessity, we resigned ourselves to hunger and thirst and asked no more.

From the docks of Nueva Gerona to el Presidio, "the model prison," was a twenty-minute journey. Along the north coast, the road cut through ridges of low-grade marble one- to two-hundred-feet high, some clothed in the solid green of stately palms and the lower luxuriant growth of the tropics, others without their cloak of greenery, ripped by time's usage, showing through to the grey undergarments of the limestone beneath. The road curved around and through these outcroppings until, topping a gentle rise, el Presidio lay before us, an ugly symbol of pain lacerating the landscape.

A ten-foot-high wire fence enclosed fifty acres of treeless grassland on which squatted immense seven-story cylinders with conical roofs, so much like storage tanks in a refinery—one storing the energy of imprisoned men, the other of petroleum, both highly combustible. There were five of these round buildings, four for living quarters, geometrically situated at the corners of a hypothetical square, and the fifth in the center—the combined kitchen and immense dining hall, used then for visits only. Off to one side, as if ashamed of itself, was a long, low, windowless blockhouse, the punishment building with its airless, dark confinement cells, which, as I was to learn, was fetid with the stink of uncollected piss and shit. To the east a hundred yards was the hospital, and barracks to house the few political prisoners working in *el Plan*. It was in a spacious, comfortable room in this hospital that Castro and a handful of his followers from the Moncada incident "suffered" through eighteen months of detention from October 1953 to May 1955 with television, library, and refrigerator to accompany them.

Outside the fence stood the administration building. Our truck convoy stopped there to wait interminably for our turn for processing. Forbidden to climb down, we relieved ourselves, and the guards' boredom, over the side of the trucks. They shouted in amusement, "If I didn't have a better tool than that I'd sit to pee."

"Brother, you'll never make a baby with that little worm."

"Stretch it, man, stretch it, or you're going to pee all over the truck."

Hours later, ravenously hungry and thirsty, we were processed through, the interviews and questions no different from the many we'd endured in la Cabaña. Pressure to join *el Plan* with promises of nirvana. Communist promises, as honest as the love of a whore.

The processed product passed out the back of the administration building, our number only slightly diminished by those conned into *el Plan* and redirected elsewhere. A fifty-yard alley, lined with barbed wire, led through a narrow gate into the prison compound. On a platform above the gate were light machine guns, and similar platforms were spaced around the perimeter of this vast enclave. Once through the gate, it was a triumphal march to our destination. Windows were filled with applauding prisoners who banged aluminum plates against the bars, shouted greetings, and welcomed us into the fraternity of the oppressed. In this flow of friendly sound and movement, weariness and hunger disappeared, our spirits rose, and we felt a stirring of pride at being there.

We stopped before Circular Three, as these buildings were called. One by one we went through the first gate into a wide passageway seven feet in height, then through a second gate which gave way into the immense interior, an empty arena soaring nine stories high to the tip of the conical roof like a roofed-over doughnut with the cells in the mass centered around the hole. In the center stood a thirty-foot "lighthouse," a watchtower reached by outside tunnel. High-powered searchlights burned atop this tower from dusk to dawn, providing the only artificial light within the circular. There were ninety-eight cells to a floor, each cell ten by five-and-a-half feet with two canvas bunks on pipe frames, one above the other. Many had three, leaving only twenty-four inches between bunks. Originally, each cell had running water. Now, the only "running water" was what each prisoner kept in his pail, collected from the showers. One cell per floor offered half a dozen *excusados,* drains to squat over, flushed every twenty-four hours when water ran in the pipes at the whim of the guards.

Under the eaves, the top floor circled the building without any dividing walls. Here, the prisoner without a bunk homesteaded his small territory to sleep on the floor, fenced about by his few possessions. Study groups met for evening and weekend classes. Protestants, Catholics, and Seventh Day Adventists held their Sunday services. Choral practice, too. It was our community center.

The arena below was where we queued for meals, played softball when not too work-weary, laundered, and assembled in brigades for work details.

For this huge hive there was only one guard who lived in the passageway between the two gates. In need, he could call for the prison commander or two hundred soldiers. But there was no need for interior guards as long as we reported on time for work brigades each morning. Except for the monthly *requisa*, this guard and two officials were the only ones to enter the circular on their morning and evening head count.

We were a self-governing community, holding elections every two months for *jefe*, chief of circular, who in turn chose volunteers for the multitude of housekeeping chores. One of the more thankless tasks was serving the food brought to each circular from the central kitchen in thirty-gallon cauldrons. It was a delicate job to be impartial to twelve hundred hungry men, and yet, for the friend, give a deeper thrust of the ladle to catch something of more substance.

There were volunteer "nurses" working nightly in the tiny dispensary under the direction of a doctor-prisoner giving injections, binding machete wounds, prescribing aspirin, and submitting the names of men warranting hospital attention. The names were telephoned to the military doctor, who trimmed the list with mathematical decision. In the eyes of the military we were all tremendous goldbricks. It was a valid deduction, as our duty was to work the minimum, none at all if we could get away with it. But among us were men truly needing medical attention, and they suffered damnation in this mathematical game of chance on the hospital list.

The doctors who treated us in the hospital had joined *el Plan* and worked under a military doctor, chosen more for revolutionary zeal than medical aptitude. Inevitably, that meant many of the prisoner-doctors were better qualified than their boss, but their hands were tied and they could do little for us.

One took his Hippocratic oath more seriously than his allegiance to *el Plan*. He presented to his boss the same X-ray of a grave ulcer case each time he wanted to protect a prisoner. His humanitarian impulse was repaid by some stool pigeon. After three months' solitary confinement, another two years were added to his sentence for "anti-social behavior," and he was expelled from *el Plan*.

Guard cruelty and senseless killings at work were so common that some prisoners resorted to self-inflicted wounds to gain the respite of days, weeks, or months in the circulars. They would whack off a finger or toe with a machete, get a strong-stomached friend to break their leg or arm with a rock or heavy pipe, rub petroleum into a razor cut to produce a spectacular infection, and commit upon themselves other horrors invented through the ingenuity of desperation. These men were few, however, and considered moral cowards by the rest of us. Most accepted conditions as they were and made the best of them.

If guard brutality on the Isle of Pines was more extreme than la Cabaña's, it was compensated for by a healthier climate. The air was wonderfully fresh and clear, and the chronic coughs of la Cabaña disappeared, as did most asthma. The men appeared tanned, hard, and strong from working in the fields. But there was the unfortunate side effect of increased appetite, and an unrequited appetite can be more painful than a cough or asthma.

A four-thirty breakfast of dry bread and a cup of sweetened milk was not much to sustain a man until the eleven o'clock lunch, delivered at work in thermoses, another piece of dry bread, a large ladle of grey macaroni, and when available, a spoonful of cucumbers. Late afternoon was the hungriest time of all, the day's hard labor having exhausted the scanty fuel of lunch while the bread, rice, and soup of supper were still hours away. Surprisingly enough, men did yeoman work on this diet, and were temporarily robust and well. Their bodies however, were drawing on reserves of health built up in youth, and their strength was peaking. The average prisoner's red cell count was 3.6 million vs. 4-5 million normal. What kept the men going were the twenty-five-pound *jabas* every sixty days with their milk, chocolate and sugar. Without this supplement, most would have been basket cases rather quickly.

Chapter 23

The day after our arrival, all six hundred of us had identification photos taken—our passport pictures, we called them optimistically—and then we were shorn of all hair and photographed again. We didn't care. We weren't going anywhere, not even out to work. A shortage of boots and uniforms kept us unemployed, living as drones in a mammoth hive, vegetating while the workers toiled.

And like a hive we had our system of communication, a small clandestine radio. When not in use, it was disassembled and so well hidden under floor tiles that the guards never did discover it. Every evening the news was copied out in capsule form and passed around for all to read. It was from the Voice of America in Spanish that we learned of an impending hurricane.

Although the hurricane season for the Caribbean is October and November, Alma began in June off the coast of Honduras. She had been charted heading directly for the Isle of Pines at eight knots with internal winds of eighty to ninety miles an hour. Pushed ahead by thirty-six hours were torrential rains, cancelling all work and giving an unexpected and welcomed holiday. Administration advised us of the storm twenty-four hours after we knew of it through our radio, and left us to cope as best we could.

Most of the open-barred windows had curtains of sugar sacks, plastic bags stitched together, and other material scrounged from work. These provided protection from tropical showers and vagrant winds, not a hurricane. We set to with sheets, blankets, towels, and clothes, lashed to the iron bars. Futile measures against the gale that later picked apart our handiwork and drove rivers into cells, while the winds fingered the perimeter of the roof, lifting off sections like so much paper. The tempest was as much within as without, and nowhere was there a dry corner.

Just before dawn, the eye of the storm brought temporary relief. Then, once again, there were torrents of water, sledge-hammer winds, and the incessant battering and thundering of roof sections slamming free. Diffused daylight showed a checkerboard roof above twelve hundred bedraggled men and their sodden belongings. Through visual Morse code we learned all circulars had suffered equally.

The hot sun and scarcity of roof helped the drying out and cleaning up. Spirits were high, thinking of nature's blow to Castro's economy. As Administration showed no sign of repairing damage, we received permission, if not their blessing, to salvage roof material from surrounding fields, rejoining the sections with those still intact. The result was a fringe open to the sky around one quarter of our roof's perimeter. Those men displaced from the top floor for lack of shelter pushed in with others, leaving the open area as a drying green and a place to sunbathe.

In compensation for our discomfort, the hurricane proved a short-term benefit to our diet. The inevitable lunch of macaroni and thin soup of supper were replaced by chicken, sweet potatoes, and squash. The chicken had been blown about and bruised, but was still a gourmet dish for us. Sweet potatoes and squash by the truck loads were dumped on the cement apron around the kitchen to be raked over and dried in the sun, salvaged from lagoons, once fields. Rice, too, in countless sacks was emptied there to dry. We blessed Alma and her bounty and prayed for the arrival of all her sisters.

Coinciding with our arrival in May on the Isle of Pines, Castro had declared a national emergency, alerting his armed forces against invasion. It was the insecure dictator's classic ploy to rally around his people in times of economic distress. While the state of emergency provided the armed forces with practical drill, it served as an excuse to suspend our visits, food parcels, and correspondence. The country was in crisis militarily (read, economically), and we were in crisis for lack of our supplementary food, the *jaba*.

If we, who had just arrived and were not yet working, were hungry, it was infinitely worse for those in the field. Those who complained the loudest were the well larded, fresh from months or years of hibernation in la Cabaña. The fatter and softer the man, the closer to starvation he will tell you he is. There was no starvation, but there was hunger. In mid-July, it was with great relief that telegram blanks were distributed to advise families of renewed visits and *jabas*.

It was the first visit for those of us who recently arrived from la Cabaña. An hour and a half ahead of time, we were dressed and milling around nervously on the arena floor, awaiting the roll call, to be searched and marched the short distance to the dining hall.

The women's gay and neat appearance belied the night they had spent on the ferry (the same tug-led craft we had crossed on), finding transportation from dock to prison, inspection of the twenty-five-pound *jaba* and another bag with the visit picnic, and finally the wait in the sun before the dining hall. Nothing was made easy for them. Later, they had to retrace their steps, not arriving home until the following morning. For two hours with their men, these heroic women slept sitting up for two nights on a boat and stood in line in sun and rain for transportation. The object of this devotion had only to walk two hundred yards. The men may have been prisoners, unmercifully treated, but it was the Cuban women who deserved the highest accolade for their silent, uncomplaining giving.

Once prisoners and families were joined inside, and having no family of my own, I could stand apart to watch this volatile coming together, the uninhibited tears of joy as they embraced, touching for the first time in months or years. Without that hateful dividing fence of la Cabaña, they could sit hand in hand, able to confide intimacies only to be whispered.

With the first flush of discovery over, the most important family news discussed, paper parcels and aluminum canteens were unpacked, preparatory to stuffing their hungry "hero," and any friends he might have without visitors of their own. Small thermoses of strong, black coffee were poured still warm, and proffered to everyone within reach of voice or hand. This was the sign that mavericks like myself might then intrude. The generosity of the Cubans was hard to refuse and stretched the stomach uncomfortably. I was adopted by many families and had to accept something from each. A refusal to eat was an insult to pride. Accustomed to macaroni, rice and soup, my stomach was hard put to suddenly accommodate a rich meal of rice and black beans, pork and chicken, salad, fruit, chocolate cake, and strong Cuban coffee. But accommodate it it did, and "the rumblings abdominal were perfectly abominable," and everyone most content.

From the wives of my *vaqueros* I heard Fidel had expropriated our house for himself, one among many throughout the island for his unannounced use. They reported that much of the ranch grassland had been plowed under to plant Brazilian coffee. Cuba had always produced the quality coffee of Latin America while Brazil produced in quantity. It was Castro's aim to cultivate both, satisfying internal consumption with the inferior Brazilian, and exporting the Cuban. Like communism, it was attractive in theory, impractical in practice. No soil check had been made. Two months later, the expensive plants turned from healthy dark to sickly green. In four months, yellow. In six, dead. Still another Castro dream for a hard-currency crop wilted into deficit.

Every visit was important to the entire prison for the messages and letters smuggled in. The same evening, news and messages were communicated to all buildings by Morse code and self-developed sign language. Letters were dispatched after dark from one circular to another in a more ingenious manner. Some enterprising soul had found an old inner tube while working in the fields. By fastening the two ends of this inner tube to two vertical bars in a window he invented a slingshot strong enough to send a weighted cord thirty yards to a window of the nearest circular. Thereafter, *el tren* ran nightly, establishing a route for notes and small packages. From outside, guards were then sent with weighted cords to throw over these lines of communication and drag them down. But we counteracted by moving the slingshot to the top floor, too high for the guards.

Six weeks after our arrival on the Isle of Pines, the workers returned one evening in an unaccustomed, jovial mood. Good naturedly, they shouted obscenities at us, comparing us to obese old women and worse, and they yelled that now we'd have to work for our food. New uniforms and boots had arrived. Our lazy days of sunbathing under a still-open roof were over. We were assigned to machete brigades cutting grass, and the very next day issued boots, khaki trousers, shirts, and the important *sombrero* to protect us from the same sun we had been courting so assiduously while unemployed.

Being assigned to a brigade, there was always speculation on which *cabo* you would draw, the old hands trying to frighten the new with tales of how many prisoners such-and-such *cabo* had sent to the hospital or solitary confinement. Ours was relatively new to the Isle of Pines and had yet to prove himself. That first morning we were more preoccupied with the cold than with our *cabo*. None of us had sweaters or jackets, and blankets were prohibited. We shivered our way to the perimeter fence to be counted once again through the gate and board the trucks beyond.

Brigades were one hundred prisoners, twelve to fifteen guards armed with semi-automatic weapons, the *cabo*, and his assistant. They carried machetes and wore the small Russian pistol called Red Star, caliber 7.65, equivalent to the American 32. There were two open trucks for us, followed by a third for the guards. It was forbidden to wave to civilians and they had long ago learned it was best to ignore us. Even the children knew. Don't feed the animals. Don't even look at them.

Packed fifty to a truck, we were soon warmed by bodily contact and the rising of the sun. At the grapefruit grove we had our first look at our *cabo*, a good looking young fellow named Estrada. Short, five-feet-eight, but well proportioned and strong. His having earned no nickname, as yet, indicated no unusually bad traits. This was reassuring to me, who had never held a machete and was nervous about my debut as day laborer. On our ranch I'd been *el gran señor* astride my horse looking down on the men clearing pasture. Now all was in reverse. And where the hell was my horse?

Estrada had no horse, but was looking down on me all the same as I took enthusiastic and ridiculously inept swings with my machete. I did no more damage to the grass than a strong wind would have done, laying it flat but intact. Obviously there was something more to machete work than met the eye, but I hadn't a

clue what it was. Others were as ignorant as I, but they weren't
gringos, and Estrada had his eye on me. One had tried to show me
how to grasp the handle to present the blade at best cutting angle
and the proper wrist motion to save precious energy on the
upswing. He had been sent packing and Estrada himself had taken
over my education. He was patient for sixty seconds before
exchanging instruction for invective, venting his entire vocabulary
on words I didn't understand. Cringing inwardly at the fear of his
machete on my back, I got it instead on my ass. Three stinging
whacks and he stalked away, leaving me to learn from fellow
prisoners. During the month I worked in Estrada's brigade, he never
addressed me another word, nor even glanced my way, a
relationship I was quite content with.

Wielding a machete, like much other work, is catching the
rhythm. Gradually the blade becomes an extension of the arm. But
any pleasure gained from regarding the swath behind oneself is
cancelled out by the uncut acres ahead and the summer sun above.
To bend double, cutting grass, nine hours a day, was blistering to
hands, back and soul. There was mouthwatering compensation close
at hand, but it required good team work to take advantage of it.
Although the young grapefruit were forbidden us, it was possible
for one or two men at a time to circle behind or below a tree, to grab,
cut open, and consume a fruit and return swinging before a guard
took notice. If caught, the flat of machete given hard was well worth
the risk. That we could consume twenty or more grapefruit a day
without indigestion showed the need we had for this food. And,
perhaps, the somnolent state of our guards in the high humidity of
July.

Two fifty-gallon drums of water were left with us each morning.
One gallon of water per man for nine hours of sweat-pouring work.
The most fortunate man in the brigade was the waterboy, usually
the one least able to work. His rounds with two pails were non-stop,
ladling out one condensed-milk can of water to each as he passed.

There was a first aid kit carried by the *cabo.* A real cut of some
depth rated a swab of iodine, a swatch of gauze to staunch the
blood, and a tongue lashing for awkwardness. Anything less was
treated with the tongue-lashing alone and the suggestion to suck the
wound like the animals we were. To work as a *plantado* (non-Plan)
was constant punishment, senseless physical humiliation ordered by
the same mentality that had mined the circulars several years before.

(Immediately following the April 1961 Bay of Pigs invasion, Castro had ordered tons of high explosives placed under each circular, ready for firing in the event of a second invasion. International outrage forced their removal in 1962.)

At last came Estrada's baptismal day when he earned the nickname *Dietético,* relating to diet or food. What it lacked in originality had meaning in depth to those of us who christened him. The problem originated with Orestes Blanco, a gentle man in his early fifties, who never should have been working in the fields. He had spent most of his life sitting behind the counter of his wife's modest *bodega* in Alquizar, a small town south of Havana.

There he dispatched groceries to his neighbors while his wife did the heavy work, wore the pants, and had the real *cojones* in the family. Those who knew Orestes pre-prison said it was she who had planted a few bombs, and she who should have been serving the prison sentence, machete in hand, probably outstripping the lot of us.

If I swung a machete like a tennis racket, Orestes swung his like a fly swatter. If I learned to eat fifteen grapefruit a day, Orestes couldn't manage two without getting caught. He had been a good *bodeguero*, a failure in the field, and he attracted Estrada's attention as strongly as the lightning rod draws lightning.

One Friday at lunch break after a bad week of fly swatting for Orestes, Estrada stood blocking our queue, arms akimbo, before the twenty-five-gallon macaroni containers. Usually we were left alone to distribute the food among ourselves, with one of our number elected for the job. The top was already off the container and the server standing by. Estrada stood there glowering, not saying a word, machete in hand. There had been incidents that morning, yet each wondered who had screwed up doing, or not doing, what. At last, in almost a shout, "Why I have to give the tit to a bunch of *maricones* like you, I don't know. But if I have to make you work, I will. From now on anyone who doesn't work doesn't eat! Got it? Understood? *Maricones!*"

With that he stood aside, motioning the line forward with his machete. Hesitantly the first man extended his plate for the bread and one ladle of macaroni, and then backed away. The line moved on, more slowly than usual. Orestes's turn came. As he held out his plate, Estrada flicked his machete twice. Orestes's hand clutched air, his plate spinning to the ground.

Those first served were spread out on the grass, boots off, beginning to eat. They stopped in amazement, mouths full of macaroni. The queue came to a standstill, and no one made a move for their food. Estrada yelled, "What's the matter? Aren't you hungry?"

Orestes's empty plate lay face down in the dirt twenty feet away. He didn't budge, just stood there mouth open, hand still out before him. Still no one moved. All eyes were on our *cabo*. Again, more frenzied this time, "What's the matter? Aren't you hungry? I said if you don't work you don't eat, and this man doesn't work," pointing at Orestes. "The rest of you can eat all you want. Now, get to it!"

Silently, spontaneously, the queue dissolved and those already served dumped their macaroni on the ground. Estrada hadn't expected this solidarity. For one tight moment he looked perplexed, like a small boy who'd had his candy taken from him. Then the instant of uncertainty exploded into an arm-waving, breast-beating tirade about the stupidity of animals and more I couldn't understand of his rapid peasant Spanish. He knew how to discipline individuals, not a hundred outraged men acting and thinking as one. And this unnerved him to an even more irrational act. Perhaps he couldn't help himself. Perhaps he felt obliged to shore up his waning authority before the guards. Alarmed at his shouting, they had run from their lunch in the shade of trees to encircle us, guns at the ready. At this point a more intelligent man would have diffused the problem. Not our *cabo*. Instead, he very deliberately strode to our two fifty-gallon water drums, turned to look at us in scorn, then bent double to overturn them, a beautiful flow of clear water, instantly absorbed by parched earth.

"*Coño!* If you don't eat, you don't drink. Now drag ass back to work pronto!"

Disregarding the hour of rest at mid-day was bad enough, but forcing us to work the afternoon through without water was sheer stupidity. He must have realized it too as he only half-heartedly pushed us the rest of the day, a bone-wearying day, fueled only by a breakfast of milk and one piece of bread.

We considered the matter closed and returned to work Saturday morning looking forward to the half day. We were wrong. Each evening, the *cabos* submitted a report to Administration and apparently our problem had been discussed. A further example of discipline had been decided. No sooner were we off the trucks and assembled in rows than Estrada called out of our ranks a young Baptist pastor, to accuse him of having organized yesterday's show of solidarity. That everyone knew it spontaneous didn't matter. The guards were always right, the prisoner wrong, and discipline had to be maintained.

In soldiered ranks we watched Estrada beat this man with all his strength—back, buttocks, arms, and legs. The pastor stood immobile until the arms that beat could beat no more. The new shirt hung in shreds on his back.

Underneath lay wide welts and broken skin from the machete flat handled, deeper cuts where the blade twisted razor sharp. The first aid kit was refused him, but he was allowed to slosh a few cans of our precious water over the cuts, a rust-colored stream staining the dust at his feet. My every muscle from calf to biceps was tense from sympathetic participation. My moral outrage of yesterday was physical today, both strong and sickening. But today I felt the stoic Baptist pastor had emerged the victor, not the exhausted *cabo*.

From the back of my mind came a bit of philosophizing from a whaler in Herman Melville's *Moby Dick*. This whaler said, "However they thump and punch me about, I have the satisfaction of knowing it is all right, that everybody else is in one way or another served in much the same way. Either in a physical or metaphysical point of view, that is. And so the universal thump is passed around and all hands should rub each other's shoulder blades and be content."

That night I asked the pastor if he prayed for our *cabo*. He replied, "I believe God would understand if I forgot. But I do pray for him. He needs God's help and understanding more than the rest of us."

I agreed, and we talked of the miserable life led by our guards. They ate little better than we did. The same breakfast, the same lunch with an additional half tin of Russian sardines, and a supper of rice and soup thicker than ours. They met us at six each morning, shared the long hours of our day, and then returned to barracks to study four nights a week. Sundays, they "voluntarily" attended political lectures, cut cane, or did other agricultural work. Paid sixty pesos a month, they had to buy their own jackets against the winter cold, and raincoats for spring and summer rains. Few could afford these luxuries, and so shared the cold and rain with us. With one three-day pass a month, they saw little of their families (since most came from Oriente Province, eight hundred miles west). Prisoners were generally imprisoned near their homes and guards were chosen from distant provinces to avoid finding friends or relatives among the inmates. A poor life these men lived with even a poorer morale. Few among us would have exchanged places.

Our high morale through the interminable years of political prison was due to the Cubans' innate strength of character and spirit, coupled with a sense of humor. They bent under affliction only to rebound with more courage and determination to resist than ever before. The worse the conditions, the better the morale. The worse the conditions, the more solidarity. Under appalling conditions and with all appropriate ceremony possible, the religious fêtes denied and prohibited by the communists were celebrated. Wherever political prisoners were confined in Cuba, the majority participated in the traditional worship of Christmas, Easter, and Passover. The dates important to Cuba's long struggle for independence were yearly commemorated with speeches, skits, and the always stirring national anthem. With *chivatos* as numerous as bedbugs, such organization was soon known by the authorities, and forewarned, religious and patriotic songs, even the national anthem, were drowned out by loudspeakers. Time and again the organizers paid for their determination with weeks of solitary confinement. But nothing the communists could do ever extinguished this spirit.

My first Fourth of July in prison was memorable. Richard Poyle and I, the only two Americans on the Isle of Pines, were invited to a skit with speeches in English and Spanish lauding the United States. The finale was an appearance by Uncle Sam in a red, white, and blue, frock coat made from sugar sacking and dyed with medicines, and a top hat of soot-blackened cardboard. He led a dozen men in our national anthem while many of the three hundred gathered there sang in Spanish. To hear my anthem sung in a communist prison brought home the meaning of every word as it never had before. My heart went out to these men, most celebrating the freedom of my country, others borrowing the fête as a show of anti-Castro. In a most inadequate reply I said, "It is my most fervent prayer that Cuba will one day soon know peace and liberty again, and that your one-starred, ill-starred banner will yet wave over the land of the free and the home of the brave."

It is still my prayer.

Following this, Poyle and I were invited to "cocktails" by the two doctors in the circular. We had received our invitations the night before, neatly penned on the back of hospital prescription blanks and enclosed in a prison-made envelope. Smuggled out with letters, I have mine still. At the top was a pen drawing of the Cuban flag and the American flag side by side, and the following words:

> Jesús Orlando Soto y Juan Almeda Carro
> request a presence of
> Lawrence K. Lunt
> to cocktails in cell 36, 2nd floor
> to commemorate the Independence Day
> of
> The United States of America, July 4, 1966

Many were in the distillery business, but for fear of confiscation in the monthly *requisa*, few aged their product more than three weeks. The doctors mixed their liter serum bottles of *vino* in among their dispensary medicines, and so matured it for months without fear of *requisas*. Their grapefruit juice, smuggled from the fields, then mixed with sugar, had been fermenting all of three months. Poyle and I were privileged to be drinking an old *vino*, broached in honor of the Fourth of July.

Chapter 24

In the early years of the Revolution, the political prisoners were still feeling their way towards establishing two separate pecking orders within the prison: social and political. Social, in the sense of seeking authority in elected or appointed posts to organize the housekeeping chores of thousands of men: chief of gallery or building, maintenance, bookkeeping, nurse, food servers. Any of these positions gave a certain power and the fringe benefits of bonus visits, and the opportunity to appropriate extra food and medicine as black market barter. Political, in the sense of seeking rank in one of several political parties of the pre-Castro years, still active outside of Cuba and just beginning to organize within the prisons: nationalists, socialists, pro and con the United States, even Black Power.

Some joined one or the other party because of friends, others because they longed to belong to something, anything, and many because they truly believed in what their party stood for. Safe in Miami, the party bosses were reaching for a mirage of power within the prisons as entrée to a future government without Castro they

169

would never see. And in the process, of course, satisfying their love of intrigue and self-importance. In the different political parties there were as many presidential candidates among these would-be Simón Bolívars as there were cockroaches in la Cabaña.

Each party had its policy on prison conduct: one refused to acknowledge as political prisoners the *Batistianos*, those of ex-president Batista's government or armed forces, wanting them separated in another prison, another demanded segregation of the foreigners, a third advocated accepting the monthly soap and cigarettes issued gratis, while an opposing faction ruled it unethical to accept anything but food and uniform.

Instead of recognizing the common enemy and closing ranks, this minority did everything they could to divide and disrupt. From within, we ourselves helped the government in the initial splintering of prisoner solidarity.

I was one of those who accepted soap and cigarettes and anything else the government chose to offer—as long as it was available to all. I did not smoke, but enjoyed giving them to friends who did. It amused me that those who refused to accept cigarettes from the government had no qualms about accepting them from me. Their reasoning escaped me. If not from the government, soap and cigarettes must come from their families with resources already tightly stretched.

The monthly five packs of cigarettes and three bars of soap were given out at work. The dispatcher of this largesse was a faded copy of the Russian commissar. On the prison organizational chart it may have looked well to see that each brigade had its political advisor, but the material he had to work with was unmalleable. We called them *abuelitos*, little grandfathers, not in affection, though they were quite inoffensive, but because they were always older men without talent for other work. When their political lectures in the field were received enthusiastically as escape from work rather than for their educational value, the lectures were stopped. The *abuelitos* became more nanny than spiritual advisor. Protests, problems, and requests were all carefully noted in their books and never heard about again. They dispensed censored mail, and accepted outgoing letters, unsealed, on the rare occasions a prisoner wrote through official channels. Gradually they became an endangered species, finally disappearing altogether. Another failed Russian product.

Saturdays were a half day of work with guard pressure off, a holiday mood, and "home" by two. We had a quick lunch of cold macaroni before jockeying for position under the showers, which ran for an hour and a half so that twelve hundred men might bathe and launder. There was a lot of good-natured pushing and shoving and ribald remarks. The sharpest was for Diosdado, a dwarf standing an even four feet, putting him at a humiliating disadvantage in this packed crowd of naked men.

To make the most of time and water, the shower was a two-in-one operation, with clothes placed underfoot to benefit from the cold, soapy water off the body. At the most, we got a minute and a half under the shower head each, then kicked the sodden mass of laundry to a vacant space to pummel it clean for another week. Then there was water from a reserve tank to rinse with, and the thing was done. Work uniforms, a towel, and a sheet all got this weekly discipline, and if not immaculate, at least there was a better smell. Few wore underwear or socks. Constantly wet from sweat, they rotted quickly, and being rationed items for the families, were hard to come by. One less thing to wash.

Every other week, there was a collective washing of the canvasses on which we slept, stretched tight on iron pipes. The strong, yellow laundry soap killed the insidious bedbug and its eggs and gave us a few nights free of their bloodsucking before survivors crawled from chinks in the wall to begin the cycle once again.

The Saturday laundry finished, ropes (made from sugar sacks unravelled and twisted into twine) were strung from every floor across the void of our huge building. It was a satisfying sight to see the heavily burdened ropes with the week's clean wash. Like regatta flags hung high following a race, they signified the weekend, rest and sleep. And sleep we did. Each Saturday afternoon, there wasn't a sound in all the circular. The prisoners, almost to a man, lay sacked out on bunk or floor, unconscious until supper at six.

Even in adversity there is happiness. Saturday night was happiness. With the pressure of forced labor lifted for thirty-six hours, feeling clean and refreshed, Saturday night was a time for visiting. A time for borrowing something to read, for teaching or studying, for joining a group around a guitar.

Whereas the great building quieted early during the week, Saturday night ran into Sunday morning with the contented hum of hundreds going about their simple pleasures. The immense empty space around which the circular was constructed muted the sounds of a thousand conversations, the various guitars, and even the violent dispute, full of sound and fury, but, in the Latin manner, signifying instant friendship when over. There was the comforting smell of wood smoke from a score of miniature fires heating milk and chocolate, or boiling a medicinal brew of bark and leaves or certain grasses to relieve some ailment.

Firewood came smuggled in from work or from the hardwood louvres at the peak of the conical roof. There were a few nerveless men who climbed the arching steel beams (Bethlehem) supporting the roof to wrench free these louvres, as much in demand for making small benches as for firewood. It was a hundred-foot drop to the ground below, and yet they risked their lives for something of small value. If they did it to help their friends, they did it also to buck the system, to feel that in destroying a small piece of their prison they were destroying a small piece of the social fabric that held them in.

For me, Saturday night was singing. Raised in a family that harmonized well together, music was part of my life. Only once had it failed me. In G-2 I tried singing some of my mother's old Scottish songs, but environment was out of tune with mood and I stopped. Now, the satisfaction of singing returned as nine of us ran through our repertoire of Spanish hymns for Sunday's Protestant service.

Saturday night was also one of the English classes I gave three nights a week. Ernesto Gómez, a young Seventh Day Adventist, was one of my students. On one Saturday evening when he didn't show I inquired of a friend and heard he'd been cruelly knocked about by his *cabo*. In his cell, I found him physically and emotionally exhausted, even questioning God's presence amidst all this injustice. "Where was God when I needed Him most?" he wanted to know.

There were several Adventists gathered in Ernesto's cell. One of the older among them told this story.

One night a farmer dreamed he was walking through his fields with the Lord. Many scenes flashed across the sky. In each scene he noticed footprints in the earth. Sometimes there were two sets of footprints, other times there was only one. This bothered him because he noted that during the low periods of his life when he was suffering anguish, sorrow or defeat, he could see only one set of footprints. So he said to the Lord, "You promised me, Lord, that if I followed You, You would walk with me always. But I have noticed that during the most trying periods of my life there has been only one set of footprints in the earth of my fields. Why, when I needed You most, have You not been there for me?" The Lord smiled and replied, "The times you have seen only one set of footprints, my son, is when I carried you."

Faith and spirit renewed with this story, Ernesto returned to work on Monday. As the *cabo* bothered him no more, there must have been two sets of footprints in his field.

Many prisoners on the Isle of Pines were young *campesinos*, strong and hard, accustomed to the agricultural work of generations. They plowed behind their oxen with a curve of wood shaped from the forking of some hardwood tree, the tip sheathed in iron, hoeing the day through their plots of malanga, yucca and corn, all the muscle-strengthening work of the land. It was incredible to see with what perseverance they worked as prisoners. It was as if it were · their own soil, in spite of everything, maintaining a stubborn belief in the value of human labor. Nobody outside worked like that any more. The regime had taught them differently. If I, or anyone else, fell behind in our grass cutting, there was always one of these good hearted *campesinos* ready to take up the slack, to double back on his own swath, meeting our slower progress, allowing us to catch up. They risked beatings, but accepted them so stoically that the *cabo* wearied of the exercise and looked the other way. It was too hot to leave the shade of his tree to be continually thumping the prisoners about.

If these *campesinos* were the hardest workers, they were also the hardest on boots and uniforms. Prison regulations, for what they were worth, stated that prisoners at forced labor warranted new outfits every three months. If not in stock, and the prisoner's old uniform unserviceable, he was not required to work until his size was available. Despite the official life expectancy of three months, boots and uniforms seldom lived so long. Sweat and rain and the gentle sabotage of ripping here and tearing there saw to that. As for their regulations, they worked us in shredded pants and shirts, boots held together with wire, and no boots at all. Barefoot in the country, men could not long avoid cuts and bruises leading to infection. This allowed a few days' respite in the circular, but with or without boots, they were returned to work, as expendable as the boots themselves.

Since early 1966, rumors of prisoner exchange gained weight as Cuba's economy grew thin. We convinced ourselves Castro was floundering and ready to swap prisoners for U. S. assistance. The world sugar price was three cents a pound. It cost Cuba eleven to produce. Sugar mills were cannibalized to keep others running. Cuba's hard-currency reserves plummeted from three hundred and fifty million dollars to fifteen million. There was discontent in the army and labor goldbricked in passive resistance. To the U.S. Secretary of State, Dean Rusk, Castro floated the idea of prisoners for the American base of Guantánamo. In our wishful thinking, there was always light at the end of the tunnel.

One August morning in this climate of expectation, the only two Americans on the Isle of Pines, Richard Poyle and I, were turned back from work without explanation. Within seconds the entire circular knew the two *gringos* had hit the unemployment list. Through the grapevine, the nearest circular had the news in minutes, and passed it on until, going full circle, back came the query from our other side, "Is it true the Americans are being exchanged?" Not wanting to be thought uninformed, our signaler replied, "*Sí.*" From contagious excitement and mob psychology, it wasn't long before Poyle and I became convinced as well.

The workers gone for the day, there was a cathedral calm in the great building, some thirty-odd men gathered round two anxious Americans, all quietly discussing what this freedom for two might mean for the thousands remaining.

In the euphoria of the moment, Poyle and I accepted bits of paper with addresses and telephone numbers. We promised to call families in the States, to write to others, and, in emotionally induced hypocrisy, to stay in touch. With notable exceptions, we were in truth friends of necessity through common suffering, momentary friends for life. We had helped each other and had lived in the shelter of each other. "Friendship was the fastest root in our heart." But once apart, yesterday's bond was today an ephemeral thing, ready to be reforged, but neither anticipated nor sought after.

In mid-morning we were called to the gate. Our possessions were few. We had given away our small but valuable supply of milk, chocolate, and sugar, and left our boots and work uniforms to others. What did we want with possessions now? We were going free. The nightmare was over.

Chapter 25

Two Americans going free! Free to walk two hundred yards to Circular 2 and immediate assignment to *Bloque 20*, the punishment brigade quarrying marble. In whatever scale disappointment is measured, ours went over the top. From nightmare months behind to nightmare years ahead. Like our soaring morale, our inflated balloon went flat. Disorientated, temporarily uncaring, we thought, "To hell with everyone and everything."

The quarry was a bite into one of the steep ridges that ran between prison and the sea. To the west, the hundred-foot-high stone face from which we quarried effectively held us in. To the north, south, and east, it was a string of guard towers armed with machine guns. Escape had never been attempted, but before the year was out four would try. The quarry had a small carpenter shop for maintenance, a modest factory for turning out cement blocks, an ancient stone crusher, and the ridge of marble. Marble is a type of limestone crystallized by pressure, heat, and water, ranging in texture from inferior granular to high grade compact. This particular ridge was granular, but when crushed and mixed with sand made excellent cement blocks.

177

Brigade 20 comprised counterrevolutionaries of all social levels: an ex-diplomat, a sugar mill owner, university professors, students, peasants, ex-buddies of Castro, and "undesirables" like Poyle and myself. A snob was hard put to know who he should snub. The raunchiest often turned out to be Batista's ex-ambassador in Paris, or his general in charge of SIM, the secret police. Some suave, immaculate type might have been a truck driver or boxer. But whatever the social background, because of the devilish work and tough discipline, Brigade 20 had higher morale and greater solidarity than any other on the Isle of Pines. If I must be prisoner, I willingly accepted membership in this brotherhood of rock-busters.

We had two *cabos*. He in charge was a light mulatto, strong, straight-featured good looks, long eyelashes, black, like his eyes, without warmth, sensual lips, that opened to bark orders, and never a smile. He was a man to avoid.

For his animal meanness he had earned the nickname, *Perro Prieto*. *Perro*, dog. *Prieto*, dark colored, also cruel. Well-christened by the prisoners, and well-chosen by Administration, he was the man to discipline the quarry. Tireless, he seldom sought shade, and made his rounds when and where least expected. Among the huge boulders, dynamited from the cliff and lying in crazy profusion below, he circled and backtracked, savagely delighted when he caught a man goldbricking.

The second *cabo* was a tough, white, bantam rooster. This little rooster, *Gallito*, was short and well put together, a bite-sized boxer. If he'd ever smiled, he might have been a man you'd like to drink with. Most of the time he was out of the sun under his shelter, four posts supporting a palm-thatched roof, a little off-center in the quarry-formed amphitheater. To relieve his boredom, occasionally he'd shuck his shirt and leave the shade to seize a tired prisoner's sledge hammer and reduce some boulder to more modest size. That done, he'd drop the sledge, regain his sanctuary and glare haughtily around as if to say, "That's the way we do it here." He seldom spoke. His muscles were his eloquence. On his own, he never mistreated us. Under orders, he machete-whipped prisoners with glazed eye and a will that left a man's back and buttocks crying for a week. Unlike most guards he had no favorites, more ignoring than treating or mistreating us. At day's end, before allowing us into the circular for the night, *Gallito's requisa* was more caress than search, in his eyes the same glaze as when he punished with machete. Shamelessly, his hands ranged higher than necessary on the inside of legs. Better endowed by nature than we poor whites, the blacks among us were even more carefully frisked.

Perro Prieto carried a small, collapsible, canvas stool to plant before whomever he chose for special vigilance, sitting and staring, impervious to heat from the sun above and reflection from the rock underfoot. This stool became the symbol of all we hated most in the man.

One day he left it standing alone among the clutter of boulders, and some prisoner, more bold than wise, but with infinite delight, urinated on the canvas seat. His three companions were so intoxicated with this defiance that they too soaked the stool. In the oven temperature the urine-impregnated canvas quickly dried and *Perro Prieto* noticed nothing on his return. The idea caught on. At last the quarry had a urinal. It was as if the stool had become a favorite lamp post for the neighborhood dogs. Whenever it stood alone ammoniacal loathing poured down many times a day. It was our hope this might continue until the canvas rotted and our tormentor should sit and fall ignominiously to the ground.

One day, the sun did not dry the canvas before his return. The still-fresh smell of ammonia and the damp canvas told him all. Only momentarily undecided, he blew the whistle slung round his neck. The guards and *Gallito* appeared on the run. All work stopped.

The four prisoners rock-busting nearest the stool were marched to *Gallito's* shelter, the rest of us herded in to one side. To the question of which of the four had pissed on the stool, only silence. Glaring at them, *Perro Prieto* slowly waved his machete at our half-moon ranks twenty yards away, from left to right and back again, interrogation in his eyes. Answered in silence, he could contain himself no more.

"Coño su madre hijos de puta maricones puercos . . . ."

An uninterrupted torrent of bile in growing crescendo ended abruptly with the thwack of machete on the nearest back, signal for *Gallito* to prod the four apart. Six guards encircled them while the two *cabos* crucified each in his turn. The remaining armed guards faced us, safeties off. With small provocation guards had killed before. We remained rooted, silently tense.

As one machete rose the other fell, a searing alternating current of tearing blows. For a moment both worked the back, then one the back, the other the buttocks and thighs, the two blades never touching or missing a beat. One blow sent the tormented stumbling right, the next turned him left, so that he didn't much move from the small circle of his macabre shuffle. Not one of the four cried out. The only sound was steel on flesh, and to each of us, the beating of his heart. The unmerciful whipping went on till both *cabos* were exhausted and the four prisoners scarecrows, tattered uniforms hanging loosely on bloody limbs. There remained only shirt fragments and shredded pants to gather round their mutilated bodies, showing angry welts and broken, bleeding skin beneath. The morality play over, the guards marched our four martyrs to the carpentry shop for first aid—a liter bottle of iodine and poor-quality Chinese gauze.

There's an anger so deep as to mute the tongue, no vocabulary to express it. We goldbricked the day out in silent fury.

A nickname had always to be found for anyone or anything uncommon. Before the wounds had been properly attended to in the circular, the story had gone around and the four were dubbed *los miaus. Miau*, the mew of a cat. In prison slang, piss. They had become "the pissers" and proudly remained so for all their prison years.

Brigade 20 had fifteen men in the cement block factory, four on the rock crusher, two in the carpentry shop, and the rest busting or loading stone. Poyle and I were set to loading trucks for the short haul to the crusher.

I was wearing the only uniform I possessed, and on my feet were the expensive pair of Italian moccasins I'd been arrested in sixteen months before. Once, I had had the mistaken notion that neither my moccasins nor I were intended for hard labor. And yet, here we were, my shoes and I, slaving in a marble quarry. I'd bought them in Florence and in the years since, we'd trod many splendid parquet floors together. I felt terrible mistreating my old friends like that, but if I were to suffer among the rocks, then they too should have their calvary, though undoubtedly more severe than mine. It was murder first degree. The rocks bit into the soles, flayed the sides, and ripped the seams apart. The second day, the wounds were suppurating bits of leather. A hopeless case. The end was near and there was nothing I could do. The third day, I was barefoot by noon, my Florentine elegance having departed this world. Their problems were over while mine were just beginning.

It was scorching work under an August sun and my compatriot gave out the same day as my shoes. Unaccustomed to physical work, and with debilitating brucellosis, he should never have been sent to the Isle of Pines. Poyle was shipped back to la Cabaña and within a month another American arrived, David Fite, a young Baptist minister from Georgia, the very best of companions. Fite joined me in loading trucks, and when conversation was possible, proffered tips on getting by St. Peter in exchange for what I had learned from Poyle on the gambling syndicates. This all-American team was split with my promotion to sledge hammer, a tool I was as little accustomed to as the machete, and which I quickly found changed weight with each hour of the day. Sixteen pounds at sunup, more like sixty at sunset. My hands, calloused first by machete, then hefting rock, had now to adjust to the sledge. New callouses, new muscles, new aches and pains.

We worked within the bite that a generation of quarriers had made before us. Bombarded by the sun above, reflected in bright marble chips below, the heat was held in by encircling arms of limestone cliffs yet to be attacked. The endless reduction of boulders to liftable chunks left us without the slightest feeling of accomplishment. Always before and above loomed the ridge of stone that all the prisoners of Cuba would little change. Work more fit for machine than man, particularly as there was no labor more inefficient than that of prisoner. We expended as much energy escaping work as busting rock. Goldbricking was not only an art, but every prisoner's duty. We became masters of wasted effort.

Rock, like wood, is grained, and with a little practice you can read the grain to find the best, or worst, angle of attack. We studied our marble boulders with as much dedication as Michelangelo studied his. If it were possible to section a boulder with one strong blow, we'd knock it about with harmless taps until a roundtrip of *Perro Prieto* forced it into two or more smaller stones.

Gathering the harvest of smaller stones for the trucks was a show of motion to produce the minimum of constructive work. Prisoner code frowned on carrying more than one stone at a time, and carried correctly in both hands the smallest can appear a heavy burden. We shambled at funereal speed until the factory bell tolled lunch or end-of-day, then flew.

181

Two water buckets circulated continuously, balanced coolie-fashion on two ends of a pole. With the waterboy came a brief rest and messages from other teams. A request for a cigarette, a newly minted joke, or the latest position report on *Perro Prieto*. There was also time off to repair a splintered sledge hammer handle with a leisurely walk to the carpentry shop. Near the block factory, the shop was always good for gossip from prison trucks bringing in sand and cement, civilian trucks taking the blocks away. Communication was well organized and the gossip received more nourishing than the macaroni. Tending to the needs of nature was still another lawful break, but not relaxing, under the binocular surveillance from guard towers, coupled with shouted doubts about our sex while squatting in the grass.

There were compensations to being in the quarry, not the least, our contact with the truck drivers. Not supposed to fraternize with us, they jeopardized their positions if they did. Letters were smuggled out for the drivers to mail on their passes in Cuba. Cigarettes and food came in, the prisoners' families paying the tariff at the other end.

By a stroke of luck, one driver came from the town of San Andrés next to our ranch and remembered something I had forgotten. I once had jeeped his sick father to the nearest doctor twenty miles away. Proving the parable of "spreading bread upon the water," the son now showed his gratitude. Whenever he could he'd toss from his truck small nylon sacks of brown sugar, a can of condensed milk, extra bread, once a chocolate bar. He in *el Plan* could get these things. I could not. He was eventually transferred and my Christmas packages stopped.

Because our place of work was permanent, we could cache a multitude of things not possible to have in the circular. When cucumbers came with lunch we made vinegar from them by adding sugar and tiny wild peppers, hot as Mexican chile, stashing it away in the block factory to mature. The peppers, found where the field of boulders met field of grass, gave black market value to our vinegar, and by our humble standards, transformed the macaroni into something digestible. Much of this was exchanged in the circular for cigarettes.

Fortunately, *Perro Prieto*'s territory ended at the block factory's entrance. Its boss was Mario, an older man of unknown rank, more interested in production than discipline, and so turning a blind eye to our shelves of fermenting cucumbers.

Another compensation was having fires to boil laundry over, a perk that came about because of the fracture of a small wheel in the factory. The machinery was old and when any part gave way only invention could repair it. Invention failed one day and left three men unemployed. To keep them busy, they were put to demolishing an unused shed. Most of the wood was rotten and permission was asked of Mario to use it for laundry fires. In five-gallon lard tins, bought from the kitchen with cigarettes, two sheets and towels could be boiled at once. Over five fires, most of the laundry of a hundred men could be done in a week. Our stuff changed color and smell from being boiled, then dried on grass, and we were saved the Saturday afternoon laundry hassle in the circular. A small thing, a great luxury.

Perro Prieto didn't much like our washing clothes. One morning, conducting head count at the factory before sending us off on our jobs, he detailed the shed demolishers/launderers to hauling stone. The laundry innovator was Tito, a strong willed Havana University student. Gentle brown eyes belied his fearless temper and the physical strength that sledge hammers had given his wiry frame. Tito banked on the hostility between *Perro Prieto* and Mario to keep his fires going, and replied, "We're under the orders of Mario, not yours."

An open provocation was unacceptable and *Perro Prieto* responded in the only way he was capable of. Out of the scabbard his machete, out of his mouth abuse. Generally, Mario took no part in quarry discipline, but hearing his name, came closer, engrossed in some machinery, while the *cabo* vented his spleen. Raising his voice, but not his eyes, Mario finally cut through the foul language.

"Tito, get to work—in my sheds!"

Perro Prieto was technically in charge of the quarry, but unlike Mario not a member of the communist party. Although his animal instincts urged him to fight, he knew where final authority lay, and with unlikely wisdom, sheathed tongue and blade. This humiliation before the entire brigade was an abscessed tooth. In repressed fury he waved us to work, as if saying, "To hell with the lot of you. I'll have you yet."

It was in character that our *cabo* should exact his pound of flesh. That same morning we thirsted in vain for our waterboy until the first splintered sledge handle took a man to the carpentry shop. He found the two carpenters trying to mend the pails, split by *Perro Prieto*'s strong boots. If we had supposed him psychopathic before, now we knew. The man was another "Captain Queeg" from Herman Woulk's *The Caine Mutiny*. That night we wrote a letter of protest to the prison director. Whether it was that or Mario's interference at party level we never knew, but the next morning there were two new buckets and a subdued *Perro Prieto*.

But the abscessed tooth of humiliation had not healed. Captain Queeg had carried small steel balls to roll in his hands when under emotional strain. Our "captain" carried a fine-grit stone for honing his already razor sharp machete several times a day. During this time of pent-up spleen the machete was seldom sheathed, more often in sudden attack on some tuft of grass or passing butterfly. This cutting tool had become his alter ego, his only friend.

Two weeks after the failure to halt the laundry industry, we were in ranks outside the circular for the first headcount of the day when *Perro Prieto* noticed Tito with an infected eye bandaged against quarry dust. Out came the machete, twirling at the end of its short leather wrist thong, a nervous substitute for the customary honing when some emotional storm was brewing. As the rabbit mesmerized by the snake before he strikes, so were we by the twirling machete and the mad glint in the *cabo*'s eye. None moved. Even *Gallito* seemed caught in the drama, watching with half-open mouth. The next maneuver must have been a practiced one, a clever twist of the wrist, stilling the twirl to flip the machete handle into the palm of his hand. With the blade stilled, gone was the spell. Chests filled with air again, feet shuffled, bodies moved, but none took their eyes from our *cabo*. With the grace of a boxer moving on his toes, he strode to Tito and in one swift swipe snatched off the bandage, throwing it to the ground to crush beneath his boot. The gesture seemed to relieve the tension that was in him, but Tito, recovering from surprise, instinctively bunched himself to fight. With strong arms, his companions held him back. The moment passed, an eternity lasting less than two minutes.

My turn for satisfying the *cabo*'s smouldering resentment came a week later. He may have not liked my nationality, the color of my skin, or the way I walked, but from the beginning he had been on my back for insignificant things. This time, for protecting my nose and lips from the sun with a white talcum-like substance from knocking together two pieces of marble. As Tito's eye patch had annoyed our "Captain Queeg," now it was my white nose and lips.

"What you got on your face, *Americano*?"

I explained.

"You gotta *sombrero* for that. You don't need anything else."

I paid no attention. In half an hour he was back, stopping before me. I was working that day with five others forty yards out from the face of the cliff where the smaller boulders lay from the last dynamiting. He stood ten paces before us, legs apart, hands on hips, staring at me. Out came the fine grit stone. The blade done to his liking, he left a butterfly fluttering groundward on half a wing.

"*Americano*, come here!"

I stopped two yards before him. He waved me closer with his machete. Everyone within sight stopped working. Once again, that detached curiosity kept me from fear. I felt only the black of his eyes without pupils, total lack of expression. Never had I seen eyes like that. Reptilian, evil. In a hard flat voice, "So you think you're tough!"

The stock prison accusation, the stock prisoner's negative in reply. The flash of machete in the sun. My hat flying off to one side.

"*Americano*, if you want to play the clown wit me, let's play."

Three feet apart, eye against eye. His were fathomless, impenetrable, emotionless. Mine, bewildered surprise changing to anger. Unaccustomed to illogical provocation, I reacted spontaneously, not remembering what happened next. My companions told me later.

I punched him twice before he reacted with the stunning flat of machete over an ear. A good place to hit, releasing a hive of bees in my head, sending my balance to hell. A blast to the nape of my neck and my knees gave way. On all fours, my head on the ground, my back was target to the flailing blade. Forty fellow prisoners, spectators to this sport, recovered their wits and as one, they dropped their tools to race in from three sides. Standing over me, *Perro Prieto* met this threat with bloody machete in one hand, his small Russian pistol in the other. The first to arrive was Tito, who had suffered too much under quarry discipline to care. Jumping my inert body, he rushed *Perro Prieto*. A sharp report, and Tito fell to the ground. This stopped the others and for a moment no one moved. What I did next before the threat of the pistol was instinct alone.

Crawling to Tito to cradle his head in my lap, I screamed my contempt of our *cabo*, hating him for bringing us all to this animal state. Now everyone was shouting insults and shaking fists. *Perro Prieto*, half crouched, waving pistol and machete, changed face before this lynch-minded mob. No swagger left, no bravado or squared shoulders. He was frightened, forgetting even his whistle. But the pistol shot, the prisoners' shouts, and a warning volley fired from a tower brought *Gallito* and other guards on the run.

The metamorphosis of *Gallito* was instantaneous. The man who had always been second, acted only when ordered and seldom spoke, became the leader. He went straight to *Perro Prieto*, holding out his hand for the pistol, pocketing it without the least sign of resistance. The other, frozen in his crouch, glared at us as if daring further mutiny.

Ignoring him, *Gallito* sent one guard for a truck and the others to hold off the crowd, then turned his attention to Tito. The blood on Tito was my own, making it difficult to determine his wound. Fully conscious, not yet feeling pain, he led us himself to a small clean hole low in his groin. Nothing to be done but get him quick to the prison hospital. From the spill of small cuts on my head, chest and back, I seemed the worse of the two, but *Gallito* sent Tito off in the back of a truck and me for repair to the carpenter shop with its liter bottle of iodine and unlimited water. I was stiff and sore, but it wasn't the physical pain, it was the moral outrage that hurt. No one much worked that afternoon and we were not pushed. Excitement was still high and another incident could have pushed us all over the top.

That night a letter signed by the entire brigade went to the Director requesting an interview and stating our refusal to work under a mentally unbalanced *cabo*. The interview never came off, but *Perro Prieto* was seen no more in the quarry. *Gallito* took over, using his machete for what it was intended, trimming grass under the tree reserved for his lunch.

A week later three civilians drove into the quarry in a dilapidated Chevrolet asking for me. G-2 wanting me in Havana, they said. I was given twenty minutes in the circular to shower and collect my belongings before being put on the commercial flight to Cuba. My neck was still swollen black and blue, cuts and bruises on my face. The civilian passengers looked once at me, travelling handcuffed to a guard, and then away.

Sitting by the window, I feasted on the panorama of sea and islands below. I had "slipped the surly bonds of earth," but not the bonds of prison. The steel handcuffs on my wrist were eloquent proof of that, and, ironically, "Made in U.S.A."

Like the beat-up Mercury on the night of my arrest, the car-that-no-one-notices was on the tarmac in Havana with three civilians waiting. A car of the Cuban secret police needs no lettering on the door to identify it for what it is. If the distinctive radio antenna is not enough, the derelict chassis is slung lower for fast cornering, and in a country running on retreads, has new tires. The driver and his companions dress in loose sport shirts to camouflage the pistol at the waist. They strut while others walk. There's a stink of oppression to them. Give a man a gun with accompanying authority and he'll stand out in any crowd. He cannot help it.

At G-2, the same routine. Confiscation of all belongings, change of uniform, and a two-man cell to myself. The only surprise was a mattress on one bunk. That night, two interrogations with Denis. Not a word about the quarry, only clumsy attempts to tie me into another case, and Denis's bullying tactics seemed lacking in conviction. Perhaps he sensed that I no longer stood in awe of either him or G-2, and worried less about their ability to destroy me. Threats were passing thunderclouds. I knew now that with God's help I could live anywhere, anyhow, without succumbing.

For two weeks I was left alone. To be quietly by myself was, I'm sure, a luxury Denis never intended.

As before, I scratched the days of November on the wall with the leaded end of my toothpaste tube. I forgot about Thanksgiving and was startled to receive my lunch and hear the guard say in a low voice, "In your country today is *el Día de Gracias* (the day of thanks). We have no *Día de Gracias* now, but, God willing, we shall again."

The door slammed shut on any thanks I might have given.

One of the lesser disciplines I had followed in G-2 was to take my food tray from the guard with my eyes on his, not on the compelling cargo of macaroni or corn meal mush. When chronically famished, no matter how bad the food, the eye is irretrievably drawn to devour it before the stomach has its chance. Only practiced discipline could keep my eye raised from this first vicarious tasting—as a trained waiter accepts a tip without glancing at his hand. It was my custom to place the tray on a bunk, still without

187

looking at it, kneel for grace, and only then examine the menu that never surprised. On this *Día de Gracias* there *was* a surprise—three pieces of bread instead of one. Through a whispered sentence and extra bread, two men had touched and shared the joy of Thanksgiving.

After two weeks in G-2 I was transferred to la Cabaña without my few belongings. I was told they'd follow. They never did. Friends supplied my needs in typical generosity and I bedded down once more on the filthy floor. Galleries were packed tighter and discipline cut deeper. Quantity and quality of food had deteriorated and must be consumed in three minutes by the clock. Instant meals. In the moats the nightly fusilades continued. I longed for the Isle of Pines.

In three days I had my wish, packed off one night to Batabano and the same tired old ferry and its tug. One other prisoner was with me, Manolo del Valle. Four guards, Manolo and I dozed the night through in the foodless cafeteria in company with the other passengers. Toward dawn, coffee and bread were sold, and from their own pockets our guards bought us breakfast. By noon I was back in Circular 2, and no work uniforms in supply, unemployed.

I returned in time for the Cuban national holiday, December 7th, the death of Antonio Maceo in Cuba's fight for independence from Spain. An anniversary shamelessly twisted into hypocritical rhetoric for Castro's benefit. A day free from work, a day for the most senseless *requisa* ever. No provocation, no reason for it.

From seven in the morning to five in the afternoon we were held in a corner of the compound under a hot sun without food or water. Homecooked delicacies from recent visits to six hundred prisoners were left in the circular. With the amorality of children, guards had strewn everything on the floor. Everything rationed outside and gathered with such sacrifice: fried chicken and pork, cakes and puddings, dehydrated milk, chocolate and sugar, all trampled into garbage. Family and religious pictures torn from the walls. The building a shambles, resembling the aftermath of battle, as if each floor had been savagely fought over. We were left with one great consolation—the bastards had not found the radio. That same night it was reaching out and we were back in touch.

My vacation lasted one week. The latest order put everyone in the fields regardless of dress. Three score of us: barefoot, boots held together with wire, in underwear alone, pants without shirts, shirts without pants. A Chaplinesque patchwork to frighten crows from some farmer's field. On the way to work, those of us in underwear were made to stand in the middle of the trucks so those we passed should not see our shame. Our shame? We'd have gone proudly naked if only to show the conditions under which we worked. The shame belonged to the Revolution, not us. *Sombrero*ed, booted, and in underwear, I quarried for three weeks till new supplies arrived.

In four days infected cuts on my legs from sunburn and flying shards of marble took me to our dispensary for penicillin shots, and out of curiosity I checked their origin. This penicillin was painful Russian without built-in anesthetic and an expiration date of eighteen months before. Most medicines came from the Soviet bloc, outdated by the time they reached the prisons, but still with a cure in them.

Although outlawed as a bourgeois custom, Christmas was kept by all Cubans in one way or another, and in spite of being a normal workday, particularly by the political prisoners. On the top floor of Circular 2, we Protestants had made a simple altar from bits of scrounged wood. A peasant, accustomed to plaiting his year's harvest of garlic into cords, plaited a grass cross. Plaited grass ropes became festive garlands with colored ampules from the dispensary tucked into their length. A crude nativity scene was sculpted from red subsoil brought to the surface by ants. With our cross and nativity scene from nature itself, no altar could have pleased us more.

The Catholics originated a more stylized setting. The only Catholic priest in prison, Father Loredo, concocted from newspaper an eight-by-three-foot "stained glass window" showing the figure of Christ. Dyed various colors from medicines, the paper was joined with starch from malanga. It produced a magical effect when hung from the rafters on the top floor and lighted from behind with bulbs "donated" by the hospital and electrical wire "borrowed" from the dynamiters in the quarry.

These two stage settings as seen against the rough backdrop of prison were islands of security consoling us all and bringing the true meaning of Christmas into our hearts. Until destroyed by the next *requisa*, men would climb to the top floor after showering at the end of the day to hunker peacefully for a while before the "window," or grass cross, drawing strength from this moment of repose. Others came later until the hour of sleep, still more before dawn and the roll call for a new day of work. The Lord was truly sharing their burden.

Christmas was also the murder of a prisoner, still another shot in the field by a trigger-happy guard shooting a prisoner squatted behind a tree. A mistake, said Administration, although the seventh that year on the Isle of Pines.

Whenever a Prisoner was killed we went hatless to work, a signal the civilian population understood. Many responded with wreaths of flowers on their gate posts for us to see on returning that evening. The Administration, infuriated by this, threatened permanent confiscation of hats if we did not work "correctly dressed." Since the hats were not worn, they were taken—and a few days later quietly returned. Too many cases of sunstroke, real or feigned, they never really knew.

Because of a foot injury I was shifted to the block factory, and so was eligible to share in the daily "Easter egg hunt." The *abuelito*, or political advisor of our brigade, having little to occupy himself with, grew a few vegetables and ran chickens in the quarry. Hurricane Alma, the summer before, had devastated the flock and their coop. The flock was replaced without the coop, and the chickens ran free, roosting in a tree at night, laying their eggs wherever during the day. Tree and laying zone being near the factory, the block makers found the time to plot the nesting habits of each bird. Without consulting the owner, who hadn't a clue to his flock's laying capacity, the prisoners decided on a fifty-fifty allocation of eggs. And posing as a poultry authority, one of the prisoners convinced the *abuelito* that depressed production was only temporary. The old man accepted his small quota of eggs, ignorant of the fowl arrangement. And each man in the factory received one fresh egg approximately every four days to barter, eat raw, or to boil with the laundry over a fire. But not content with just sharing their eggs, these generous chickens entered into a second cooperative with us, their daily supply of stale bread from the kitchen. Until some over-greedy character subtracted one entire sack on a Monday, and Tuesday saw the whole brigade eating bread pudding. Blatant grand larceny, obvious to even the old man. The bread went to the hens after that.

Chapter 26

In January 1967, we read in the party newspaper, *el Granma*, that the Isle of Pines was henceforth to be called la Isla de Juventud, the Isle of Youth. Rumors said prisoners would be returned to Cuba, leaving the island to youth brigades to toil "voluntarily" in the fields. Agriculture schools were to be built for students from developing countries, and our circulars converted into dormitories to house them. We wondered who would quarry the marble.

As rumor strengthened, discipline weakened. The afternoon count into the trucks became sloppy and four prisoners decided to take advantage of this, hiding in the cement storage shack for a later escape. Four of their friends muddled the tally by being counted twice into the trucks, slipping over the sides to clamber in again at the back. Before the circular, the head count was muddled again and the missing four remained undetected. Impossible, however, to fool the two officials at evening roll call with each standing before his cell. They counted, conferred, and counted again, departing as if satisfied. Twenty minutes later, back they came with the building roster and thirty armed soldiers, ordering us to the arena while the soldiers combed cells. It was well after midnight before all twelve hundred of us had passed muster and the four fugitives identified.

All work was suspended while the quarry area was searched with dogs, and the marsh between quarry and ocean where a dog's scent failed was burned by flame throwers. Light planes circled overhead. Not a trace of the four. We were glad of the holiday they had unwittingly provided and kept our fingers crossed for their success. On the fourth day the search moved further afield and work resumed with renewed vigilance. *Gallito*, held responsible for the escape, had been relieved and a new *cabo* took over.

A week passed and still no sign of our friends. Hopes for them rose. And then a civilian student brigade cultivating cucumbers became suspicious over the remains of a camp fire near their field. Soldiers and dogs were called in and a half-hour search led them to the exhausted prisoners.

Many months later, I heard their story. The four left the shed at dusk, clothed in sport shirts made from mattress covers and work pants dyed green from boiling with grass. Prisoner boots and hats presented no problem, being identical with those worn by all Cubans. They followed a road through the swamp to the shore a mile away, then west towards the port of Nueva Gerona by swimming round rock promontories and climbing others. The fishing fleet was anchored in the river that led to Nueva Gerona, and it was their hope to reach one of these boats. A day's spying from the river bank dissuaded them from this. A bustling patrol boat checked incoming and outgoing traffic, crew and cargo as well. They slept the second night at a garage in an abandoned Greyhound bus being cannibalized to provide unavailable spare parts for its still-active comrades. Able to break into a small cafeteria maintained for the mechanics, they found bread, ham and sugar, but to their disgust no coffee to brew on the hotplate.

Then came their craziest scheme. Without food or knowledge of the terrain, they struck out for the almost uninhabited south coast through forty miles of rough rock and scrub growth. Once there, to build a raft and float to Mexico's Yucatán Peninsula, or be picked up by some passing freighter. Sleeping the day and walking the night, they stumbled through the points of the compass, making large circles of their path. On the seventh night, St. Christopher, the patron saint of travelers, took pity and set their feet towards a *carbonera* where a peasant and his son were making charcoal. Sympathetic to political prisoners, this man shared his poor rations and brackish water and recommended northeast to a huddle of houses near the coast where they might find some small craft and help from the peasants. St. Christopher was off on other business and the four soon strayed, hopelessly lost. Three days later they were discovered and spent the better part of six months in la Cabaña's solitary confinement.

In February 1967, visits were cancelled and little by little work stopped in the fields until only we in the quarry were in business. We made only a pretense at keeping ourselves occupied, the guards as uncaring as ourselves. An open secret: the Isle of Pines was folding.

In March, the quarry closed and the exodus began, one thousand prisoners every other day. Easier and more efficient had the omnipotent Castro pulled a "Red Sea" on the shallow strait of Batabano, sending us over on foot. But jammed together we came and jammed we returned. Some to be sent to the notorious prison of Boniato at the other end of Cuba, some to la Cabaña, and others to the newly completed concentration camp at Taco Taco in my province of Pinar del Río. It was Taco Taco for me.

Taco Taco was near the south coast on the rich delta land of rice and sugar cane where mosquitoes were the size of horseflies and horseflies, sparrows. Everything flourished there except the prisoners on their interminable diet of macaroni and cornmeal mush. The agricultural work was hard, the heat extreme, and food inadequate. But accustom an ox to small and inferior rations and he will continue to labor without much bellowing or protest.

Now came the surprise we'd been hearing rumors about. The khaki uniform of political prisoner was to be changed for the blue denim of common prisoner. Sweating in the sun outside the administration building, we listened to the commander of the camp confirming this. Denim for khaki today, now.

Awaiting our turn to be called inside, we heard the consequences of refusing. Grunts from stomach pummelling, cries of pain from body blows, the thud of dead weights hitting the floor. Impressive orchestration, deciding many vacillating men into an acceptance of the new uniform. And I was one of them when my turn came. Suddenly all sorts of good reasons came to my mind for wearing the blue. What difference did it make, the color of one's uniform, if one's convictions remained the same? The commander had said our pants and shirts would be distinctive from the common prisoners' with a stripe down the side. The change was inevitable. Why not make life easier by accepting now? So I reasoned as did many of my companions. Sickened and tired by two years of violence and humiliation in the shifting sands of prison life, I took the easier of two routes in a mixture of shame and relief. Only in retrospect was it clear this change of uniform was the thin end of the wedge driving most of us into *el Plan*.

Hesitantly climbing the steps of the administration barracks, I was afraid. Partly the unknown, partly the knowing a real going over followed refusal. Before me were piles of blue uniforms stacked on the floor, behind them six muscular soldiers, legs apart, arms folded across chests, their eyes threatening with, "Are you man enough to take me on?" The moment of truth. You either gave your size and had two sets of clothes tossed at you, or refused and were dragged into the next room for "physical interrogation." If that didn't convince you, into solitary with all the time in the world to reconsider your errors. I gave my size and walked out the back with the others who'd "bought." Bought only temporary relief.

Apparently I was at Taco Taco by mistake. In thirty-six hours I was packed off in a patrol car for la Cabaña. In the final *requisa* on the Isle of Pines I had lost sheets and blanket and personal belongings. At Taco Taco another *"requisa"* had further depleted my baggage. Now, at la Cabaña, a third *requisa* in as many days took its toll and I was left with toilet articles alone, minus Gillette blades, of course. Not only had they taken all of my personal things, but now the two blue-denim uniforms I'd suffered in shame to acquire only a day and a half ago. I was back again in khaki. Four months later came the uniform change for la Cabaña, and for the second time I accepted the blue.

When the Isle of Pines changed from concentration camp to youth hostel, the Minister of the Interior changed from repressive Ramiro Valdés to the more benign Sergio del Valle. The inhumane handling of political prisoners was recognized as mistaken and rectified for all but *los plantados*, those who refused to change khaki for denim. There was more emphasis on attracting men into *el Plan* with pretty promises not always honored. One of the carrots was the chance to work on open farms, as opposed to concentration camps like Taco Taco. As a "political undesirable," I was not eligible for this.

I was, however, eligible for a group used as window dressing to entice *los plantados* into the shop. Two hundred and fifty of us were moved to gallery 32, a "suite" of five inter-connecting galleries: three for double-decker bunks, one with showers, toilets, and laundry tubs, the fifth a dining room with cement tables and benches. At last! A place to read, write, and study that was not a sagging bunk. And three times a week for an hour we were released onto the battlements to sunbathe on the old Spanish cannons and throw the eye to Havana and the ocean beyond.

One of my new companions was ex-colonel Cantillo, Batista's chief of SIM, the secret police, tall and spare, handsome, a kindly face, quite unlike the stereotype of a man once in charge of this organization's excesses. He had to walk carefully in prison. More than a few prisoners would have enjoyed avenging some friend's death at SIM's hand. He kept to himself except for a time as my student in English. Unable to concentrate, he soon dropped out. Although condemned to death, he eventually went free to the States, rumored to have ransomed his life with a part of his ill-gotten gains stashed out of Cuba.

Another in gallery 32 was a handsome six-foot-two mulatto, Roberto Guevara. In 1953, with Castro arrested for insurrection, Guevara had been warden of the prison, and, had he only known it, held history in his hands. When Batista ordered Castro poisoned, Guevara substituted the lethal dose with something harmless and saved his life. On coming to power, Castro showed his gratitude by making him his aide-de-camp—and official pimp. Greed rerouted into his own pocket gifts intended for the boss, and the price of discovery was eight years in prison.

Jorge Nelgado, an ex-army major, was said to owe his life to having sold arms to Castro in la Sierra Maestra—and to being the father of Raúl Castro, Fidel's brother. Nelgado had been military commander of the district in Oriente Province where the Castro ranch was and knew the family well. By self-admission, being beast himself (*Soy una bestia*), short and squat, toadlike, he might well have serviced the Castro mare, renowned for being perpetually in heat. If only a tithe of his Castro family stories were true, the promiscuousness in which this family lived would allow for much of Fidel and Raúl's aberrations.

Raphael del Pino was of our gallery, roommate of Castro's in Havana University and close companion until finally falling out politically. He believed Castro could have been anything he set his mind to, with a phenomenal memory to complement a notable intellect, but a lust for power greater than any ideology.

Another fellow-prisoner, Mario Chanes, had been with Castro in his initial bid for recognition at the 1953 Moncada attack, shared twenty two months of prison on the Isle of Pines, exile in Mexico, and the 1956 "invasion" of Cuba. Mario spoke highly of Castro's organizational abilities and powers of persuasion, but said an ungovernable temper led him into errors of judgement that later he was incapable of admitting or rectifying. (As of this writing, Mario still vegetates in prison after 30 years, the object of a madman's spite and pettiness.)

Two of our lot merited psychiatric care. One, a manic depressive, had retreated into a dark hole where none could reach, a pathetic wall-starer, a physical Tarzan quietly living in his own broken world, forced there by excessive guard brutality on the Isle of Pines. He talked to no one and blankly refused any overtures of friendship. He kept himself and his clothes clean and neat, neither wrote nor read, and had no diversions other than lying in his corner bed staring at the wall. His mother never missed a visit, passing the two hours holding her son's hand without a word, complete indifference on his face, hopeless, sad anxiety on the mother's.

The other *loco* was quite the opposite, a gregarious, overfriendly puppy, constantly under foot, but tolerated for his good nature. He too had broken on the Isle of Pines while living above tons of dynamite under each circular, set to explode at Castro's orders during 1961-1962. After electric shock treatment, applied by common prisoners instructed solely in the mechanics of throwing switches, he entered a new life of changing personalities. First, as "doctor" with all of us as patients. Then, with a scarcity of rations in prison diet, he switched to "cook," though lacking the essentials of his trade. His next metamorphosis to "taxi driver" was more successful. He was forever being flagged down to send on errands, deliver messages, or summon someone to a game of chess or checkers. "Taxi" was kept happily busy, only deserting his profession for *siestas* and food. He took himself, and was taken, seriously. His world was small but happy.

A dog finds its corner, a cat its chair. The prisoner stretches a piece of string between two nails as a towel rack on the wall to establish place, to give a sense of permanency. Every move to another gallery, cell, or prison meant securing property rights to a bunk, preferably near door or window, and the corresponding wall or ceiling space. But this settling in meant finding tools.

"Hey, Pipo, are you the guy with the chisel?"

"You dumb bastard! Do I look like a guy with a chisel? Can't you see I'm trying to sleep? Sure I got a chisel. I got two chisels. One to loan to jerks like you and one to keep for myself."

"*Bueno.* let me have the one you keep for yourself—please."

And pushing my luck a little further, "Pipo, you know you are my best friend in all the world—how about loaning me your hammer too?"

"Larry, I've already told you what I think of *gringos*. You think I run an American hardware store? It's over there in my underpants. Now, for the love you bear the mother you never had, go away and let me sleep—and bring them back."

The chisel was a twelve-penny nail with point flattened into a cutting edge by patient grinding on the cement floor. A hammer was any piece of metal, torn from a bed, the plumbing, or whatever lent itself to prison ingenuity. With Pipo's nail and an eight-inch piece of pipe, I banged holes into "my" wall for bits of broom handle as pegs to hold my two sugar sacks of *pertenencias*: clothes, books, and provisions for the stomach. Around each stick I rubbed soap into the crevices to prevent egg laying by cockroaches and bedbugs. My territory staked, I returned chisel and hammer to Pipo's underwear and asked what other tools he had. His reply was descriptive and unrepeatable.

Although reading, writing, studying, and teaching filled my days, I agonized over the two-and-a-half-year separation from my family and the disquieting thought of my sons maturing without knowing their father, nor I them. So little contact between us. In fourteen months on the Isle of Pines, no embassy visits and few letters. Now all this changed. My narrow horizon broadened and my heart filled. Each month I saw the new Belgian Ambassador, Mr. George Elliott, generous with his time and interest on my behalf. Once more I received correspondence, books and magazines. And from renewed family contact I realized the difficulty of reasoning well to correctly assess my position when too-long isolated in prison thinking.

The Swiss Embassy, and my family through the Belgians, were urging me to join *el Plan de Rehabilitación. Reeducación* had become *Rehabilitación* for reasons best known to our *reeducadores*. The government had convinced the two embassies that *el Plan* was the only door to freedom, and that if I were not a part of it, none could help me.

Raúl Roa, the Foreign Minister, parrotted to the Swiss and Belgian ambassadors what Sergio del Valle, Minister of the Interior, had told him: that I was a troublesome prisoner, always in conflict with the guards, and continually writing disparaging letters about the Revolution. None of this was true, but unfortunately the two embassies and my family believed it.

My sister Faith sent messages urging me to rectify my behavior, mentioning my "proud spirit" as a deterrent to springing me. I replied to her:

"You talk of my proud spirit as a stumbling block to extricating me from prison. A proud spirit, if such I have, is something inborn, an integral part of one, not so easily discarded or bent to conform to adverse forces. In the present circumstances it is this proud spirit that sustains and carries me along. I believe it would be nigh impossible to fully comprehend unless having experienced the indignities, physical and mental, that the communists are so clever at. I personally do not pretend to have suffered to any great degree, but the insidious corrosive effect of daily wear and tear can be fatal and needs be held off by some anti-corrosive. A belief in God, courage, spirit, what-have-you. Drop this guard and you have a man such as I do not want to be. My family are all profoundly dear to me but I have discovered something else of immense importance as well, which cannot be explained, but only understood. An inner tranquility and faith transcending the meanness and pettiness of the present life enabling me to endure prison in a right and honorable way. You cannot lose your self-respect here, and a proud spirit need not be abrasive.

"I have been reading a book by an English prisoner of war in Italy, who wondered of his ability to meet freedom, fearing he had been unmanned by captivity. I cannot help but feel he lacked a proud spirit.

198

"By quoting the Indian prayer, 'Do not judge me, O Lord, until you have been two moons in my mocassins,' I am glad you do not judge me. Only one who has experienced the deceits and vileness of the communist prison system can so do. No always easy to think and act rationally behind bars, but the good Lord occasionally helps—and my proud spirit. Please leave me that."

I had the experience of other foreigners ahead of me in *el Plan*, who had never reached the carrot held before them. I continued to hold out.

To induce us into *el Plan*, many stratagems were used. One was magazines in any language, allowed one month and the next forbidden, those we had, taken away. "Now if you'd join *el Plan* this wouldn't be necessary," they'd say. One month, books in English and French permitted, two months later, only those in Spanish. Sometimes no books at all. The same with correspondence. Following a deluge of letters, a long dry spell. They knew the written word in familiar script was tonic to the soul. Their psychological games kept us off balance, but were not the determining factor that forced us into their rehabilitation program.

Official laissez-faire with books and correspondence usually went hand-in-hand with better food. During one of these upswings we had enough bread to amuse ourselves by tossing surplus into the moat outside our windows to watch the soldiers' chickens fight. One enterprising man fashioned a line and hook to try his luck at "fishing" a particularly aggressive rooster. The bait was a ball of bread and macaroni. The rooster took the bait, but protested so vocally at being reeled in that a guard patrolling the far side of the moat fired a warning shot into the wall above our window and stopped our fun. Frustrated at "fishing," the same man tried "hunting" and rigged a clever device to electrocute the rats on their nightly invasion of our galleries. Too large and strong, they got no more than a hefty shock, but enough to scare many of them away.

Those not into "fishing," "hunting," or studying, used their hands in prohibited manual labor of their own invention. Toothbrush handles, and anything else plastic, were melted to multi-colored blobs to work into jewelry. Paper beads were rolled from the glossy pages of magazines, the Soviet bloc monthlies being the glossiest—and the dullest. Colored towels were unravelled, the yarn woven into baby clothes with knitting needles made from heavy wire. Jute strands from sugar sacks were knitted into sweaters or twisted into lengths of rope for clotheslines. From canvas bunks came heavy thread for weaving belts and miniature hammocks for storage space above one's bed. For much of what one needed the materials were at hand—if one but had the eye to see them.

In Cuba where the shops' display cases were empty and many of the families' cupboards bare, the prisoners' handiwork, once smuggled out, often represented income when sold or bartered. Later, when tools and ingenuity became more sophisticated, this prohibited work became an important revenue for many families. Outlawed silver pesos were smuggled into prison for conversion into ornaments, and then smuggled out again and sold at fifty times the value of the original coins. Even guards brought money in to have made into rings for themselves or their *novias*.

Another thriving industry was the making of dominoes from melted plastic sacks, numbers painted in with Mercurochrome, and dice, of wood. Castro had outlawed dominoes, forever the Cuban pastime, and decreed chess the national game. He claimed seventy percent of the population as aficianados, a statistic more valid for dominoes than chess.

Chess is a quiet, reflective game, while dominoes, in the hands of Cubans, becomes an explosive hairy-chested sort of thing, often leading to blows, upset feelings, and enormously offended individuals. Notwithstanding, for the recriminations of Tuesday, all is forgotten on Wednesday and together the same men are once again happily rolling the dice, muttering spells in the language of the game, and noisily inventing unlikely antecedents for partner and opponents alike.

While Castro was pleading with the people to save electricity, we were making electric elements from bedsprings, or coils, to fashion stoves and submersible water heaters. This subtracted nothing from the comfort of the few beds with springs, while adding much to the luxury of having hot water and cooking facilities, and utilizing an enormous amount of current, but we weren't paying the bills.

We used our stoves for everything. When guards drank grapefruit juice we cadged the skins, boiling them with sugar to make marmalade, and made pudding from rice or old bread to improve our diet. We squeezed macaroni into pulp and dried it in the sun to produce a paste for pseudopancakes, and so was cornmeal mush mixed with malanga starch. When no longer serviceable for water, a lard can atop a stove became an oven for toasting bread, baking puddings, and what we optimistically called "cake," made from the same ingredients as above with an egg or two added. These came from men on special diets, often preferring swapping eggs for cigarettes. Our pleasure was more in the making than the eating, and our crude stoves gave endless gratification.

Chapter 27

At five centavos for the captive population on the street, free for prisoners, *el Granma*, party voice, was published daily except Monday and distributed liberally throughout the prisons. It proved a great boon to us with toilet paper in short supply. Two of its six pages were devoted to international news. In 1967-68, this meant the problems of Afro-Americans and their riots, American atrocities in Vietnam, opposition to that war within the United States, and guerrilla activities in South America. Two pages of sports were dominated almost exclusively by blacks, and on winning some international event, the article was moved to the front page. The rest of the paper belched the people's enthusiasm for "voluntary" labor. Everywhere, norms were being fulfilled, often in excess. Pictures in *el Granma* of grinning men and women and children at work were proof that all was well.

There was one small section, half a column, that gave insight into what was really troubling Cuba, the parasitical problem of bureaucracy. Heading the article was a photo of the culprit at the public whipping post of the day, accused of the inefficient management of some cooperative, nepotism, or misappropriation of funds. If not these anti-social delinquents, the photo was of ruined, imported merchandise, lying outside, overgrown with weeds, and bought with Cuba's dwindling supply of dollars. The accompanying article deplored waste and criminal negligence and called for help in determining blame. We read this avidly and proposed candidates of our own from the prison staff, guilty of stealing our belongings in *requisas*. We wrote letters, had the families mail them and, needless to say, they were never printed. We expected nothing else, but we'd had our fun.

In December 1967, Castro suggested to Washington an exchange of any hundred political prisoners in Cuba for the remains of Che Guevara, killed two months previously in Bolivia. The Bolivians refused to return the martyred body and our hopes dissolved. Simultaneously came a request from the Swiss Embassy for suit and shoe size of all Americans. Once more my hopes flew high. Nothing happened and once more I hunkered down to wait.

I had settled too easily into this way of life, living from day to day, visit to visit, with long-term planning necessarily based on that elusive date of release. There were so few decisions to make that those I was compelled to face seemed disproportionately large and heavy. A letter from my wife asked if I thought our son Antonio, just sixteen, should be allowed to motorbike to camp in England, or go by train. A simple decision of yes or no. I mulled it over for days, thrilled at being a part of family planning again, but indecisive in a way I'd never been before (finally I replied motorbike, and so he went).

My indecision over this small incident bothered me and brought from my subconscious annoyance at my acceptance of being caged. In a new light I looked around me, wondering if a physical escape were not possible, as it had been spiritually. Was my proud spirit atrophying? Was my adjustment to this abnormal life a mark of mental illness as suggested by the philosopher-psychiatrist Dr. Erich Fromm?

I had never seriously considered escape, though on the Isle of Pines we had all discussed it. Of the dozens who walked away from work in the fields, many were shot with only a handful making it to freedom. The odds against success were high and I was not a gambler, but still I wondered why I had not the nature for evasion. In self-defense, I asked myself if my tough friend Paco, a three-time escapee, would have my nerve to ride bareback a Brahma bull or bucking bronc? For the pure joy of it, to ride the leavings of an Atlantic hurricane in a twenty-two-foot sailboat? From trust and experience, to ride the winter air currents in a light plane over the eleven-thousand-foot Continental Divide of the Rocky Mountains? I talked to Paco about this, and at all three suggestions of riding beast, water, and air he threw up his hands. He feared horses and ocean and could put no trust in invisible air currents. Yet he had the courage to try an escape through three hundred yards of two-foot drainage pipes, unsure where or how he was going to surface.

I realized then that courage has many faces and few can wear them all. As many kinds and degrees of courage as there are and people on this earth, there is to each his share, for different circumstances. I felt better for this introspection and went back to looking through my bars, not at them.

Chapter 28

Until the spring of 1968, we had been free to study what and how we wished. Now Administration decreed studies would be programmed by the prison. Those who could teach would lead the others through simple mathematics and Spanish grammar. Everyone, a professor or a student. And three times weekly we had *el círculo político*, political studies, a light shampooing of the brain from reading and discussing Castro's long and contradictory speeches. Faithfully printed in *el Granma* at the expense of a page from the international section, organized study and new regulations chipped away at the promised freedom within our gallery. Those refusing were transferred to another. Those of us accepting this new regime remained where we were, knowing silently we were being led towards *el Plan*, while denying it out loud.

To teach was to preach what the communists wanted. I refused and became a student of Spanish grammar. Four college graduates among us taught two hours a day, five days a week at a sixth grade level. For one third of us, no mental strain, while the others struggled to stay afloat. Once a month a *reeducador* gave written tests and conveniently looked the other way while everyone helped each other score. The goal was statistical, not educational.

Los Círculos Políticos were taken even less seriously than the classes in mathematics and Spanish grammar. A week before the monthly test a mimeographed sheet was circulated with forty-five questions on Castro's latest ranting. Ten of these would appear on the quiz, so that with very little memorizing, one could hardly fail. The difference, however, between just passing and scoring high was the sauce one added to the dish. Knock the Americans and praise Castro, your score was pushing 100. Do as I did and prefix everything with "according to Fidel" and you just barely passed. To the question on the meaning of "revolution," I quoted Emerson: "Armed revolutions invariably replace old injustices with new, throw more elements out of balance and bring in new injustices." And I added, "except the American Revolution." I was not a great success.

As a lure to joining the organized school, the first conjugal visits were scheduled. For many this was an emotional bomb and the determining factor to join. The Director of la Cabaña himself announced the conjugal visits, explaining that if a prisoner had no wife he might invite some "serious woman." No elaboration on how serious the woman must be.

Lacking facilities for conjugal visits in la Cabaña, the men were trucked to el Principe, the prison hospital organized to handle this. Beforehand, a great deal of marital advice was freely given, and doubts cast upon the ability of the older bucks to adequately perform, with many friendly offers to stand in for them. Preparations began a week ahead: careful washing and pressing of clothes, particular attention given to the underwear, the plucking of grey hairs from chest and eyebrows, and the assuring of an adequate supply of talcum powder and deodorant.

This pre-mating dance with such a great fluffing of feathers seemed ludicrous to us non-participants, but we encouraged the show with much vicarious pleasure. When the great day arrived the men were nervous, their sense of humor strained. On their return, exhausted and irritable. But all agreed it was worthwhile.

For a few, the conjugal visits presented problems. One of these was Toldo, who had had his eternal love for Olga tattooed on his hairy chest by a fellow prisoner only to discover later she was as unfaithful to him as he would have been to her had the situation been reversed. When María del Carmen agreed to be his "serious woman," Toldo felt obliged to alter the tattoo in favor of this new imperishable union. Applying aspirin, salt, lemon juice, and much painful elbow grease, Olga disappeared forever from his life and chest, leaving an ugly scar as a testimonial to the fickleness of women—and men. With the unreserved optimism of one in love, Toldo persuaded the tattooer friend to apply his art again. A sewing needle, dipped in a mixture of Mercurochrome, indelible ink, and soot, etched María del Carmen into his life—for better or worse—until aspirin, salt, and lemon juice should them part.

Another created his own problem. Martínez was close to sixty, but where women were concerned, clung tenaciously to his twenties, boasting outrageously of his sexual prowess. Corpulent, with sagging face muscles, he resembled a Saint Bernard, imparting some of this to his wife with whom he had lived contentedly for so long. She came to la Cabaña's regular monthly visits, never having been told they'd been changed to fortnightly. Her husband's faithful mistress of happier days came in between. Señora Martínez was short and round, the rival, tall and thin, not unlike a sausage hound. Learning of the conjugal visits, Martínez scheduled his mating program in the same way, alternating wife and mistress. Most would have been a nervous wreck at this harem juggling, but not Martínez.

Martínez had been among the first arrested in 1959, enduring nine years of forced celibacy. His first kenneling of the sausage hound had him preening even more carefully than for his wife. A friend in our dispensary confided to him in the greatest secrecy that there was a new heart stimulant just in with side effects of stimulating other organs as well. "Even better," he whispered to Martínez, "It's American." The friend assured a memorable performance with one pill. Martínez suggested two. When the day arrived, he swallowed the pills half an hour before departure, frisky as a puppy. Boarding the paddy wagon, he was less exuberant, and according to his companions, something more than drowsy on arriving at el Principe. The somnolent and mortified Don Juan staggered into the arms of his bewildered and worried lady. The lunch she brought went untasted. The doctor she requested for her dying suitor brought only guffaws. While the mistress wept, the lover slept. The "heart stimulant" was a strong sedative. We had to get our kicks where we could, even at the expense of our aged Don Juans.

209

Not for kicks, but of necessity, we made some chores into recreation. One of these was the twice yearly rejuvenation of our mattresses. Stuffed with waste and rags, they grew harder and thinner with the months. When no longer able to find lump-free areas to sleep on, it was time to rip them open, wash the ticking, and pick apart the well-baled stuffing. To obviate the monotony of rejuvenation one had only to establish the focal point for a good gossip by emptying the stuffing on the floor. In three minutes there were half a dozen pitching in and as many more kibitzing on the side. On one occasion my mattress yielded an uncommonly fine array of colored rags and conversation.

Pedro recognized a bit of red that reminded him of the dress José's wife wore when she went dancing with him, José being out of town. José held up a checkered scrap.

"This must have come from the bikini of Pedro's wife, the one she wore to meet me on the beach while Pedro was cleaning house."

Jesús, coming upon a shred of burlap sack wondered sadly, "What can Mario's wife possibly be wearing now? She had only this one dress made from a sugar sack Mario once gave her."

Mario, on finding a square of pink cotton, retorted, "I didn't realize, Jesús, your wife wore underwear."

Another suggested, "Let's all of us donate our mattress stuffing to Pito to make a miniskirt for Chiquitica," Pito's enormous wife of some two hundred pounds.

Thanks to an hour of innuendos and helpful marital advice, my mattress was restuffed to a two-inch softness. In four or five months it would again be a good communist inch.

Chapter 29

August 1968, was a 200-yard leap toward *el Plan* through several gates and walls to Patio One. The "patio" had once been a narrow, 75-yard-long street, deep in the old fortress, flanked by storage galleries. Conversion from storing hardware to storing prisoners was a matter of installing cold water pipes and punching holes in floors for sanitary needs to connect with the storm sewers. Twelve-foot walls constructed at each end converted the street into a patio. On the other side of one wall were over two thousand military prisoners, unhappy teenage deserters from the army, a product of the Revolution. Their conditions were deplorable—overcrowded, subsistence-only diet, machete discipline, and infrequent family contact—a captive force at seven pesos a month for everything from agriculture to construction.

For the first time, we non-Plan shared territory with *el Plan*, each on his own side of the street, each with his corresponding degree of amenities. Proper showers and toilets for *el Plan*, spigots in the walls and holes in the floor for us. We were no longer the window dressing.

With the move, we hoped our organized studies might sink quietly into oblivion. Wishful thinking. The red balloon of

211

reeducation had been inflated by the *reeducadores* without lungs enough to get it off the ground. Now they had an eager minion to do it for them. Claró, a Spaniard who joined *el Plan* soon after being arrested, was one of those unhappy individuals looking for position in life and seldom finding it. Of small stature, he had the hairy chest of a man without the *cojones* to go with it. A former accountant in Cuba's Banco Nacional, he was intellectually equipped to organize and manage the reeducation courses. He took his job seriously, ran the school with an iron glove, and was harsher than any guard. We called him *Napoleoncito*.

The little man went in for charts. He loved them. Schedules, names, absentees, grades, and his favorite, the progress chart. After a month of this unpopular efficiency, the students posted a progress chart of their own, an ascending graph indicating the time and place of Señora Claró's infidelities, a cruel but well-merited response to *Napoleoncito*'s infidelities to the prison code of honor. The offending chart only enraged the man to tougher discipline, turning in more names than ever to the administration, suggesting visit cancellations, and even solitary confinement. This excess of zeal had adverse effects on the school and the Director was forced to deflate *Napoleoncito*'s authority. His few friends had deserted him long before, and with his authority curbed, he cut a pathetic figure in the solitary confinement of his own choosing.

One of our galleries was designated as the schoolroom. To *Napoleoncito*'s disgust, one quarter of it was requisitioned by the kitchen as storage for an unexpected shipment of potatoes for the guards. With our chronic interest in any food not related to cornmeal mush or macaroni, potatoes represented a gourmet dish. The schoolroom became an unusual center of interest, and class attendance soared while the potato supply plummeted. Every stove in every gallery was boiling potatoes and for days no one touched the macaroni. Inevitably the sergeant was alerted, a salvage squad sent in, and the tuber festival was over.

A few months later, our schoolroom was preempted as dormitory for an influx of men from other prisons. *Napoleoncito* tried unsuccessfully to keep his school going in the patio, but having lost the Director's blessing, made no headway. We were put to work instead, assembling pasteboard boxes for Havana's bakeries from sheets of cardboard—factory marked and cut for folding. Within two days the daily quota had to be revised. According to the first statistics, production fell before we'd even started. A large part of the factory cutouts traced on the cardboard had not been cut at all, and no amount of folding, twisting and tearing could make bakery cartons out of them. A lowered quota, easily met, traced a more satisfactory line on the progress chart. But the graph, showing relation of material received to finished product, was so out of balance that the distraught *reeducadores* removed the offending chart.

The faulty material continued to arrive. We put together what we could. The rest we converted into fans to move the stifling air, or laid them between the wire springs and our mattresses to fill the sag and make our beds more comfortable. A small mountain of finished cartons grew until storage space became a problem. Calls were made to numerous ministries. No one knew who had made the initial order, who they were for, nor how to halt the flow. No one wanted our cartons and yet the raw material still arrived, and we continued putting more under our mattresses than into production. *Los reeducadores* lost interest in something they could not control and stayed away until, inexplicably, the flood ceased. The stacks of bakery cartons were never retrieved and in time flattened back into their original shape before being eventually burned.

Sharing a patio with *el Plan*, we shared the advantages of more frequent visits and *jabas*, but also the disadvantage of their more stringent discipline. One aspect of this was mandatory attendance at the public trials, a mirror of those held throughout the island by the CDR, the local defense committees, for the minor peccadillos of civilians. A few went to gloat at the humiliation of their companions. Most went in disgust.

Infractions of the penal code were judged by three military personnel, and ranged from fighting, smuggling contraband, lack of respect to guards, urinating in the patio, homosexuality, or anything else that might contribute to lowering the standards of *el Plan*. Generally, sentences were loss of visits and *jabas*, sometimes solitary confinement.

Regarding homosexuality, the great illogic of the Latin attitude toward it was extraordinary. It was no disgrace to be the active partner, while the passive friend received scorn and condemnation. In these trials the "male" received a verbal wrist slapping, whereas the "female" lost visits, *jabas*, and was transferred to another gallery. There was a good deal of inter-gallery transfer.

I too had my day in court. From a visit, I brought back two cheese sandwiches, thinking to share them with a friend. My sandwiches were confiscated at the post-visit *requisa*. Having brought such foodstuff in before, I protested, only to be told that cheese was not allowed.

"Well," I replied, "If you are so hungry, then take my cheese sandwich and welcome."

I thought no more about it until I saw my name on the next trial list. My crime? Disrespect to a guard and the introduction of contraband into prison. On the day of the trial my friends occupied front-row hunkering space before the "tribunal," three chairs, and a table in the patio. In his four-minute lecture, the lieutenant in charge worked in "the dignity man" three times. First, at my "accusing" the guard of taking the sandwiches for himself. "The dignity of revolutionary man does not permit him to steal." There was a coughing fit from the front row of spectators and a scowl from the lieutenant. And again, "It goes against the dignity of man to introduce contraband into prison when that man is in *el Plan de Rehabilitación.*"

"*Señor Teniente*, I am not in *el Plan* and cheese sandwiches cannot be considered contraband when I have 'introduced' them before without a problem."

"Whether you are in *el Plan* or not doesn't matter. There is no dignity in bringing into prison a product not available to all."

The man was hooked on that word *dignidad*. And, of course, after that he was dubbed *Dignidad*. Magnanimously, I was let off with a reprimand and allowed to retire—with dignity, I hoped.

That evening my friends and I were still laughing about my day in court, and the question was raised about one cheese sandwich's degree of dignity, and do two have more than one, and hadn't I gotten off too easily considering there had been butter on the bread? Butter was not permitted. Prison sense of humor turned intended humiliation around.

In August 1968, I was pulled back to G-2 for the fourth time: sixteen days of rest and relaxation. There was a short interview the first night on why didn't Beatrice come to see me, why didn't I join *el Plan*, and how was my health? He knew the answers: my wife had not yet come because the Cubans refused to guarantee a visit with me, *el Plan* held no benefit for a foreigner, and my health was as good or bad as any other prisoner's. He dismissed me with a *"Bueno,* we'll talk again tomorrow."

"Tomorrow" never came and I used the funereal quiet and seclusion of G-2 as a welcome respite from the constant clamor and crowding of la Cabaña. I lived well enough within myself among my turbulent fellow prisoners, but usually with help of book or paper and pen. My bunk was the only calm refuge, and to lie still in thought with open eyes was to invite a neighbor's concern for my mental health. To lie still with eyes closed was to invite sleep. So this fourth round in G-2 was welcome, almost a spiritual retreat. Had Denis known, he'd surely not have left me quiet for such a time.

While I was in G-2, Castro's most controversial political prisoner, Hubert Matos, and a group of twenty followers began a twelve-day hunger strike in el Principe, forcing their transfer to la Cabaña and the treatment accorded all political prisoners. Matos, Castro's first military governor of Camaguey Province, had resigned from the army on October 19, 1959, in protest against the communist trend. Arrested two days later, he faced a kangaroo court and was sentenced to twenty years. Now, nine years later, he led almost six hundred *plantados* on a hunger strike of seventeen days to protest living conditions, insufficient food, and poor medical attention. Once again they won their rights, but the benefits slowly evaporated into unkept promises. To regain these, a year later in September 1969, still another hunger strike was staged by over eight hundred *plantados,* and completed thirty-six days later by five hundred.

These were not the ballyhoo of an Angela Davis hunger strike in an American prison, a doctor in attendance and "fasting" on orange juice, milk, and crackers three times a day. This was living on water alone without medical assistance.

Depriving the body of food over a long period forces it to start living off itself. Its reserve of fat gone, the muscles are consumed, sometimes atrophying. The brain lacks an adequate supply of blood from a weakened heart. Vitamins and other medicines were necessary for these men, but the families were not allowed to send them. Castro was little concerned over his political prisoners' health as long as they did not embarrass him by dying. He was forced to nurse these troublesome and emaciated bodies back to minimal health or lose face internationally. Once the strikers were ambulatory, however, the special diets of milk, fruit juice, and meat were revoked and convalescence wobbled on with the customary cornmeal mush and macaroni.

The suffering of these men through successive hunger strikes finally bore fruit for all. We began to receive one hard-boiled egg or small fish with the evening meal, a wider variety of medicines in the dispensary, and for the first time, superficial dental care and visits from an oculist, both sorely needed in our increasingly toothless, eye-strained community. And yearly typhus and tetanus shots were begun.

With these improvements, and for propaganda reasons only, the *jabas* of *el Plan* were raised from twenty-five pounds to fifty pounds every two weeks. One mother said, "To give my son fifty pounds every two weeks I should have to collect the stones from off my field."

As we settled into "seven years of plenty," a parade of new prisoners passed through la Cabaña on their way from G-2 to other prisons. Now there was no choice of joining *el Plan* or not. On being arrested for political reasons everybody was automatically "Plan." The only difference between these new political prisoners and common or military prisoners was the distinction of having committed a crime against the state. A young delinquent caught breaking public pay phones—breaking, not robbing—was political. A soldier caught leaving the country in a raft was political, not military. The common crime of theft became political when the thief was married to the niece of Cuba's president, Osvaldo Dorticos. This unfortunate man was a dentist, sentenced to four years for stealing two electric fans from the government clinic where he worked, one for his wife, one for his mistress. He had foolishly taken them both home. His wife had discovered the second fan's destination and, in a fit of jealousy, turned him in. She had started divorce proceedings, his mistress had forsaken him, and the government had impounded his beloved MG sports car. As he pointed out a little wistfully, it had been stupid of his wife for she had lost a perfectly good husband with the only MG sports car in Cuba and an excellent electric fan as well, made in China.

A few from the present government also passed through, punished for "thought deviation." Usually they were kept well

216

away from our contamination and sent to farms maintained for them alone. Being thrown in with us, their intellectual enemies, was an added turn of the screw.

Such was the case of the prosecuting attorney, Armando Portillo, a man soft from eating too well at the expense of others, arrogant as prosecutor, a Uriah Heep in prison, humble and self-debasing, the kind of man who cannot meet your eye. Before the Revolution he was an insignificant provincial lawyer prosecuting Juan for putting his pigs into Ramón's malanga patch. This was his preparation for becoming Castro's voice demanding firing squads and generations of prison years for hundreds of men and women. His greed for a better house had led him to falsely accuse a vice-minister of counter-revolutionary crimes, anticipating possession of the property once the minister was convicted. His skill at prosecuting porcine vandalism in the country was not enough for big-city intrigue and he was caught in the web of his own weaving. Like Cantillo, Batista's chief of the secret police, Portillo had to walk with eyes in the back of his head.

Hippies on drug charges were also our temporary companions. With so little on the streets to amuse the young when free from "voluntary" labor, they turned to drugs and drink, increasingly in proportion to repression and material scarcities. Drugs were normally a civil offense. One case was decreed political because José Martí, Cuba's George Washington, had been involved. Martí's brooding face and figure are in every city park and town, in every school and many homes. There was a Martí bust in a small park fronting the home of one of these recently arrived hippies. He and two of his friends had asked permission of their *Comité de Defensa* to plant and tend a garden around this bust. *El Comité* gave their blessings, delighted with this revolutionary zeal. The small garden flourished and *el Comité* considered an agricultural award for these long-haired pariahs of society. Unfortunately the little garden grew too luxuriant, attracting the attention of one who knew the difference between flower and weed, and the counterrevolutionary plot of marijuana was uprooted before it could mature. *El Comité* was mortified, the families placed under observation, and the hippies packed off to prison, accused of defaming a national figure.

Pot, provided by families or guards, was smoked as much in prison as on the street. If marijuana were unavailable, there was

217

always medicine from the dispensary to inhale or crush and add to cigarettes. Even the ubiquitous aspirin was said to give a smoking high. Those who made these short escapes had only transitory pleasure, bringing debilitating frustration in its memory. With mental muscle flabby from disuse, alone, and with no signals from their minds, I had seen them turn in desperation to beating their heads against a wall.

For a few weeks we had four soldiers with us, convicted of evading military service to escape their country. From Cuba's north coast they had set out in two tractor inner tubes lashed together. A Russian freighter sighted them in international waters sixty miles out and alerted the Cuban coastguard.

In February 1969, the captain and first officer of the Cuba joined us. With this new and prestigious Spanish-built freighter, the pride of the Cuban merchant marine, they had planned to defect to the Key West naval base. A third officer, entrusted with the secret, had turned them in.

A champion bicyclist was caught defecting in Czechoslovakia. Another, a student studying in Poland, elected to remain there with his Polish fiancée and was forcibly returned to Cuba and la Cabaña. All sorts came and went with stories to belie a thousand times Castro's claim of "Cuba, free territory of the Americas." How could anyone support the Castro regime except from a privileged position of self-interest, youthful delusion, inertia or fear?

In September 1969, the protective shell unconsciously formed through four-and-a-half prison years was shattered with the news that Beatrice and my oldest son, Antonio, were coming to Cuba. I had not seen Beatrice in four years and the family relationship had been held together with the glue of postage stamps. Tens of thousands of words smuggled out, a symbolic embrace with every letter. I had come to think of home as existing in a world behind the one I knew, and my present setting as a place with drives and emotional values that none at home could ever understand. We lived in different dimensions, different rhythms. At this intrusion of my wife and son, my fragile defense disintegrated, leaving me vulnerable as I had never been before to the rawness and reality of my confinement, suddenly and terribly aware of life passing me by. I had seldom dwelled on these months and years subtracted from my life. I had transcended imprisonment and disregarded time. Now those years were to materialize before me in a son last seen at seven, suddenly become eleven.

One afternoon, on my sixth transfer to G-2, I knew where I would be seeing my wife and son. I had hoped for a happier setting. Happier was the cell, however, than on my last time there. A new towel and soap, a new mattress, pillow and pillow case, and *two* sheets.

Despite this luxury, I could do nothing but pace the afternoon away. I brushed my teeth. I chafed at not having had my hair cut the week before. I brushed my teeth again. I worried over Antonio's attitude toward me and envisioned having my arms around him and his mother together. I spent the afternoon between misgivings and emotional highs, hoping and fearing at the same time that the door would open and I'd be led out to see my wife and son. Until dusk fell, I couldn't relax, and that night was one of the few in prison when I could not sleep. At one moment I anguished at the idea of the meeting, willing it postponed. I had so desperately looked forward to it, and now that it was near I panicked and wanted it preserved just out of reach, a dream to be realized, but not just yet. In retrospect, it was myself I feared, not my wife or son. I wasn't sure I would measure up to their respect and love. And I so desperately wanted to.

That was Monday. Tuesday came and went. I had seen no one but the guard who handed in the food. I ached to ask when I should see my family, but I held my peace. No guard would know, and anyway would not have answered. Wednesday morning brought doubts, then the fear that the whole thing was a hoax. I cursed the cruelty of the prison axiom, *never tell a prisoner anything.*

Sometime after Wednesday's macaroni the door swung open and I was motioned out. At last! Upstairs for a shave and haircut and clean uniform. Now groomed for presentation, there was the regulamentary wait in the cell. Gone was the fear that I might not measure up and any wish to postpone. Now I was anxious for, not over, the reunion. Still again I brushed my teeth and wondered how much longer I had to wait.

When my escort picked me up it was four years I'd been waiting. To the same visiting room with the same dirty carpet and frayed furniture, the sad paper flowers. I saw none of that. I saw only a woman holding a small boy's hand, her warm, happy smile, and his very serious, worried frown. She said something to him and let go of his hand. A tentative step toward me, and then as I knelt, a rush to my outstretched hands, and his small arms were hard around me. Over his shoulder I looked into the eyes of my wife, and four years disappeared. Then to an already full heart came the happy surprise of seeing our much beloved Aunt Marie-Thérèse. The Belgian Ambassador, Mr. George Elliott, was there, a man from the Protocol Office of the Foreign Ministry, and, of course, Denis, my interrogator. Between Beatrice and Antonio, I sat on a couch, an arm around each. He spoke little English and had forgotten Spanish, so I was pleased he understood my halting French, and I his. Of our conversation, there was no disciplining it. Begun on one track, it soon detoured to another, a tangle of talk with beginnings, no ends. It was enough that we were together.

Beatrice and Marie-Thérèse had brought a feast of sandwiches, cake, a thermos of tea, and another of ice cream. No one had told Antonio that drawing-room manners did not extend to his father's interrogator. Before anyone could stop him, he was politely passing sandwiches to the man from Protocol and Denis. Protocol brought a hand half-out of his pocket, then refused. Denis looked coldly away. The hour and a half alloted us disappeared like a leaf on the wind. But during the two weeks my family would be in Cuba, we were to have five visits. One down, four to go. I had seen my wife, son, and aunt, and should see them again. I was the happiest of men and returned to a cell without walls.

The following visits were a joyous repetition of the first. Beatrice, Marie-Thérèse, and I took up from where we had left off four years before, with no sense of strangeness between us, only the good rapport of people very close to one another. I drank heavily of this tonic so long denied me, intoxicated with my love for them and the love and understanding I felt in every word and look from them. Those hours revitalized me as nothing ever had before. What untold strength there is in love and family.

With Beatrice, it was renewal of all that had first brought us together and the ties of a happy marriage. With Antonio, it was the beginning of a relationship that had yet to form. In the wonderful innocence of an eleven-year-old, he accepted his father without restraint. Those child's arms around his father's neck gave the spiritual strength of all the prayers I'd ever said. The strength of those arms was the strength of love and trust, one of God's rare answers to a questing heart. Had there been any reserve remaining on my part, it instantly dissolved at hearing the one word I had subconsciously longed for: "Papa." Four letters denoting a world of things we never consider. All the wonder of love leading to conception, gestation, birth, and maturing. I was unprepared to hear "Papa" and marvelled at the music in it.

For my son's unreserved acceptance of me, I gave full credit to his mother. She had kept alive the father image by including me in their nightly prayers, with stories of our times together on the ranch in Cuba, seeing that each boy had a photograph of me in his room, urging letters to me in their illegible French, and translating my letters in French into something more clearly understood by their young minds. When we finally met, I was already known and not the stranger I might have been. Antonio's naive acceptance of my status was clear. In a school questionnaire he gave his father's occupation as "prisoner."

At the end of two weeks my family returned to Belgium and I to la Cabaña. The happiness of finding myself again a husband and father, a touch of normalcy in my life, carried me along on the crest of the wave. Within forty-eight hours my wave peaked, and without warning dropped me into a depression such as I had never envisioned. Suddenly I lost hope and faith. My evening prayer gave no solace and the phrases I'd so laboriously put together in solitary confinement had no meaning. Someone else had concocted this insipid hymn of thanks to One who did not listen. How could I ever have believed in the intangibles of faith, in the substance of things hoped for, the evidence of things unseen (Hebrews 11-1)? If faith were the evidence of things unseen, I had no faith for I could no longer see through the bars, only the misery they enclosed, and the dreary, useless years ahead. The adrenaline which flowed in such copious quantity for my two weeks in G-2 had run dry, leaving me without will to care, or even make the simplest decisions. I wanted only the drug of sleep. Fortunately, euphoria's excess brought mental exhaustion, and I slept deeply for a day and a night, and intermittently for another twenty-four hours, holding off the opening of my eyes to the brutal reality around me.

In uneasy dreams, I reached out to my wife and sons, a distance that could be reached no matter how far away. Over there beyond the sea, one could sail or fly to it, eastward, to the beech forests of Belgium. It wasn't yesterday or tomorrow. That was another and crueler distance. There was no way to get there. In my depression I wanted only tomorrow with the promise of something better, anything but today. Unexpectedly, a flame of terrible longing flared up to show how artificial my prison adjustment had been. The hard, grey, cement world of la Cabaña became overpowering, and arms around my family as unobtainable as yesterday or tomorrow.

The mood passed and I was caught again in the rhythm of prison life, able once more to see through the bars and derive meaning and solace from a faith greater than understanding. The memory of that brief, saltless interlude frightened me and gave insight into the hell that people experience without faith or hope. But though I could identify better with those who had broken, I had no clue as to how one ventured into this bleak land to lead them out.

The concern felt for the depressed is like the pity the free person feels for the imprisoned, a pity that amounts to awe because the free person cannot imagine how he himself could possibly bear such suffering. But prison so adjusts its man that it and he can come to terms. Nature comes to the rescue with measures of spiritual and moral adaptation and relief which the free person naively fails to take into account. And so it is with the greater part of our depressions. We come to terms with them. Nature has her seasons and we have ours.

Chapter 30

1969 was officially called *El Año del Esfuerzo Decisivo*, the year of decisive force. The Cuban people at once changed it to *El Año del Gran Pedo*, the year of the great fart. In February of The Great Fart, under the urging of the Swiss and Belgian Embassies, I joined *el Plan*. I moved from one side of the street to the other, my attitude remaining behind. But I continued answering examination questions with "according to Fidel."

With much false optimism, 1970 was officially called *El Año de los Diez Millones* in reference to a hoped-for record sugar crop of ten million tons. No agronomy expert believed this feasible, but Castro was infallible, denying the hard facts of nature. By bringing forward part of 1969's sugar harvest on the balance sheet, the announced figure for 1970's crop came to six and a half million tons. Through his own propaganda the infallible Castro had proven fallible. His credibility fell.

In March 1970, I was dismayed to hear myself called on the loudspeaker with nine other thirty-year men. We were to collect our belongings and report to the main gate. I expected the worst, a move to G-2 or el Principe, as three were ex-Castro men imprisoned for attempting his life under the aegis of the CIA: Dr. Rolando Cubela, a once-trusted major of Castro's, Alberto Blanco, and José Luis Gallareta, my old friend from Protocol. A fourth was Raphael del Pino, another ex-Castro *compañero*. The rest were similar hard cases, all under the stigma of the CIA. Not a very promising group.

The pre-transfer *requisa* was unusually severe with particular attention to books. Boarding the paddy wagon, I looked back on my confiscated library in English and French with the regret of losing old friends.

Patrol cars escorted us, an unusual precaution for only ten prisoners, through the tunnel under Havana harbor, and west along the main artery on the sea wall of el Malecón to a red light. Left meant G-2 or el Principe. Straight ahead could mean the intimidating prison of Cinco y Media, any one of several concentration camps like Taco Taco, or open farms. We held our breath for the change of light and our fate's direction. The prisoner nearest the door and its small window thought we were in the left lane of traffic, confirming G-2 or el Principe. Interminable uncertainty, and expecting the worse (a prison axiom), we instinctively braced ourselves for the left turn. The light changed and the truck eased ahead. We breathed free once again and began conjecturing as to where we were going. An hour of familiar landmarks half-seen through a tiny window finally indicated a minimum security prison, the former women's reformatory of Guanajay.

Guanajay was blinders and hobbles removed. Absence of the overpowering la Cabaña walls gave free reign to the eye over green fields, trees, and distant hills. And an unbarred door to our sleeping quarters allowed us to rove the many acres of the prison compound, enclosed by an easily scaled eight-foot wall. The sense of freedom was undiminished by guard towers spaced round this wall. With no armed guard at our door, I could walk in and out as I pleased, lie in grass midst the clean country smell, smoke an evening pipe beneath a tree, and best of all, find a quiet corner in which to be alone. Only to smell the smoke of burning leaves, I made a small fire of last year's foliage from the mango trees. As close to freedom as I had been in five years. Heady stuff to hand a man right out of la Cabaña.

Not all prisoners in Guanajay enjoyed this emancipation. There were seven hundred *plantados* enclosed in two-story buildings of three-man cells within the inner compound, released to the sun two hours a day. In *el Plan* there were sixty-five of us, our function being to serve *los plantados* in kitchen, office, warehouse, maintenance, and truck gardens. They the drones, we the workers. Catalogued "rancher" on the prison ledger, I was assigned to agriculture, riding herd on the vegetables grown for the penal colony between the high wire fence enclosing the inner compound and the outer wall surrounding the entire prison.

It was so immensely satisfying to be in the country again, hands in earth—weeding the onions, tomatoes and lettuce. Ever since leaving the Isle of Pines three years before, I had longed to sweat the filth of prison from my system through this kind of work, to have the touchable realities of nature around me.

With the five-and-a-half-day week at agreeable labor, time flew by faster than ever before. It was evening when it had just been morning. It was the week's filthy clothes to wash Saturday noon when it had just been the clean clothes of Monday morning. The hands, cleansed of the indelible red earth in Saturday's laundry, took on the farmer's grime again on Monday. A good grime, as the work-produced fatigue at the end of each day was a good fatigue. The hours and the days were swallowed by the onion and tomato crop. These harvested, cabbage and malanga became the time symbol. This self-perpetuating vegetable calendar ruled our lives, a most welcome master after the dreary zero of la Cabaña.

Eight of us tended the acres of vegetables with one soldier-overseer, a peasant in his fifties, face and hands furrowed from work and sun, and friendly eyes that called you neighbor instead of prisoner. He carried a machete, but to discipline the weeds, not us. To my proposal that weeds could be utilized as compost, he shrugged. "*No vale la pena,*" he said, an attitude of "It isn't worth while," endemic throughout Castro's Cuba, typifying the general feeling towards the Revolution, and explaining the disastrous state of the economy.

In May 1970, there was another of Cuba's periodic "national emergencies." This time the counterrevolutionary organization, Alpha 66, had sunk two Cuban fishing boats near the Bahamas and taken the crews hostage. Castro blamed the Americans and organized one of his "popular protests," a four-day demonstration before the American Embassy, occupied by the Swiss caretakers. The mob carried hand-lettered signs with one of the crudest reading, *"Nixon, tú eres creado con la secreción del excremento humano."* (Nixon, you are made of human shit). And the *x* of *Nixon* was changed to a swastika in the Cuban Press. This was the Castro who never tired of talking about the dignity of his Revolution.

These emergencies always heralded new waves of arrest, harder discipline both in and out of prison, and in my case, a loss of the freedom I had so enjoyed. While the majority of *el Plan* continued to work, I was transferred with twenty others into the inner compound, *plantado* territory. Our only duty, three times a week, was to attend *el círculo político* to study Castro's speeches, so frequent and long that we never lacked material. My taste of comparative freedom had been all too short, but even in the inner circle, behind two barriers instead of one, there was compensation. Our splinter group of *el Plan* could mix each day with *los plantados* during their patio time to renew old friendships and play softball. We were allowed to cultivate private plots of tomatoes and lettuce. I could have *Time* and *Newsweek* and most of the books I wanted. Correspondence flowed in and out with fewer restrictions. Prison life was improving, but only for a handful of us.

In October 1970, *los plantados* refused to accept the new regulation of stripping to the buff for the pre-visit *requisa*. An army unit was called in to quell the subsequent riot with the result of broken bones, lacerated bodies, and concussions. Soldiers flayed away with iron chains and heavy cables, teasing their leashed German shepherds with a bite or two of prisoner, while restraining them from outright slaughters. A prisoner who resisted became a punching bag and ended in submission, or in a truck to the hospital. *Los Plantados* were locked into their cells, and in the manner of collective punishment, we were locked into our quarters and the men in the field in theirs. The untended vegetables were left to rot in the ground. Our individual tomato and lettuce plots were torn up, and for "security" reasons all the trees within the inner compound were cut, even one magnificent two-hundred-year-old *ceiba* tree, which had given such welcome summer shade. It seemed as if the Director's rage had not been satiated with the blood and broken bones of prisoners, but must run its course in disciplining nature too.

For two weeks we were locked inside, our privileges only gradually restored. Finally, nightly television in the visiting room began again for *el Plan*. To my surprise the Thursday evening Sector 40 show, an hour-long documentary on G-2 cases, produced my story. To wring entertainment from it, the producer had been forced to add bikini-ed girls in swimming pools, cases of empty Vat 69 bottles, a convertible I had never owned, and a host of other inconsistencies. Corn without the pop.

One of the few programs of interest on Cuban television was the half-hour evening newscast. Like the party paper, *El Granma*, it was necessary to read between the lines. If the government was urging everyone to volunteer longer hours at cutting cane, we knew the harvest was in trouble. Then an earthquake hit Perú and Castro asked from every Cuban a "voluntary" contribution of a pound of sugar from their quota "for their brothers," it was a forewarning of tighter rationing. And so it was in mid-1970 when the civilian sugar ration of six pounds a month was cut to three and our weekly ration stopped.

We preferred our news from my *Time*, *Newsweek*, or the *British Economist*. During the periods of sufferance when I was allowed such things, I shared them with at least a dozen friends, who in turn shared them with a similar number. Groups were organized to hear certain articles translated into Spanish. Notes were taken for discussion groups. Both the prisoners of the far right and left pirated material for their monthly bulletins, handwritten, plastic wrapped for more mileage, and as slanted in their reporting as Castro's *Granma*. Directly or indirectly each magazine was enjoyed by several hundred men. Resewn, a magazine might reach the hospital of el Principe inside some prisoner's shirt sent there for treatment. From then on I lost track and never knew how far they travelled, although once I heard a *Newsweek* of mine had reached a prison a hundred and fifty miles the other side of Havana.

In May 1971, we had the first and only Russian inspection of a Cuban prison. Our buildings and grounds were given an unaccustomed cleaning. We were ordered to be correctly dressed and shaved for the great day. Diagrams were posted showing how the bunks were to be made (a forty-five-degree angle on turning down the sheet). New towels were issued to be hung on each bunk (and taken back again after the inspection). Years of mold were scraped from shower stalls and white paint applied. Newly whitewashed fifty-gallon drums were scattered round for trash.

When the day arrived, the Director led around a pod of three Russian civilians and a uniformed Cuban woman as interpreter. Pushing closely behind was an obsequious clutch of Cuban officials. Standing by our bunks, we of *el Plan* were first to be inspected. The elder Russian chose prisoners at random to ask the same of each: name, civilian occupation, sentence, and were there any complaints? He was a large man with a kindly face until you caught the eyes—business only, don't waste my time with trivia. I had no wish to waste his time, but the Director pointed me out as the only foreigner there. That's when I met his eyes. Instead of giving my name to the interpreter's stock question, I asked to whom I might be talking: a delegate of the Red Cross, United Nations perhaps? The Russian understood my Spanish for without allowing time for interpreting, replied in his own language. With icy eye, the woman said to me, "Just a tourist." With that he turned and left. The Director looked unhappy.

By hand signals from our windows, word was spread of the Russian inspection. *Los Plantados* reacted immediately with their aluminum cups and plates, raising a din on window bars to be heard for miles. As the committee made its way across the compound, insults were shouted and rolls of scarce toilet paper thrown like streamers. A few, conversant in Russian, added what offense they could. It was a magnificent reception for the detested atamans of their island. Without their tanks and Migs, the Russian invasion was brought to a standstill. Indecisive, the inspection team stopped, an excited Director gestulating toward the noise and sending a minion for the guards. The Russians conferred, and turned and strode for the gate, their Cuban coterie strung out behind in disorganized retreat. A heartwarming sight, even knowing collective punishment would be the price.

To our surprise it was *los plantados* alone who paid. A *requisa* that same evening stripped their cells bare of books and all the small, material comforts a prisoner collects. Although locked in their cells for three months, their satisfaction in routing the Russians counterbalanced the punishment.

My life of inactivity came to an end in early 1971 with the construction of a carpentry shop. Multi-colored progress charts were hung on walls. Pine from Chile was stockpiled. Additional personnel from *el Plan* were brought in, and we were declared carpenters on a salary of forty-three centavos an hour, less thirty pesos a month for food and uniforms. A nine-hour day, paid for eight. The odd hour was called *educativa*. Not for us, for us it was *voluntaria*. During *la hora educativa* we read manuals on the machinery and tools we were to use. The sergeant said it didn't matter that not one of the manuals applied to what we had. We'd study them anyway since his orders were to give written tests before production started. After a week's studying, the tests were given, and to the sergeant's delight, everyone passed with honors. Small matter to him that two or three texts circulated openly during the exam. He wanted favorable statistics and proudly marked his carpenters' scholastic progress on the chart. The black grease-pencil slash against an orange and green background shouted that everything was fine.

With each assigned his place on the assembly line to produce clothes cupboards for students, the carpentry shop was inaugurated. The first cupboards were unacceptable because of doors that did not fit, an unprofessional cant to one side or the other, joints that didn't conform, and other unorthodox defects. To the detriment of the progress charts, the rejects multiplied. The Ministry of Light Industry, for whom we labored, lowered our output quota to protect themselves, and as we learned the mysteries of our equipment, the graph on the progress chart angled upward. Becoming more dexterous with our tools, we more easily met the quota, and to avoid having it raised, slowed our tempo. We found time to make all sorts of products for ourselves and friends: clothes pins, nail files from sandpaper, wooden shower clogs, pipes, and chessboards. Someone devised a folding chair that could be cut in the shop and smuggled piece-by-piece for assembly in our quarters. We were very busy, but not always for the Ministry of Light Industry.

If our carpentry shop was typical of Cuban industry, it was not difficult to understand the growing shortage of consumer goods. To increase exports for necessary hard currency, Cuba was forced to cut back on home consumption. So that when a government campaign failed to convince the Cubans that smoking was detrimental to their health, rationing forced tobacco onto the black market. The prisoners' four packs a month could only be augmented by smuggling through the families, and the carpenter shop solved the problem temporarily by producing slingshots.

The visiting room was on the second floor of the administration building thirty yards from our shop. With a slingshot or two slipped into the visit, prisoners could shoot packages of cigarettes to us to be passed back later. When the guards caught on and collected more of the booty than we did, the game was no longer cost effective. So we turned to producing cigarette holders so that each cigarette could be smoked to ash. Those who couldn't wait their turn for our sophisticated holders made do with an ordinary pencil. With lead removed from the center and the eraser from its metal casing, the casing just held a cigarette and the hole left in the center provided draw. The carpentry shop was an invaluable asset to prison life.

I preferred *la cachimba*, a pipe, with the feel of a well-shaped piece of wood in hand, the comfortable ritual of tamping tobacco into the well-grained burl of a tree. With every puff of smoke I felt in harmony with my surroundings, even prison.

For the most part, pipe smokers made do with their allotment of six cigars a month, finely cut and mixed with cigarettes. In the unlikely event one was given or found a cigar stub, the method of rejuvenation was to simmer it in sugar water, dry it in the sun, fine-cut it with a razor blade, moisten it with coffee, and then it was ready to smoke.

I was more fortunate than most, sometimes receiving the Cuban-export pipe tobacco from the Belgian Embassy. And Beatrice occasionally sent the fragrant Dutch tobacco, Clan, in its Scotch-tartan plastic pouch. I gave the empties to my friends for cigarette stubs. When they took them to visits, their wives seized on them as small change purses to carry in the hand, as supplement to their dull wardrobes. Sad comment on Cuba's consumerless society.

Even matches were rationed, providing an insight into the devil-may-care mentality when necessities were lacking. After weeks of razor-splitting each match in two, each prisoner was unexpectedly issued two boxes. Carried away by this windfall, a rocket enthusiast constructed a model of an Apollo from three empty toothpaste tubes stuck end to end and painted with the American flag. Friends donated their wealth of matches as propellant. With patience, the head of each match was severed and stuffed into the empty tubes. For maximum public, blast-off was arranged to coincide with the *plantados* patio. One Sunday morning there were several hundred to applaud the launching of this eighteen-inch Apollo standing on its pad, a six-inch fuse of kerosene-soaked string trailing from its tail. Castro-style, an ironic speech was given on the glories of the Revolution, and the fuse was lit. The launch exceeded all expectations with its proper bang and whoosh that even Administration heard. The rocket rose to a respectable fifty feet before falling apart to cheers. Guards came running, windows flew open in the Director's office, and the Officer of the Day arrived to investigate. Still warm, the U.S. flag yet visible on the scorched paint, the valiant toothpaste tubes were solemnly gathered up and taken away as evidence—of indomitable spirits and high morale. A collection of matches was made, one from every man, and the missile architects had more matches in the end than when they started.

In August 1971, *El Plan de Rehabilitación* was changed to *El Plan Progresivo*, though we could see no progress whatsoever—and the Cuban economy grew more chaotic by the day. Our daily protein of one hard-boiled egg or a bit of frozen mackerel was substituted with shark, an unpalatable fish by any standards. To save Russian-supplied petroleum, there were electricity cuts each night throughout the island and even water was rationed in towns. Juvenile delinquency became too great a problem to ignore, and Castro devoted an entire speech to it, recognizing that over fifty percent of his common prisoners were between the ages of fifteen and seventeen. Promises of better things *mañana* were postponed to next month, next year. The ruling class continued fat from their special stores, while *el pueblo* hitched in their belt another notch.

In this climate of want, I got news that Beatrice and our three sons, accompanied by Tante Marie-Thérèse, were coming to Cuba for two weeks. This time, there were no doubts or reservations over being jolted from "my way of life." Only the great happiness that I was to know my family once again.

There was no one to oversee our hours together in a comfortable reception room in Guanajay, and at each visit Beatrice could bring a *jaba* of unlimited weight. At a time when *jabas* of twenty-five pounds were allowed only every three months—tremendous liberality! And I took advantage of every pound. I was a *gringo* benefiting from the Cubans' effort to impress the Belgians.

Antonio was thirteen, Michael twelve, and Larry ten. Very much the elder brother, Antonio had the situation well in hand. As befitted his being self-appointed head of family, he was first to throw his arms around me. Then, catching my hand, he said to his slightly awed brothers, "Come and greet your father."

Before this man they could not well remember, having last seen him at ages six and four, they were uncertain just what to do. Once again the elder brother took charge.

"Papa, this is your son Michael. Michael, this is Papa. And this is your son Larry. Larry, this is Papa."

The ice was broken, and amidst shy grins from the young and laughter from the old, the two youngest came confidently into my arms. The three boys set off in a babble of French and English, only Larry holding to French. No sooner were two of us off on one topic than an interruption from another turned the conversation. No strangeness between us, only the naturalness of small boys telling their father the importance of the pet goat in Belgium, the difficulties of school, and the miracles of shells to be found on Cuban beaches. Their young lives were brimming over with important happenings and they must tell me all. Larry asked what I would do when released. To my reply that I wasn't sure, he said, "You can always come and live with us."

Beatrice and I had been favored with two conjugal visits, giving us a further chance to close the gap of years. For these visits one ward in the small prison hospital had been converted into four bedrooms with baths. A militia woman met each wife or girlfriend to give a token frisking. The four bedroom doors opened off a small hall, and from a typewritten list the militia carefully checked off each woman's name against the room assigned her. Only when each was locked into her room were the men allowed into the hall. Consulting her list even more carefully, the militia unlocked one door at a time to motion in the corresponding mate, relocking afterwards. With the Latin custom of married women continuing to use their maiden names, the list sometimes got confused. It had happened before that Señora González Rodríguez had been paired off with Señor Rodríguez González—perhaps with mutual delight, but more probably with a startled neigh from the lady.

My two conjugal visits were scheduled for eight A.M.. Beatrice came to the first embarrassed at queuing with three other women for a programmed bedding down. A degrading performance for many of the wives until habit forced its acceptance as a normal and even necessary part of their lives. They brought overnight bags with their feminine needs and another with coffee and sandwiches. Beatrice's only baggage was a thermos of tea and a heavy sack of packaged goods from the States and Europe to augment my prison diet. Were we going to eat all that in our three hours together? the militia wanted to know. The other three women were staring in fascination at the unaccustomed riches being searched for contraband: a whole cheese, dried fruit, dehydrated meats, jars of Nescafé and other delicacies. Timidly, one asked Beatrice if she worked for the government. To her mind there could be no other explanation for having access to such luxury. Learning that Beatrice was Belgian and her husband American, the Cuban ladies turned voluble in questions on fashion "outside." It was not often at first hand to hear of the prevailing styles in Paris or New York. On learning the mini-skirt was out, one looked smuggly happy over her long skirt returning to fashion, the other two disconsolate over their hemline too high. The militia tugged down her short skirt, but too many years of rice and beans made the maneuver impossible. Regretfully, she called a halt to the gossip to show the women their rooms—not forgetting to check the list carefully beforehand.

The reality of three hours alone with my wife for the first time in six years, the unaccustomed intimacy and tranquility, it was all too difficult to grasp. I wanted to hold each minute in my memory to bring out later when all of this should be only a dream. But minutes were no more to be held than hours, days, or years. The minutes became the mosaics of time segments, of lighter or darker hues depending on the mood. The mosaics formed the pattern of those happy hours and only the whole could I remember later.

At the third family visit Beatrice and Marie-Thérèse were bubbling over in suppressed excitement, and as soon as the first round of chatter with the boys was over told me why. The Foreign Ministry had called the Belgian Ambassador to say that Major Manuel Piñeiro, First Vice-Minister of the Interior, wanted to meet with Señora Lunt. Piñeiro was in charge of international intelligence and an appointment with him was as important as with Castro himself. Puzzled at the reason for this meeting, Beatrice and Marie-Thérèse went to the Hotel Havana Libre, former Havana Hilton, where Piñeiro had his office. An armed guard waited in the lobby to escort them to his twenty-first-floor suite. Piñeiro had studied in the

States and married an American communist. He spoke perfect French and English, but insisted on Spanish with my wife.

"Señora Lunt, I suppose you would like to have your husband back? Well, perhaps it can be arranged if you can convince your husband's friends in Washington to intervene with the Portuguese government for the release of a Cuban arrested in Guinea."

"You would exchange this Cuban for my husband?"

"No, I did not say exchange. If our man were released, we would release your husband. A humanitarian gesture on both sides."

"Who is this Cuban held by the Portuguese?"

Pedro Rodríguez Peralta, an ex-captain of the Cuban army (emphasis on the *ex*), helping the people of Guinea in their fight for independence from Portugal."

Beatrice had the presence of mind to ask for this in writing to show the American government.

"Señora Lunt, between gentlemen one's word is enough."

Marie-Thérèse, Beatrice, and I discussed this new hope and agreed that any exchange would be a slow process. The remaining visits disappeared in plans for the future, the first time we had allowed ourselves this self-indulgence. No dates were mentioned. Next month or next year. It was as if a terminal illness had been found to be curable after all.

Chapter 31

My indefatigable family on both sides of the Atlantic tried one scheme after another to free me, and always came up against Castro's steel-wool beard.

In 1968, my brother John prevailed on Dr. Christian Barnard of South Africa, the pioneer in heart transplants, to offer one month demonstrating his technique in Cuba, the necessary equipment to be sent with him and donated to Cuba on his departure. A month's instruction by the world's foremost heart surgeon and invaluable medical equipment—against my one hundred and forty pounds of bones and flesh, unsuitable for soup, soap, or lard. The bargain of the year, but Castro said Cuba had no need of Dr. Bernard's expertise.

That same year, my family approached the Chicago lawyer, Constantine Kangles, with personal ties to Castro. Kangles had once sprung from an American jail a Mexican, Antonio de Conti, arms supplier for Castro's 1956 "invasion" of Cuba. And Castro's only son had lived with Kangles during the Batista purges. Despite their close relationship, another blind alley.

Castro had once said to Kangles he had no need of money.

"Look, I've cut my salary from seven hundred to three hundred and fifty pesos a month."

Kangles pointed out that in reality he was probably getting the equivalent of twenty thousand pesos a month.

"Consider all your bodyguards, houses, boats, choppers, etc. Just look at your pocket with cigars lined up like matches. I have to pay ninety-five cents apiece for those at the Hilton."

Castro appeared astonished.

My family had approached the Cuban government from every angle. Through the Mexican Foreign Minister, President Barrientos of Bolivia, western embassies in Havana, the Vatican in Rome, the royal families of Belgium and Sweden, even friends of Celia Sánchez, Castro's secretary and ex-paramour. My sister Faith had talked with an exiled Cuban, Humberto Truevas Rojas, whose ex-wife was currently the mistress of Ramiro Valdez, Minister of the Interior. This woman had used her influence before to get people out of Cuba, and it was thought a foreign bank account in her name might have effected my release. A family friend, and ex-Foreign Minister of Brazil, was asked to intervene with President Allende of Chile. Too much interest in my case. I had become a collector's item in Castro's mind, whose value could only rise. He held onto me.

George Smathers, ex-senator from Florida, agreed to use his influence in Panama to bring Castro around. He demanded a $10,000 retainer and a $50,000 contingency fee. But the Panamá Canal negotiations had just begun, taking precedence, and in deference to a request from the White House, this was dropped.

To excuse Cuba's intransigence, a completely false picture was presented to all who tried to help. They said my case could not even be considered until I changed my attitude and ceased being a leader of rebellion within the prison. And the Cuban dictator remained impenetrable—until his army captain, Pedro Rodríguez Peralta fell prisoner in Portuguese Guinea-Bissau.

Captain Peralta had headed the Cuban military mission advising PAIGC, the Guinea-Bissau nationalist guerrilla movement. Wounded and captured in November 1969, he received a sentence of eighteen months from the Portuguese army. Although President Caetano rejected pressure from Washington, Brussels, and Rome to affect a Cuban-American exchange, he did set aside the initial light sentence, held a new trial, and gave Peralta ten years. In March 1974, through Vatican arm twisting Caetano finally agreed to the Peralta-Lunt exchange. But before it could be acted on Caetano was overthrown and the new regime reneged. Going further yet, the provisional government under acting-President Antonio de Spinola decreed an amnesty for all political prisoners.

Washington objected and Spinola blocked Peralta's release with the excuse he did not fit the role of a Portuguese political prisoner. Leaks to the press led to headlines of American meddling in Portuguese affairs. "Meddling" was Vatican cables urging Spinola to hold Peralta until I was turned over to the Swiss in Havana, also a letter from the White House indicating President Nixon's "extreme interest" in the case, and my lawyer's, John Wainwright, presence in Lisbon to coordinate the blocking of the Cuban's release. The Cuban Embassy in Lisbon channeled funds to the Portuguese labor unions to demonstrate before the military hospital where the Cuban was held, demanding "the unilateral release of Comrade Peralta." Spinola retreated before this challenge from the left and announced Peralta would be freed when the Guinea-Bissau guerrilla movement released Portuguese captured during the thirteen-year war.

I read of Peralta's release on September 15, 1974 in *el Granma*. I was greatly disappointed, but not terribly surprised. Nine years of prison had conditioned me to unfulfilled hopes.

That same month, the first U.S. congressmen visited Cuba since the breaking of relations in 1961, Senators Pell of Rhode Island and Javits of New York. Pell raised my case with Castro. "Castro's immediate reaction was to pound his forehead with his hands and say he never wanted to hear the name Lunt again."

Despite his distaste for my name, in January the following year, Castro once more took the initiative, suggesting that if the United States released Puerto Rican nationalist Lolita Lebrón, he would turn me free. Lebrón was one of four Puerto Ricans, who in March 1954, to draw attention to their cause, had fired pistols at random from the spectators' gallery in the U.S. House of Representatives. Five congressmen had been wounded. This offer came through the East German lawyer, Wolfgang Vogel, who in 1962 engineered the exchange of the American U2 spy-plane pilot, Francis Gary Powers, from the Soviet Union for Rudolf Abel, top Soviet agent in the United States.

On January 24, 1975, the left-wing FALN, a Puerto Rican radical group, planted a bomb in Fraunces Tavern in New York, killing four, wounding fifty-three. The Department of Justice refused to reward violence with clemency and backtracked on recommending Lebrón's release. My exchange was temporarily blocked.

Again through the East German Vogel, President Ford agreed in 1975 to a Thompson-Lunt swap. Robert Thompson was a naturalized American jailed after conviction in 1965 of passing secrets to the Russians while an Air Force intelligence clerk. Pressured by the Russians, Castro consented to the plan, but reneged when Ford publicized CIA plots against his life. Thompson and Lunt remained on ice.

Chapter 32

In January 1974, Guanajay Prison was needed for packing common prisoners into, and we politicals were transferred back to la Cabaña. After the relative freedom of Guanajay it was difficult to adjust to the stark confinement of high walls, no distance to lose the eye in, and no softness of grass underfoot. One hundred yards beyond the moat I could see the tops of Australian pines, now thirty feet high, seedlings nine years before. If the pines had changed, the old fortress had not. It was still infested with bedbugs, cockroaches and rats. A heavy rain still backed up sewage onto gallery floors, and the stink of repression was the same. Misery, like fear, carries its own smell, and the massive coral blocks of la Cabaña, raised into place two centuries before, were impregnated with it. Only total annihilation could cleanse this.

And so began the most difficult period of my fourteen years in prison. One hundred and fifty of us were quartered in gallery 26, actually two inter-connected galleries. Save for twenty-five, we were mature, responsible men with at least nine years behind us. Twelve had served fifteen years and were still under sentence of death. We wanted only personal tranquility and survival within a system we

239

could not change, unworried about a future we could not control. We knew how to live together, respecting the other's privacy. We had learned self-discipline, patience and tolerance, and loaned a hand to friend and unfriend alike. Mutual trust and consideration were what made life tolerable.

Into our ordered existence where the communists could not reach, they loosed twenty-five delinquents, newly imprisoned for common crimes. They were there to stir us up, a further punishment for men already punished quite enough.

The leader was *Tiburón*, a nickname from the shark tattooed on his back and thigh. Five-feet-ten of solid muscle, skin that had never seen the sun, a plain face with friendly brown eyes when smiling, devilishly malignant when not, sly like a fox (without its intelligence), and threatening or conciliatory depending on the odds. He did a hundred push-ups morning and afternoon without a drop of sweat, and daily measured his biceps with a red braided string he wore around his neck. Muscles were all he cared about, being number one in brawn. He invented the game *cojones*. *Cojones*, a man's balls, very macho. *Los cojones* didn't figure in the game, but being macho did. One stood hands on hips, legs wide apart, belly muscles tense. Another, head down as battering ram, charged from twenty yards. The two men usually ended in a heap on the cement floor, laughing and boasting and rolling around in mock exhaustion until two more were ready to try. *Tiburón* forced everyone in his group to play, pairing them off by size. When he thought some were playing soft, he'd make them do it over again—with him. If one got hurt, *Tiburón* cradled him in his arms, laughing away his frustrations for minutes after.

Tiburón kept a slim, underdeveloped seventeen-year-old for himself, *Juanita*, the feminine of Juan. *Juanita* did *Tiburón*'s laundry, picked up his food, shaved him, and shared his bed. None of the others could touch or ask anything of this slave. One who tried his sexual favors was sent to the hospital in *el Principe* with broken ribs.

This gang was the puppet of the *reeducadores*, manipulated to demoralize us, or worse if they could. The behavior of these men-children was determined by frustrations, unconscious drives, and *machismo*. Together they were victims of herd poisoning, escaping into a kind of frantic animal mindlessness. Individually they were quite different, each with his raison d'être, a personal identity and a great sense of insecurity. One alone could be likable and even reasonable, but his loyalty lay with the pack and any gentleness he might show alone was instantly replaced with hard aggression on rejoining his buddies. For these veteran street-men fear and tension were an addiction. Inactivity was a restless interlude before the high of the next fight or excursion into enemy territory.

We of *el Plan* ranged in ages from early forties to the sixties. Unschooled in street fighting, it was difficult to know how best to deal with twenty-five muscular teenage punks. They set the pace and we improvised from day to day according to their mood. We lived in orderly fashion in one gallery, the delinquents in disorder in the other. The days were quiet as they slept them through, only coming awake at dusk to sing, drum up-ended pails, and dance with one another. There was seldom a night without sexual jealousy provoking a fight, often with homemade knives or sticks of soft pine with razor blades embedded in them. Scars were worn with pride as were tattoos covering much of their bodies. A life-sized head of Santa Bárbara was top fashion on back or chest with sharks a close second. Many had tattooed variations on "only a mother's love is free of treachery." Hearts and initials adorned biceps, pectoral muscles and buttocks. One stocky, good-looking boy, an aggressive homosexual, had a serpent whose head began at his penis and twined down one leg to the small toe. Another tough had a swastika tattooed on each eyelid. His paramour in *el Príncipe*, a half brother, had the same.

When night fell they used both galleries for fighting, both real and sham, for running races, playing tag, and hide-and-seek among and over our bunks, throwing water bombs, and when they could, stealing. When they caught an old man alone at the urinal between the two galleries and tried to gang rape him, we decided we'd had enough.

One of our group was Gilbert Simon, a black American of solid body and principles. A handsome man over six feet tall with eyes instant barometers to his mood, his deep supple voice an instrument of power. He'd been a champion boxer and at another time and prison had gained the delinquents' respect by flooring the leader of their inter-prison pack. A studious man, never looking for a fight, he was ready to defend himself and others when provoked. Together with ten of the youngest and strongest among us, Simon gave an ultimatum to *Tiburón*. Our gallery was off limits to them unless invited. To our surprise, *Tiburón* accepted this in seeming humility. To compensate, however, for what must have been loss of face, the noise increased ten fold next door.

A few nights later, they politely asked if they might entertain us with a skit. We agreed and they staged a mock trial with all the proper nuances of communist justice. The female judge was impersonated by the prisoner with a serpent tattooed on his leg and penis. Mascara applied with soot, a wig from an unravelled sugar sack dyed in Mercurochrome, miniskirt and blouse made from mattress covers, and exaggerated breasts completed the ludicrous get-up. The smallest of their group, a good looking kid of some five feet and eighteen years, marched in as prisoner between his guards, two six footers brandishing broom handles. The charge was read, buggering Castro's brother Raúl, and the prisoner escaped. He jumped onto the judge's lap and began fondling her enormous breasts. Ecstatically the judge clasped the prisoner in her arms, and in an aside to the audience, said, "I can't bear hanging another innocent man, but the quota must be met."

The trial proceeded to its foregone conclusion of "Whether innocent or guilty, you shall be hung until dead." A rope was swung from an airvent in the ceiling and the prisoner dangled "dead."

Another night, it was a ventriloquist act. A muscle-bound weight lifter—one of those with a shark tattoo on his back, "no one knows how I suffer" on his chest—sat on a bench with the "prisoner" of the previous skit on his knees. A little girl this time in frilly pantaloons and a wig of watersoaked, raw macaroni molded to her head.

The "little girl" asked why it cost Fidel more to talk three minutes on the telephone with Nixon in the White House than to talk all night with the Devil in hell. Back came the answer that when Fidel talks with the Devil it's a local call. Not the brightest of humor, but we enjoyed it and encouraged their skits, Apache dances, and all else they invented as constructive occupations for their troubled minds. We congratulated ourselves that we had weaned them from their aggressive animosity.

We were wrong. Either orders from above, or biding their time, with our defenses down, the chicanery began again. It began one night with stabbing a man in the buttocks while at the urinal. They brought their fights into our gallery, and though we managed to throw them out, the threat of invasions was always there. They'd creep in at night to yank a sheet off a sleeping man, running away with it barking like dogs. We posted one of our number twenty-four-hours a day and went in pairs to toilet or shower. They blocked the door into the patio to trip or jostle the older men—always the weak and defenseless. Our pleas to the Director to have them removed were met with, "There's no room for them anywhere else." Their knife fights, often requiring a patch-up in the dispensary, went unpunished, while an occasional fist fight among ourselves promptly got a week in solitary. *Tiburón* and others were frequently called out by *los reeducadores*, the only reason to receive instructions on how to bedevil us and hand in their "progress reports."

After one long year of this, two ex-Castro men could take no more personal harassment. They decamped one day into the patio with all their belongings, refusing to return unless the delinquents were removed. The delinquents stayed and the ex-Castros went to solitary.

Having lost two of their principal targets, the gang was directed onto four Batistianos, still under the death sentence after fifteen years, and me. The cowardly bullying of the older men continued, but for the first time they tried provoking fights with me.

One evening I was sitting on my bunk breaking up a package of cigarettes to mix with pipe tobacco when from behind, always behind, came a whining voice asking for a smoke. An open hand appeared over my shoulder with a swastika tattooed on the palm, a razor blade held between two fingers. I should have been afraid, but instead became angry. I picked up the chessboard on which I was mixing my tobacco and moved to another bunk where two men were playing checkers. Like most of his kind, the man was a coward, willing to try me alone from behind, but not with two others beside me.

Later, I decided to talk with this fellow, although it was difficult to find him away from the pack. One afternoon, I saw him sitting alone against the patio wall, eyes closed, head thrown back to catch the sun. Squatting beside him, I said, "Do you want a smoke?"

With the instinctive reflexes of the hunted, his hands dropped to the ground for quick leverage, his body tense.

"Huh?"

"Do you want a cigarette?"

Accustomed to forceful acquisition, not voluntary largesse, he weighed the possibility of a trick, found the scales in his favor, and without a word, took the three cigarettes from my hand. From his pocket he pulled an empty matchbox. Directly over it, so as not to lose a single shred, he expertly broke the three into six equal parts, deposited five inside, the last into his mouth. In the habit of men the world over without a match, he patted his pockets, looking quizzically at me. Without hurrying, I prepared my own smoke first, lighting it and tossing the match away. Immediately he stiffened. A hard look came into his eyes, disappearing when I held out my pipe for him to light his half cigarette. He relaxed and we sat in silence smoking. With his first hunger for tobacco satisfied, the taste deep in his lungs, he glanced at me. I suppose he thought I was doing this from fear, or because I wanted something from him. I did want something, a small insight into what made him tick.

"Why did you ask me for a cigarette like that the other night? That's no way to treat a fellow prisoner."

He answered with a shrug, and in a tone of self-pity, "You guys never want to give us nothing. You always got more than us."

"Don't give me that. We all get the same quota of cigarettes, and if we seem to have more it's because we ration ourselves."

"I can't do that. My *brothers* would take them away from me."

"Leave them. Ask for a transfer. Make yourself some real friends."

I'd said the wrong thing. Whatever faults his companions had, they represented a group he belonged to and somewhere in the pecking order he had his place. They were his *brothers*. Without them he was nothing. He turned hard and the first signs of aggression appeared.

"What the hell do you know about friends? How do you think I can get a transfer when they put me in here to take care of you guys?" He didn't seem to think he'd told me anything unusual and went on. "You think I like being locked up with you guys? I wanna be with my real *brothers*."

And he raised his right hand with the dime-sized swastika in the center of the palm. To my question of what significance the swastika had for him, he answered, "Doesn't mean anything. It's just identity."

He had never heard of Hitler or the Nazis. Nor had he ever heard of his mother or father. He had been raised in a Havana orphanage, whose founder, a Señor Valdez, gave his last name, and little else, to all who passed through.

The guard's whistle blew, the half cigarette long ago reduced to ash. Not wanting to be seen with me, Valdez jumped to his feet and quickly walked away. He went a few paces and he stopped, pivoted on his heels, patted the match box in his pocket and half raised a hand in salute, perhaps even in thanks. We never talked again and he never asked for another cigarette.

Anti-American graffiti in Mercurochrome began appearing on the gallery walls. One of our group, with the addition of the letter *n*, changed the delinquents' *Cuba sí, Yankees no* into *Cuba sin Yankees no* (Cuba without Yankees no). The Mercurochrome war of words continued until, failing to antagonize me on the national level, I began to be shoved and tripped in the patio. Two friends, standing guard for me while I showered, were attacked by five of the pack. Because of restricted space they could hold them off till I joined in and the fight became a draw. Another day I was hit on the back of the head by someone hiding between two bunks. I awoke two hours later in the dispensary to be trucked off to el Principe for X-ray. After that I was fortunate in a self-appointed bodyguard, Gilbert Simon, and could walk in peace.

But I was fed up, and for the sake of all of us I complained to the Belgian Ambassador. Within a week, the Ministry sent a major to interview me. Delinquent aggressiveness changed to indifference. Sleep came more easily again, nerves unwound, and our twenty-four-hour-a-day vigil relaxed. *Tiburón* and five of his buddies were transferred and life returned to pre-delinquent normal.

Chapter 33

In early 1975, we experienced one of the periodic swings of the pendulum. Complete indifference to our health changed to sympathetic consideration. The only dental care through the years had been extractions (without anaesthesia). Few could smile with a full mouth and almost all needed extensive bridge work. For the first time cavities were filled. Impressions for plates and bridges were taken for which the families paid. Prisoners, once shy of snaggletoothed smiles, now grinned wide in flashing splendor. One, who had labored long to correct my French pronunciation suddenly had to correct his own. Another, after sixteen years of unattended dentistry, had his sunken cheeks filled out with a complete set of false teeth. Before the first post-denture encounter with his wife he was practicing smiles before a mirror.

Dentists were not the only specialists we could see. There were rhinolaryngologists and other tongue-twisting names that few could understand. Many of the peasants had never envisioned so large a catalogue of ills, and even less had access to such medical attention. That all of this was available by simply putting your name on a list was too much for some. They signed up for every doctor who came through. I bet the doctor who compiled these lists that if he announced a gynecologist he would get at least a dozen names. I lost the bet by two.

The services of a psychiatrist were offered too, and he was inundated with men wanting a shoulder to lean on. Suspecting he was an arm of G-2, none of the right people subscribed and he was discontinued.

Cuban vitamin pills were prescribed for all who wanted them, though by the time they reached us many were decomposed. We Americans asked the Director for permission to get vitamins through the Swiss Embassy. Permission was denied as Cuban products were already available. At one visit from the Swiss I responded by giving them several of the decomposed Cuban vitamins still in their sealed plastic, and also some of the good ones. I learned later they were not much more than brightly colored sugar pills.

Some medicines were not always used for what they were intended. The ingenuity of the Cubans discovered milk of magnesia an adequate substitute for deodorant when that went off the market. Demand soon exceeded supply and the government was forced to take evasive action. Orange food coloring was added that did no harm to the stomach, but stained the clothes. The food coloring was in short supply and soon gave out, and the Cubans went back to milk of magnesia. The government added it to the list of "by prescription only," and doctors prescribed it liberally. A losing battle for the government. They stopped producing it. Substitutes were found, but never one as good as milk of magnesia.

For a few months we actually believed the Ministry of the Interior was concerned over our health. We should have known it was only temporary whitewash. This was the year that Cuba joined the Human Rights Commission in the United Nations.

Chapter 34

Senator McGovern came to Cuba in the spring of 1975 to give Castro a fraternal *abrazo* and assure him he was working in congress to reestablish relations. President Ford came close to reestablishing commercial relations in 1976, but Castro spoiled it by spilling his vodka over Gerry's new Cuban policy with his Angola rumble. Relations were postponed until the following year with simultaneous openings of Interest Sections in both capitals.

Carter became president in January 1977 and was dubbed *el carterista* by the Cubans—"pickpocket" in Spanish. The hope was the new man in Washington would pick Castro's pocket of his Russian credentials. Carter's strong stand on human rights gave us new encouragement, as did the rash of visits that followed. Senator Church came to Havana. Barbara Walters of CBS came to Havana. Church to discuss mutual problems, Walters to interview the Prime Minister on television. Her handling of Castro in the three-hour interview was masterful, and did wonders for the morale of the political prisoners and the man on the street. None had ever dared before ask such questions of this megalomaniac. Her innate acting ability and quick intelligence were more than a match for a Castro unaccustomed to open questions by the free press. Surprisingly the program was aired not once, but twice, and printed almost verbatim in *el Granma*. One deleted question in the newspaper was Walter's, "What do you think of your sister Juanita's statement that you are a monster who should be destroyed?" He two-stepped around that one.

With this interview we mistakenly saw a new permissiveness, but it was only token, and like the Chinese "democracy wall," soon closed down. I had tested this permissiveness at a visit with the new Belgian Ambassador, Victor Allard, and a Belgian Senator of the Christian Democrat Party, Raymond Scheyven. Interested in prison conditions, Mr. Scheyven asked many searching questions, all of which I answered frankly. My candor was quickly repaid. Visits every forty-five days with the Belgian Ambassador were cancelled on one pretext or another. Mail, magazines, and books were withheld. Bursitis treatments were stopped with the excuse that I was cured. I had misbehaved and I would pay.

The new prison of Combinado del Este near Havana was nearing completion, and with our transfer there, la Cabaña was to be converted into a museum. It wasn't, of course. It was needed for the Revolution's waste, the overflow of prisons throughout the island bursting at the seams with untold thousands of political, military, and common prisoners.

When finally transferred to Combinado del Este in January 1977, it was an agreeable surprise. There were three four-story buildings for prisoners, each designed for twelve hundred men, a hospital, kitchen, warehouse and a two-story visiting building—family visits on the ground floor, conjugal on the second. Painted in different pastel shades and attractively landscaped, the buildings were grouped around a baseball field and track ring, almost bringing it off as a modern college campus.

There were no restraining bars in evidence. The bars were on the cells inside. All were prefabricated with outside walls of vertical cement louvres, giving a light, airy appearance, well-architectured for a tropical climate. Enclosing this thirty-acre quadrangle were a fifteen-foot-high double-wire fence and a six-foot-wide alleyway between for patrolling German shepherds. The guard towers every forty yards were armed with machine guns. One electrically operated gate penetrated this double fence. And outside the gate lay the sprawling administration building.

While I know of no insect, bird, or beast that wittingly builds detention cells for its own kind, Combinado del Este had been built, and was still being built, by prison labor. Two months after our transfer, the construction of a punishment block was begun and completed in record time—by Cuban political prisoners. This one-story structure, designed to Soviet plans, with its low-ceilinged, windowless isolation cells and rough cement bunks, we dubbed the "Human Rights Building." Manipulation of man by man is classically attributed to the capitalists, but no one does it better than the communists.

For the first time, we political prisoners were thrown together with American prisoners held on common charges—blacks and whites escaping criminal charges in the States by skyjacking commercial planes to Cuba, and a cross section of whites intent on making a fast buck on the marijuana run between Columbia and Florida. These last, in boats and planes, had either fouled up on navigation, or been illegally coerced in international waters or skies to land in Cuba. One of the white skyjackers, Lester Perry, held from 1970 to 1980, was never tried. And rather than face a sentence of over fifty years in the States, Perry elected to remain in Cuba when released. On fleeing their country (the U.S.A.), the blacks had thought to find a better social climate, but without exception had been sadly disillusioned. The United States, through first the Swiss then later their Interest Section, looked impartially after the needs of all Americans with periodic packages of underclothes, hygienic necessities, and magazines. They never, however, petitioned Cuba for the release of the American common prisoners, as they repeatedly did for the last four remaining *políticos*, myself and three others.

I was assigned to a six-man cell with four others. One was a Cuban-naturalized American of my own age who had owned a fishing boat in Miami, then found it more lucrative clandestinely freighting Cubans to the States at a thousand dollars a head. His boat had malfunctioned one night and he'd been caught. His mixed bag of friends ran from delinquents to the oriented political left. His troubled mind, inflamed by spirits from another world, made him a difficult cell mate.

251

Another was a thirty-year old Puerto Rican who had skyjacked a plane to Havana in 1966 to escape a federal warrant for his arrest. He never explained his crime. Of no propaganda value to the Cubans, he had been jailed. A self-professed homosexual with theatrical tendencies toward suicide, he had studied with the Jesuits in San Juan. Although he called himself an atheist, his knowledge of the bible was encyclopedic. He was an unhappy, unbalanced kid, a minus to our group.

There was a Turkish doctor in his forties with Cuban citizenship, arrested while escaping Cuba in a boat with his eighty-year-old mother and ten others, a great blimp of a man who preferred eating to all else, but kindly and an easy companion. His only recreation was reading medical texts, two books on English idioms, and polishing his boots.

My fourth cellmate was a sixty-year-old Hungarian, a real weirdy with a deviousness that belied his white hair and kindly Santa Claus face. An intellectual, who had served the Nazis in Hungary during World War II, fled to Cuba after the war to become a Cuban, studied for the Catholic Church and been defrocked for reasons unknown, taken up teaching, and eventually counter-revolution. He had a good word for no one, and so no friends. Two redeeming qualities made him possible to live with: he was orderly and clean.

We were an unhomogenous group, but got along by respecting each other's territorial rights in the ten-by-twenty-foot space. When reading or conversation palled, I often lay in my third-floor bunk, smoking my pipe and studying the spider population homesteading where wall met ceiling. I came to feel a part of their cobwebby world, augmenting their catch with insects of my own hunting.

Vertical cement louvres on the inside cell wall led into an airshaft, giving cross ventilation and excellent communication between the four floors. With the louvre edges chipped away to allow a hand through, communication was not only vocal, but, aided by a stout cord, parcel post. Books, magazines, and cigarettes passed freely back and forth, as did a notebook with the nightly newscast from one of several clandestine radios. Although the architects of Combinado del Este never intended it, the airshaft became the nerve center of our building.

The outside cell wall was of vertical cement louvres with a barred door opening into a corridor that ringed the entire floor, broken up by several steel gates to facilitate prisoner control. Cell doors and corridor gates were electrically operated from a control center and patrolling guards carried connecting phones when wanting to open a door or gate. Within a month, some prisoner devised a method of short-circuiting the solenoid activating each door. Armed with two wires, anyone could open his own although a corresponding light in central control indicated it open. If quick about it, two neighboring cells could short-circuit simultaneously to swap friends for visiting, chess or whatever before the guards were alerted.

Each floor had its dining room, used for lunch, supper, and each evening, two hours of television. A roving cart provided room service for breakfast of milk and bread.

Apart from fortnightly visits, the only other escape from one's cell was the twice-weekly hour and a half in the sun, an hour and a half of patio cement underfoot, cement building to the north, south and west. To the east, the vivid green of grass, palms and hills through a high wire fence meaning "don't walk on the grass."

Our only patio sports were jogging, sunbathing, and a baseball game with homemade ball. A volleyball court lacked the net, and a basketball basket, the ball. The manicured baseball diamond and track were for the common prisoners in the other two buildings. For mind and body exercise, I fast-walked a figure eight. To walk in circles lopsides the sole of boot and mind. As I went round, I hung the washed-out thoughts of yesterday on the clothesline of today—together with the once-white sheet, shorts, and towel.

With time, Administration and prisoners became more organized in the strangeness of this new prison: Administration, in coping with the frequent electronic malfunction of doors, and other unforeseen bugs inherent in any new establishment, and prisoners, in setting up their intercommunication system, probing the security system for weaknesses, and getting to know new guards. Our guards were mostly young kids doing their three years of compulsory military service at seven pesos a month. Few were happy with their lot, many malleable to our "domestication."

One of them liked to practice his twenty-seven words of English with me. I was a bad influence and introduced him to my *Mechanics Illustrated* magazine. On night duty, he always asked for it to pour over the advertisements, particularly intrigued with the Marlboro cowboy and horse. I wanted to give him the magazine, but he said it would only get him into trouble. If caught with such American "propaganda," he'd be accused of "ideological diversionism" with a year at forced labor on some rehabilitation farm. He loved horses and took in the rodeo in Havana on one pass. When I asked him about it, he'd seen nothing of the rodeo; he'd been too busy taking advantage of sandwiches and beer sold without limit. He ate all he could and brought back more "for the dry season."

In August 1977, loudspeakers were installed inside the punishment block, the "Human Rights Building." A psychiatrist visited daily to observe the effect on a man in a five-by-eight-foot cement cell of radio music in alternating intensity from five in the morning to ten at night seven days a week. Even fifty yards away this constant music at inconstant pitch shortcircuited our nerves, causing a mental somersault at each intensity change. In the first week, five were driven to hysteria and removed to the hospital. In the second week, Raphael del Pino committed suicide in one of those brutal cells. Del Pino, a Cuban-naturalized-American, had staged a hunger strike protesting Castro's demand that he renounce his American citizenship. While Administration gave out that he'd strangled himself with his socks, we thought it too convenient a death for Castro's once intimate companion, who could no longer testify to Castro's infidelities to friends and cause alike.

Del Pino's death, suicide or murder, forced a modification of this musical torture. The loudspeakers were moved from inside "Human Rights" to the roof, and others were installed above our building. The doves and sparrows, accustomed to our handouts of breadcrumbs and macaroni, fled this infernal rhythm as we would have liked to. Our protests only increased the volume.

As suddenly as this exercise in sound began, it stopped. But the loudspeakers remained in place, intermittently broadcasting music and news programs at moderate volume. Only on religious or national anniversaries was the volume turned up to drown out the prisoners' patriotic speeches, the singing of Cuba's national anthem, and Christmas carols.

Once again, there was a change of uniform, to black pants and smock. Pocketless, the first thing we did was add our own. It was the same uniform Russian prisoners used, a cheap material that after half a dozen washings turned grey and shapeless. Russian underpants were issued too, dark-blue flyless bloomers. Had all Russians underpants like these, we wondered if they sat to pee.

In August 1977, the United States and Cuba established Interest Sections in each other's capitals, mini-embassies without an ambassador. In November, we had the first of monthly visits from Tom Holladay, one of our consuls, a real breakthrough for us, making us feel closer to a final solution.

I had had my batteries recharged by a visit from my brother John in April of this same year, and in December came an unexpected interview with two American congressmen. Richard Nolan of Minnesota and Frederick Richmond of New York took pictures, tape recorded our conversation, and asked Castro for our release. Castro responded by freeing the oldest among us, Frank Emmick, sixty two with a cardiac problem. For the remaining four—Everett Jackson, Claudio Rodríguez, Juan Tur, and myself—Castro wanted the four Puerto Ricans—Lolita Lebrón and her co-terrorists. The congressmen did their best, but the climate was not yet right for freeing Puerto Rican terrorists.

In early 1978, a complicated three-way swap involving four governments was set up by Vogel, the East German spy broker, and Representative Ben Gilman of New York. The prisoner exchange involved Thompson again (the American spying for the Russians), an Israeli pilot downed in communist-controlled Mozambique, and an American student imprisoned in East Germany for trying to smuggle a doctor and his family into West Berlin. The negotiations were well started when my lawyer, John Wainwright, filed a brief in a Washington court arguing that Thompson should not be released unless I were included. The legal grounds were shaky, but the State Department urged Congressman Gilman to include me, and the court action was withdrawn. Castro, however, was not letting me go unless Lebrón was in the package too. The American government was now willing. Lebrón, without her three accomplices, refused.

Vogel then began on still another swap. Gunther and Chistel Guillaume, East German spies arrested in West Germany in 1974, against Anatoly Shcharansky, imprisoned in Russia as a dissident, and myself in Cuba. The Russians preferred to hold onto Shcharansky.

As I was hoping for my personal exchange, there was cause for general hope as well. In September 1978, Castro gave a television press conference in Havana with selected Cuban-American reporters. For the first time he discussed his political prisoner problem and indicated a willingness to release the majority through a dialogue with the Cuban community-in-exile in the United States, a political forum favorable only to Castro and those Cubans-in-exile who saw political and material advantages for themselves. The futility of any discussion was evident when the plan to release political prisoners went ahead independently of any dialogue. No dialogue was necessary. If Castro wanted to clean out his concentration camps, he had only to do it, not discuss it. Over three hundred political prisoners wrote an open letter to Castro rejecting his propaganda ploy. In effect they said, "We do not negotiate our liberty because our principles are not negotiable."

At the same time, the Ministry of the Interior began interviews to determine how many political prisoners intended leaving Cuba. As only a prisoner's immediate family could be included in the exodus, all bachelor prisoners became targets for single women seeking matrimonial exit visas. And many divorced men remarried their ex-wives to get them and their children out of the country. Magnanimously, some bachelors married women they had never seen. Others had their pick of women from thirteen to seventy-five with guarantees of a dollar bank account once out of Cuba.

One *señora* over fifty came to marry an eighteen-year-old, a friend of a friend. At her wedding in the administration building she found another prisoner, witness for the groom, more to her age and liking, postponed the wedding to rearrange the necessary papers, and promised the daughter of a friend to her almost-groom. Each week had its spate of weddings, more pragmatic than romantic.

Together with the Ministry interviews, written and oral psychological tests were programmed. Doubting the motive behind this, many refused to participate, gaining a week or two in "Human Rights." One who did participate still gained time there for his unappreciated sense of humor. Asked if he had ever had homosexual experiences with other prisoners, he had replied, "No, never with a prisoner, but with the director of the prison every Sunday afternoon."

Adding fuel to the fire of our optimism, superficial medical checkups were instigated. I had been having dizzy spells, considered a vitamin deficiency by a medical friend, so thought to have this corroborated by the military doctor. Without getting out of his chair, he diagnosed my problem as mental and said he'd arrange an appointment with the newly reinstated psychiatrist. I thanked him for his time and told him not to bother.

A black prisoner suffering from anemia had his blood tested, only to be told by this same doctor there was not only nothing wrong with him, but in fact he had the blood of an Anglo-Saxon. No man after years of prison liked being told there was nothing wrong with him. We all cherished malfunctions of some sort. And to compound the doctor's gaffe, this black didn't know what an Anglo-Saxon was. On finding out, he was furious and vowed terrible revenge. No white blood for him.

With hopes so high for a general amnesty, or whatever Castro had in mind, there was a rush to learn English among the domino-playing crowd. Now that they anticipated a free ticket to the United States, they wanted instant English, the pre-packaged, ready-to-use variety, something to be bought for a few cigarettes, but without having to forgo their dominos. One came to me for a hundred of the most important English words. He believed that, once memorized, they would lead to his first Cadillac and colored television set. I sent them back to their domino games and they seemed relieved. After all, they weren't yet free. Liberty was still *mañana* so let *mañana* take care of itself.

We four American political prisoners received an unexpected Christmas present from our government in January 1979, an interview with four congressmen, headed by Representative Ben Gilman of New York who had tried a year earlier to include me in a three-way prisoner swap. After talking with Castro, they were optimistic over exchanging us for the Puerto Rican "Gang of Four," Lolita Lebrón and her friends. This brief meeting with fellow Americans so concerned with our welfare seemed tangible evidence of our impending release, and my customary indifference to time turned to an unrest such as a captive migratory creature must feel when the season to move on is at hand.

And then in March, two months later, came five visits in one week from my sister Hilary and her daughter Hil. For six years they had been trying for a Cuban visa! As in my brother's visit, these two women, not seen for sixteen years, charged my batteries to overflowing. During the happy hours spent together my mind was in suspended animation. Only later in my cell did the playback of all we had discussed make sense. Among the books, dried fruit, and pipe tobacco Hilary brought me was hidden a small transistor radio with spare batteries.

To have my own radio was more than hearing world news first hand. It was to hear classical music, the voice of my president, and commercials for everything from the wonders of the latest detergent to the classic beauty of Detroit's endless sameness of rolling stock, Madison Avenue blah saturating the air waves. I loved it. It was exciting and I exhausted two sets of batteries before rationing myself to news and music.

Chapter 35

The idea of freedom becomes an obsession with each passing year in prison, and when it arrives is a traumatic break in what has become a way of life. It is frightening, a jump into the unknown, as a transfer from one prison to another is upsetting. Years behind bars with few important decisions to make atrophies the decision-making muscles and modifies one's reasoning. Freedom is always possible next month, not this one, *mañana*, not today. Prison is an unconscious putting off of the inevitable, like a return to childhood where postponement is better than confrontation. In prison, events are thrust on one, and if not against one's moral precepts, accepted. There is little chance for deciding. So when that long-seen mirage of freedom is announced as attainable and real, the first reaction is doubt with a tinge of that old fear of change and the unknown. *Mañana* has become today.

After evening head count the cells were open until ten. The locked gates on each floor at the central stairwell were the community center, like the local drug store or pool hall of some small town. Conversation and messages flowed easily up and down this vertical Main Street.

On the evening of September 6, 1979, "*Oye*, second floor, someone tell Larry that Bruno on the fourth floor wants to talk with him. *Rápido*, it's important."

Bruno Salas Ledo was a recruit of one of my recruits, and we'd not met until la Cabaña. We'd studied French together, he'd taught me chess, and shared his mother's visit when I had none of my own. In prison lingo we were "brothers." Our ways had parted, but not our friendship, when I joined *el Plan* and he remained *plantado*. Of slight build and hair, he was full of nervous energy and smoked too much—when he could. I couldn't have had a more loyal friend.

I was playing chess in my cell when Bruno's message came. I didn't like having my chess game interrupted, even from one of the men closest to me in prison.

"Yah, I know, he probably wants to bum a cigarette. Tell him I'll call back when I've checkmated this chump I'm playing with. Bruno's the chess champion of the building, so he'll understand."

"O.K., but he says it's important."

"It'll be even more important in half an hour. Thanks for the message."

In three minutes the messenger was back.

"Bruno says you've never checkmated anyone in your life, and that you're a dumb son-of-a-bitch if you don't want to hear the latest about Lolita and Larry."

The mention of Lolita Lebrón was enough to make me forget the chess and everything else. I told my friend not to move the pieces around and I'd soon be back to finish him off.

The game was never finished. When I got to the stairwell the crowd let me through to the locked gate for maximum communication. I yelled up two floors, "*Oye*, Bruno, what's so damned important that you have to screw up my chess game? If it's for something to smoke, you can shove it. Now, tell me, what's my girlfriend Lolita gone and done?"

"It's not what Lolita's done, it's what Jimmy's done. Just got it on the radio. Carter's pardoned Lolita and her three boyfriends. You're going free, *viejo*, free! You got me?"

Like a blow to the solar plexus. Bewildered and numb, I heard my voice as if another's. "Don't kid me, fellow. No jokes. You can't believe the commie radio."

"No, Larry, no! I heard it myself on The Voice of America. It's true. Carter's opened the door for the Puerto Ricans and expects

Castro to do the same with you four. Congratulations, *chico*, congratulations! Now, let's celebrate with our *cachimbas*. Send up some of that pipe tobacco you've got hidden under your bed."

"You bastard! I knew it! You're only telling me this lousy joke to fill your pipe."

"No, *viejo*, I'm only kidding about the tobacco. It's really so. You're a free gentleman—well, free anyway. When you see Jimmy, remember to tell him about me. *Por mi Dios*, I hope I'm not far behind you." (After twenty one years in prison, Bruno was released in September 1986.)

The reality of my freedom was weighted with the doubt of prison years, a doubt heavy enough to stifle the elation I should have felt. It wasn't tomorrow, next month, or even next year, but NOW!

Confirmation on the Cuban television came soon afterwards, allowing a little of that pent-up euphoria to escape. But not much. Humiliation after humiliation, abuse after abuse, injustice after injustice were in the balance. Mistrust of Castro was too deeply ingrained to let the floodgates flow. Mental self-discipline, on the defensive for fourteen years, effectively dampened my reactions. When the ultimate day arrived and the need for restraint evaporated, feelings that so desperately wanted out were blocked. To yell, to cry, to sing, to turn somersaults over the moon. Habit was stronger than this turbulence of imprisoned feelings, allowing only a cautious glow with friends gathered round.

Then came another radio report. Because of bureaucratic delay the Puerto Ricans could not be released till September 10th, four days later. I equated this with a similar delay for us and postponed the celebration I should have had right then. With the reprieve of delay, I planned nothing that night and went happily to bed.

At three twenty the next morning I was shaken awake and told to be ready to leave in five minutes. Five minutes after fourteen years! I had possessions of small street value, of inestimable value in prison. My radio, pipe tobacco, shaving cream, a whole list impossible to proportion out in five minutes. I said I'd be ready in half an hour, and I was, despite the lieutenant's fuming, threats and jibes.

Waiting on the ground floor were the other three Americans: Everett Jackson of California, Claudio Rodríguez of Puerto Rico, and

261

Juan Tur, born in Tampa, Florida, raised in Cuba. We smiled and shook hands, saying nothing. This pre-dawn September morning was cold. I'd left my sweater behind and shivered in my uniform, grown thin from too many washings. But the cold felt good, like the sun coming out after a long rainy spell. In silence we followed the lieutenant and four guards around the perimeter of the baseball diamond to the main gate and on through to the administration building. There was no moon, but more stars than a person could ever count, and instinctively I concentrated on picking out the ones I knew. Behind us to the east, false dawn brought into stark relief Building One, my home these last twenty months. In handcuffs, I had often walked this route for interviews and visits. Today, no handcuffs.

As I shed my uniform for light-blue pants and a blue and white striped sport shirt, I felt the first strangeness of the day, the first awareness of some momentous change. The metamorphosis of grub to butterfly? Guarded by two nodding soldiers, we waited on wooden benches until seven when the first office personnel arrived. A captain showed surprise that the Americans had not yet picked us up.

"*Muchachos*, what are you doing here? You're in the hands of your Interest Section now. If they don't want to collect you, that isn't our fault."

Three hours later, still on our bench, I said, "Hey, Juan, do you suppose this is some kind of a joke? Maybe they dressed us up like Sunday just to take our pictures."

"No, not possible. It's some transportation snafu, or these idiots have got the wrong date, or someone forgot to call the embassy. These bastards are so dumb anything could have happened."

"Bastards, *sí*. Dumb, no."

At eleven we were given a lunch we had no appetite for, then moved to an outdoor amphitheater. At least there we could watch the traffic, always expecting the beautiful black Chevrolet station wagon of our embassy. I grew tired of stretching my eyes and stretched out instead on a bench to try and sleep. The good feeling of the early morning had vanished. I was tired, hot and dirty, and I was pissed off.

I awoke an hour later to hear a guard saying, "*Vamos, Americanos*, your taxi's waiting."

It was three thirty, twelve hours since since we'd dressed civilian. I looked eagerly for the embassy car and saw only a Russian paddy wagon before Administration. Nothing strange in that, and I idly wondered what unhappy souls it carried. My eyes still turning corners, my heart sank as I realized the paddy wagon was for us. Inside the van, each locked into his cage, I thought, "Oh hell! This is going to be G-2, completing the circle, back where I began this nightmare."

And so it was, but this time quite a difference: civilian dressed, two-to-a-cell three times the size of the others I'd been in, with real beds and innerspring mattresses instead of wooden planks, and an adjoining tiled bathroom! No water in the pipes, but a tap on the judas window brought a guard, a courteous! guard, to give drinking water or escort us to toilet or shower. We each received a package of cigarettes every morning, books in English and Spanish from their library (stolen from prisoners), and chicken or another meat on our trays twice daily.

I slept and read, read and slept. I relieved the boredom of the windowless cell with a shower twice a day, and its corresponding round trip down the hall, that long, brilliantly lit, white passage lined with the silent, bolted, iron doors of the cells I knew so well. The doors that hid so much misery and pain, doors that had closed chapters on so many lives, hateful symbols of oppression and injustice.

Chapter 36

Nine days later, at noon on Saturday, September 15th, we were led to an interrogation room. Two majors and another without rank awaited us. The rankless one was the movie prototype of communist secret police, accentuated by a Stalinesque blouse of olive green, buttoned to the neck, the first Cuban I had seen dressed like this, if Cuban he were. His short and pudgy body, balding head, and well manicured hands suggested softness. The strength was in his eyes: steel blue, hard, and unblinking behind rimless glasses. He did not identify himself.

In Spanish he asked us to be seated, and in the firm voice of a commanding officer, he said, "This afternoon you will be turned over to Immigration for deportation to the United States next week. This is a humanitarian gesture by the Cuban Government and we hope you will accept it as such. Do you have any questions? No? Then you will return to your cells until called."

We had not uttered a word. There was nothing to be said. No hand was proffered nor expected. Was that all there was to being freed after fourteen years? Where were the trumpets sounding, brass band playing, American flags waving? There should have been tremendous elation in my heart, an outpouring of emotion strong enough to be felt by everyone I loved wherever they might be. Instead, nothing. This unknown man might just as well have announced a supplemental sentence. In silence we filed out and back to our cells, unresponsive to this momentous truth.

Half an hour later, we were called again, this time for the van in unlocked cells. Immigration was a comfortable three-bedroom house in the once-fashionable residential district of Miramar. The once-immaculate elegance of these expropriated homes had been replaced with decay and neglect. The exception was Immigration's house, freshly painted, cared for garden, and the miracle of plumbing that actually functioned. The neighboring houses were given over to Soviet bloc technicians and their families, or to schools and dormitories for children taken from their parents for the week, returned on Saturdays mentally shampooed.

G-2 turned us over to a lieutenant and a corporal of Immigration. We were shown the house and then two refrigerators stuffed with cans of Cuban fruit juice, Cuban cheese and butter, an enormous Polish ham, Bulgarian pickles and jam, and more delicacies still. This exorbitant display of plenty in a land rationed to the penultimate hole in its belt, was only for our snacks! Breakfast, lunch, and supper were brought in from outside, hot, plentiful, and good. *Did we want anything else?* asked the lieutenant. We looked at each other in disbelief. Thinking nothing ventured, nothing gained, I suggested a bottle of rum and cigars. We got them, although the price was excessive, pre-paid in blood, sweat and tears—and years.

With no restrictive fence, we were requested, not told, to remain within the garden. That first evening, sitting on the front porch with a glass of rum and an excellent cigar, the lieutenant's transistor radio playing, we could almost have been in the Havana of old. But where were the lighted streets and houses, the happy, laughing pedestrians, the traffic, and all the unrestricted movement of an early evening that makes a city live? The streets were dark, the houses ill lit, if lit at all, and only an occasional bicycle or foreign technician's car went by to interrupt the tree frogs' concert. Not even the wonderful sound of children's laughter. We were surrounded by children and yet we heard no games being played, no songs or shouts of joy.

Monday morning the corporal found us in the back garden and said we had a visitor. It was Jay Baker, one of our vice-consuls, who had often visited us at Combinado del Este. She was there to shepherd us to the embassy for passports and lunch with the personnel. Later, she said, we'd drive to the small airport in Varadero for a five-o'clock flight to Miami on a chartered State Department plane. It was an emotional moment, walking out the door of Immigration's halfway house to freedom, into an American embassy car where Cuban officialdom could no longer reach.

At this point a major, three captains, and a lieutenant arrived in two cars. A problem had arisen. We could not leave Cuba in sport clothes, but must have suits, white shirts, and ties. This imposing array of rank had come to measure. I couldn't have cared less whether I gained my liberty dressed or naked. But if accepting their finery expedited matters, I was for it. At least I would have something to hang in an empty cupboard in the States. While Jay Baker waited, the lieutenant produced a measuring tape, the major recorded this ultimate interrogation in a notebook, and the three captains looked on.

Free of our tailors, we drove in growing excitement to the embassy, less than five minutes away. Juan Tur's Cuban wife and daughter were there, to be leaving with us. They each carried one suitcase of clothes, all they were allowed to take from their home of twenty years. Instant passport pictures were taken and the necessary forms filled out. The sheep complex had yet to be shaken off as we complied with the necessary paperwork, not even reading what we signed. In retrospect, it seemed a slow-motion, silent movie of the twenties and about as far removed in time, none of it quite real. I had a sense of jet lag, a weariness beyond the hour on the clock.

A bottle of champagne was produced by Wayne Smith, head of mission. Toasts were drunk, a pizza consumed, and back we went to the Immigration house to collect our suits.

Our hearts were too full for conversation in the embassy bus as we drove toward Varadero through the tropical loveliness of an island that even Castro couldn't much desecrate. Trailed by two cars of G-2 to monitor our departure, we reached the field in good time for our five-o'clock flight. Rum and soft drinks were offered at the small terminal where we waited. What a strange *adiós* from Castro to four men and two women he had mistreated for so many years—beaten the former, browbeaten the latter. As five o'clock came and went, we could not keep our eyes from the sky to the north. When we did catch sight of the plane it was on its final approach from the west. It could have been any plane landing on any runway, but for us it was the wings of an eagle.

As we had expected only State Department men on board, I was totally unprepared to see my brother John first out of the plane. My mind in limbo, nothing surprised me any more, not even my beloved brother's magical appearance. Together having enjoyed and shared so much of youth, it seemed quite right he should share this moment, too. I felt in our *abrazo* the love and support of all my family through all the years. My brother's touch gave substance to a dream, and though still on alien soil, I felt the truth of freedom. The melancholy slime of prison years sloughed off like dead skin. I felt clean. Past horrors were as distant as East from West. In the depth of my soul I had long since known this would happen. I had known it and yet kept it from myself. I wanted no more disappointments. It was a long-seen mirage miraculously reached and found gloriously real.

Following John from the plane were my lawyer, John Wainwright, stalwart fighter for my cause the last seven years, two political officers from the State Department, Ralph Brainbanti and Jeff Smith, Governor Hershler of Wyoming, Representatives Gilman of New York and Leland of Texas, and Gilman's aide, Bob Becker. That we were all there at that particular place and time was due to the efforts of many people over many years, but in particular to the stubborn persistence of Representative Gilman and John Wainwright in prodding and cajoling sleeping bureaucrats in Washington.

The few formalities between the State Department men and Tim Towell of our Interest Section were completed in minutes, the G-2 huddle observing from a distance. Boarding the plane, I wondered how many of those G-2 men would have secretly liked to be with us on that flight.

A spontaneous cheer from all aboard filled the cabin as our plane lost touch with this piece of geography that concerned me no more, except for my prison companions left behind bars and barbed wire. The coast of Cuba receded to the south and the setting sun showed the first Florida Keys to the north. Eighty minutes after leaving communist territory we landed in the United States.

At the Miami International Airport we walked into the glare of television cameras and the kind of instant notoriety that is full of sound and fury, signifying nothing, and then is heard no more.

"The Last American Political Prisoners Freed From Cuba"

"Americans Survived Brutality, Deprivations in Cuban Jails"

"From Cuba With Joy"

Such were the headlines the following day.

The next morning, my brother and I flew to Washington where my wife Beatrice, our second son Michael, and my two sisters waited. John and I were held on the plane until the other passengers had disembarked so that Beatrice and Michael could come aboard for a first encounter before meeting the press outside. To have my arms around my wife and one son was the ultimate reality, the essence of all I'd lived for and endured. Words were superfluous, a poor medium at such a time to bespeak the exhilaration of the heart.

To Larry Lunt
With very real regard and respect
Claiborne Pell

Senator Claiborne Pell (RI) and Larry Lunt (1979)

To Larry with the greatest respect & admiration. May you now be blessed with peace & a family time
Sincerely
Malcolm Wallop

To Larry – Your courage touched me deeply. Your faith and tenacity serve as a guide for us all. God Bless you as you pursue the course of your life. Warm regards
Al Simpson U.S.S. (WYo)

For Larry Lunt, Your courage is an outstanding example for all of us. Best wishes for the years ahead
Dick Cheney

Senators Malcom Wallop & Alan Simpson (WY), Larry Lunt, and then-Representative Dick Cheney (WY) (1979)

270

Epilogue

Sudden freedom was not the emotional bomb I'd expected. Different all right, but a close and loving family helped the adjustment. Without their emotional feedback it would have been difficult.

In Washington, at my sister Faith's house, there was a joyous family reunion for two days before each went his way. Beatrice and I stayed on for ten days. I had many courtesy visits to make on The Hill to thank congressmen and senators instrumental in my release. Aside from Ben Gilman and a host of others, there were two in particular to whom I owed much, and still owe: Dick Cheney, Representative from Wyoming, and Claiborne Pell, Senator from Rhode Island. Requests for talk shows and interviews poured in. TV crews camped on the sidewalk outside my sister's house for chance shots and a chat. Instant notoriety, instantly forgotten. There was a thirty-six-hour stint in the Bethesda Naval Hospital for a check-up. There were hours of debriefing. There was a full and satisfying schedule that exhausted me into twelve-hour sleeps.

To live in a clean and gracious home with flowers about—to hold a knife and fork, breaking the prison habit of eating only with a spoon—the food! The wonderful food. To walk out a front door into a quiet, tree-lined street with no one's permission—I felt almost guilty of attempted escape. To ogle the endless aisles of supermarket wonders—who could ever want or need this variety of foods? I wished I could send the entire store to the Cuban families I knew—plastic jugs of milk and fruit juice, the used jugs thrown away to pollute our earth when any Cuban would save them for a thousand reuses—the paper and plastic bags, carelessly given for the smallest of purchases. Extraordinary waste all around me. And the cars! So opulent and large, chromium status symbols as alike as a litter of pigs from the brood sow in Detroit. I didn't yet want to try driving. It still felt right to be a passenger on this flight into reality. Prison was, far away, except at night when grey dreams the color of confining walls dropped me into the past.

Freedom had happened too fast. I wanted time to acclimate, to make decisions, to find my way. My decision-making muscles had atrophied. I stumbled around in uncertain daze, more willing to follow than decide.

My first priority was wife and children. Beatrice set herself to spoiling me with love and good Belgian food, and soon brought me back to par in every way. My two older sons, Antonio and Michael, inspected me for horns, and finding none, accepted me wholeheartedly as friend and father with all the warmth I'd longed for. The youngest, Larry, had trouble with this instant father, and couldn't bring himself to call me dad as did Antonio and Michael. He was friendly but wary, feeling his way into a relationship he was unsure of. Not for several months could he bring himself to call me dad. And when one day, spontaneously, it popped out, he was embarrassed. His brothers' laughter brought him round and his reticence evaporated.

The first months of freedom were pure euphoria. Time had no meaning. Each day was the promise of new discovery, a rebirth of all my senses to surrounding wonders. The simple pleasures, so taken for granted by the free, were all novel and exciting: the smell of pine woods, the feel of grass under bare feet, the spring song of birds. Miracles would never cease. Life was so bloody great!

But great for being free, not for the wealth of material luxuries that surrounded me. Actually this bothered me. I'd just come from fourteen years of prison values where the plastic casing of a Mennen's deodorant stick would be converted into a case for cigarettes. Suddenly here I was in a world of consumers. Consumers being consumed by an urgency to overindulge in everything from instant mashed potatoes to instant gratification. I was appalled, and not a little disturbed by all I saw.

Mae West claimed that too much of a good thing is terrific. Maybe for her. My first unshackled months *were* terrific, but there came a time when restlessness crept in. Living half the year in Belgium, the other half in the United States, I began to write. To pour out unbidden thoughts that stumbled from my subconscious faster than I could record them. Prison thoughts. On men I'd shared so much misery and pain with, on those who had died there, others still there, on the jailhouse philosophy I'd built for myself. My memories kept coming. So many experiences without descriptive words for some. Just as well, maybe. Some are best forgotten.

Civilized society seemed superficial, frivolous and complacent.

The right to vote. So many of our elected officials are roundly cursed by a near majority of our citizens too lazy to cast a ballot. There are herds out there by the millions yearning for this privilege denied them. Murphy's Law: those who can won't, while those who can't would.

And conservation, conserving our wasteful way of life at the expense of nature, the future of future generations. We are so greedy and uncaring, like children entrusted with a precious toy they don't know how to care for. So many blessings granted to us and far too many taken for granted.

I don't blame my fellow blunderers for this blindness. It is in our nature to need a shock before our fragile freedom can be appreciated. But we learn so slowly—and so badly.

Prison had modified my sense of humor. What had once been fun and funny seemed less so now. An over-larded human blimp munching on a jelly doughnut appeared disgusting. The too-obvious humor of Bob Hope bored me. Having shared a small part of the world's miseries had changed my outlook and perspective. Before, I would only have been intent on self-gratification: backpacking, skiing, tennis, and writing too. Now I felt the need to repay the good fortune I'd been born to. Without renouncing sports or writing, I found equal, or more, gratification in working for the homeless of Tucson, Arizona. Prison gives an insight into the hopelessness so many of the homeless feel.

If prison years had been an exaggerated loss of time with family, there were compensations. I had matured into a more caring and understanding person. I was no longer satisfied with just living for myself and family, but somehow must justify my privileged niche on earth. We have become more cynic than believer through Washington and Wall Street's affluent effluence seeping through the shredded ethics of our moral code. But prison gave me a simple remedy for our rush to suicide with everything from deforestation to drugs. Very simply, it is a respect for nature and our fellow man. I know it cannot be. We are too rapacious and self-centered. But those of us who care must make the effort and hope that sanity will yet win through. If enough of us throw our pebbles, the ripples could turn to waves.

Afterword

I can think of no one for whom I have more respect than Larry Lunt. Not that I agree with him on everything. He thinks Kennedy's "no-invasion pledge" at the time of the Missile Crisis was a matter of snatching defeat from the jaws of victory. I thought Kennedy's handling of the crisis masterful and the no-invasions pledge devoid of costs since we didn't plan to invade anyway. On the other hand, had I been Larry Lunt, sitting on an exposed mountain in Cuba, I might have been hoping against hope for an invasion and felt the same way he did.

In any event, a few divergences of opinion of that kind in no way diminish the tremendous admiration I have long had for him. I also was in Cuba before Castro came to power, serving as Third Secretary of Embassy from 1958 until we broke diplomatic relations in January of 1961. I did not know Larry Lunt at that point, but I knew of him. Who did not? There was no one more highly regarded in the foreign community than Lunt, known to be a gentleman and a man of high principle in every respect.

I was on the Cuban Desk back in Washington when he was arrested in 1965 and thus was aware of the various efforts—on the part of the Belgian government, his family, and the Swiss (encouraged by us)—to have him expelled rather than imprisoned. Who can say? Perhaps the

275

result would have been the same even had he said nothing at his trial. There had seemed to be some hope, however, that Castro would simply deport him. But Lunt had not stayed in Cuba on a lark. He had agreed to stay and to work for the CIA because he loved Cuba deeply and deplored the path along which he saw Castro to be taking her. Thus, despite the possible consequences, of which he was of course perfectly aware, he chose to speak out forcefully at his trial, pleading guilty to the basic espionage charge but demolishing the more absurd accusations of the prosecutor and pointing to the injustices he saw around him. The court was not amused. Rather than deportation, he was sentenced to thirty years at hard labor, a fate he accepted with his usual calm dignity.

For the next eleven years, I kept track of Larry through various Belgian diplomats in Moscow and Buenos Aires, where I was on assignment, and through friends on the Cuba Desk back in the Department of State. Once or twice there were rumors that a deal might be struck to bring about his release; nothing came of them. When in 1977 I returned from Buenos Aires to become Director of Cuban Affairs, Larry and a number of other Americans held on charges of a political nature were still in prison. To get them out became one of the foremost objectives of the Carter opening to Cuba. Several were indeed released in 1978 and as they made their way back to the United States, all had high praise for Larry Lunt, who was described as their "spiritual leader," a man of great patience and kindness, but of iron will, courage and total integrity, a man looked up to by virtually all his fellow prisoners. American and Cuban alike.

Freeing Larry and the other three last remaining American prisoners became something of an obsession with me. Surely fourteen years behind bars was enough. Castro had hinted in late 1978 that he might be more disposed to release our four if we paroled Lolita Lebrón and three other Puerto Rican independence activists who had been in prison more than twenty years. In memo after memo, and, after my transfer to Havana in July of 1979, in cable after cable, I pressed for that parole, and for other efforts to free Lunt, Everett Jackson, Juan Tur, and Claudio Morales. On September 7, the wheels began to move. The Puerto Ricans were paroled in the United States. On September 16, I was told by the Cuban government that we could pick up Lunt and the others the following day. They were free to return to the United States. As I note in my own book, *The Closest of Enemies* (W.W. Norton, 1987), seeing Lunt and the others walk into the U.S. Interests Section on September 17 of 1979, having a glass of champagne with them and then watching them head for the airport, their long ordeal over, was one of the high points of my three years as Chief of Mission in Havana.

I remember remarking to Lunt over champagne that day that I hoped he would write a book. I am delighted that he has now done so. It is the kind of book one would expect of Larry Lunt. The anger and pain come through, but in quiet understatement, not, ever, through strident ranting. Indeed, its poignancy lies more in what it leaves unsaid than in what it states outright.

It is a book which reflects Larry's love for Cuba and the Cuban people. One of its most moving passages is his tribute to the Cuban women who stood by their men in prison, sharing their own scarce rations with them, often traveling days for their once-a-month visit, and enduring with dignity the taunts and humiliating procedures of the prison officials. Lunt saw a great nobility in them, and he was right.

Despite all he suffered, Lunt emerged from prison an unembittered man. He was deeply angered by the wanton cruelty of some of the guards—angered because their behavior diminished all men. But he saw goodness in many others and it did not escape him that their lot was a harsh one also. A lesser man would have hated them all; Lunt continued to see them as fellow human beings.

Lesser men would have been destroyed by fifteen years in the worst of Cuba's political prisons. Lunt came out of the experience not only intact but if anything a bigger and better man. When he was not breaking rocks, he studied Spanish, gave English lessons, and thought long and hard about the human condition. Even in prison, he was guided by concerns beyond himself. As one former prisoner put it to me: "Lunt always thought of others first; if you were hurt or in trouble, he was someone you knew you could turn to. He was a rock."

In his quiet unassuming way, Larry Lunt doubtless intended this book simply to be the chronicle of one man's experiences in Castro's prison system. What it is, however, is much more than that. It is a tribute to the indomitable human spirit and to the author himself, who represents that which is good in humankind. One cannot read this book without feeling somewhat more optimistic about the future of our species.

Wayne S. Smith
Washington, D.C. June 1, 1990

(Regarded as the State Department's leading expert on Cuba, Wayne S. Smith was Chief of the U.S. Interests Section in Havana from 1979 until 1982. He is now Director of Cuban Studies at the Johns Hopkins University's School of Advanced International Studies.)